The Turing Test and the Frame Problem

AI's Mistaken Understanding of Intelligence

ABLEX SERIES IN ARTIFICIAL INTELLIGENCE
Yorick Wilks, *Series Editor*

The Turing Test and the Frame Problem
AI's Mistaken Understanding of Intelligence

Larry J. Crockett

Ablex Publishing Corporation
Norwood, New Jersey

Printed in the United States of America.

Library of Congress Cataloging-in-Publication Data

Crockett, Larry.
    The Turing test and the frame problem : AI's mistaken
understanding of intelligence / Larry J. Crockett.
        p.   cm. — (Ablex series in artificial intelligence)
    Includes bibliographical references and index.
    ISBN 0-89391-926-8. — ISBN 1-56750-030-7
    1. Turing test.   2. Frames (Information theory)   3. Artificial
intelligence.   I. Title.   II. Series.
    Q341.C76   1994
    006.3—dc20   93-9050
                                                      CIP

Ablex Publishing Corporation
355 Chestnut Street
Norwood, New Jersey 07648

Contents

Preface

Part of what it means to be a researcher is to identify what appears to be a relationship that others either have not noticed or have not fully appreciated. Both the Turing test and the frame problem have been significant items of discussion for more than 20 years in the philosophy of artificial intelligence and the philosophy of mind, but there has been little effort during that time, as I read the literature, to distill how the frame problem bears on the Turing test. I believe that there is an important relationship and that this essay articulates that relationship. Of course, I must leave it to the reader to judge whether I have argued convincingly that such a relationship exists.

In a larger sense this essay is also an attempt to explain why there has been less progress in artificial intelligence research than AI proponents would have believed likely 25 to 30 years ago. As a first pass, the difficulty of the frame problem would account for some of the lack of progress. One could take this to mean that the progress will simply be much slower than originally anticipated because the problems are much more complex. An alternate interpretation, however, is that the research paradigm itself either is destined to be less productive than we might have hoped or must undergo radical change. In general terms, the view advanced here is that the future of AI depends in large part on whether the frame problem will fall to computational techniques. If it turns out that the frame problem is computationally intractable, if there is no way to solve it computationally by means of a program operating on formally defined constituents, which is AI's understanding of intelligence, then I suspect an increasing number of writers will reach the conclusion that AI embodies a fundamental misunderstanding of intelligence. In fact, that is the view I tentatively advance here.

In short, I defend the view that the Turing test is a good test for intelligence but that no computer will be able to pass the test unless there is a solution to the frame problem. Against those, such as Gunderson and Searle, who say that passage of the test would not necessarily signify that a machine was thinking, I argue that a computer passing the test would have to possess a solution to the frame problem and that such a solution should convince us that thinking is in fact occurring. Against those, such as Dennett and Turing, who imagine that passage of the test is just a matter of time, I argue that it is not at all clear that we will be able to solve the frame problem, and, as a result, it is not at all clear that a computer will ever pass the Turing test. In fact, I think the prospects for a solution to the frame problem are not good.

A number of people have read the entire manuscript and deserve my thanks. Among them are Keith Gunderson and Douglas Lewis (philosophy), and Michael Kac (linguistics/computer science), all of the University of Minnesota. Lewis reads manuscripts more closely than anyone I have ever met. Gunderson, a member of the Minnesota Center for Philosophy of Science, in particular graciously and helpfully commented on my critical assessment of his well-known views. We have had useful conversations about these issues for a period of 10 years now, and he has encouraged me to continue attempting to explain why I think he is mistaken. Yorick Wilks, Director of the Computing Research Laboratory, New Mexico State University, who is the editor of this Ablex series, read the entire manuscript and offered a number of insightful suggestions. My colleagues at Augsburg College, Minneapolis, Bruce Reichenbach (philosophy), John Benson (religion), and Larry Ragland (computer science) read parts of the manuscript and offered valuable suggestions. For several years, as well, I have had a number of useful conversations about related issues with my colleague Noel Petit (computer science). Last, but perhaps most significantly, I have tried out my ideas on a number of undergraduate and graduate students at Augsburg, and they have been remarkably helpful as I attempted to grope my way to some clarity with respect to these subtle, slippery issues.

Larry J. Crockett
June 1992

CHAPTER 1

Introduction: Interpreting the Turing Test in Light of the Frame Problem

It has been more than four decades since A. M. Turing (1950) published his article, "Computing Machinery and Intelligence," which proposes a conversational test to answer the question of whether a computer can think. Turing's paper not only advances a practical test but also constitutes a theoretical fountainhead for both classical work in AI done as early as the 1950s and AI-influenced philosophical discussions of mind and psychology occurring during the last 40 years. Examples abound of the paper's enduring influence over the years. For instance, saluting it as a "classic," A.R. Anderson's 1964 anthology, *Minds and Machines*, places Turing's paper first, perhaps following the ancient Semitic practice of placing the most important literature in a collection first. In his introduction, Anderson claims that more than one thousand papers were published in the period from 1950 to 1964 on the question of whether machines can think, with many referring to Turing's paper. More recently (1987), the entry for "Alan Mathison Turing" in the *Oxford Companion to the Mind* extols the test named for Turing as the best test we have for confirming the presence of intelligence in a machine. On the other side of the philosophical aisle, John Searle (1980, 1984, 1990) and Keith Gunderson (1971, 1985) have advanced arguments against the adequacy of the Turing test for a number of years.

More recently still, the Computer Museum of Boston hosted the Loebner Prize Competition in November of 1991. The goal of the

1

competition was the development of software that would pass a "modified version of Alan Turing's 1950-era Turing test" (Zeichick, 1992). Competing programs included Ann, which purportedly possesses the knowledge of a 7-year-old child, and Wittsgenstein (note the play on the name of the 20th-century philosopher Ludwig Wittgenstein—no 's'), which allegedly holds forth ably on the genteel subject of burgundy wine. While there is no claim that a program has passed the full-fledged test, Ziechick's claim is that "we're not far from having imitative programs that can pass a limited Turing test with ease and do well on an unrestricted test, as Turing proposed it" (p. 5). Given this four-decades-long history, it seems fair to conclude that the Turing test has been the focal point around which a great deal of discussion, as well as a fair amount of programming, have turned in the last 40 years for what would be sufficient to convince us that machines think.

An undercurrent that is never far from the surface of debates over the Turing test is the fact that the debate is often a debate between disciplines. As is true in the cases of Searle and Gunderson, philosophers often have been suspicious of claims that a relatively straightforward test such as Turing's could confirm the extraordinary claim that a machine thinks. Researchers in various scientific disciplines, by contrast, have often welcomed the test as obviously the right way to answer the philosophers. In fact, Turing designed his test in part to limit the seemingly endless haggling over terms, definitions, and distinctions that scientists often accuse philosophers of substituting for "real science." As many scientists see it, they can justifiably point to the test when the philosophical question is asked, "How would we know that a computer is thinking?" and they can then profitably return to the research designed to produce such a machine. Indeed, the philosopher Haugeland (1985, p. 9) is sympathetic to this approach: "By accepting the Turing test . . . scientists can concentrate almost entirely on the 'cognitive' aspects of the problem . . . [and] they can dispense with messy incidentals and get on with computational psychology." Instead of limiting the philosophical wrangling, however, Turing's introduction of his Imitation Game as a test, as we will see, has generated its own decades-long history of argument and counterargument.

Turing was not as consistent as we might like in defining the question for which his paper purportedly advanced a practical decision procedure. In the first sentence of "Computing Machinery and Intelligence," he writes that he will take up the question, "Can machines think?" Before the first paragraph is out, however, he exchanges this question for two questions associated with the Imitation Game. When we consider these substitute questions, nevertheless, they still involve the issue of whether machines think and — even more importantly — how we might satisfy ourselves that a machine is thinking. The Imitation Game, as a result, remains Turing's pragmatic answer to one pivotal question: what evidence would enable us to distinguish genuine machine thinking from cleverly engineered, machine imitation thinking?

Despite repeated attempts to dismiss it, the Turing test has proved to be a remarkably resilient proposal in the philosophy of mind and in philosophical discussions of artificial intelligence. Just when philosophical opponents conclude that it has finally been vanquished, Phoenix-like, it surfaces again, with defenders offering new defenses. This essay, in fact, constitutes in part just such a new defense. Perhaps the most spirited defense of the test published in the 1980s was offered by Daniel Dennett. Dennett's (1985) "Can Machines Think?" is something of a traditional defense of the test, however, because he suggests that his general orientation to the argument that ordinary conversation would be a good test of thinking in machines goes back as far as Descartes. Dennett's principal argument is that writers who dismiss the test have both overestimated the powers of current computers and underestimated the demands of conversing in a natural language. Such detractors of the test, as a result, believe that a computer might pass the test but that passage would not by itself indicate that the computer is thinking. Against such detractors, Dennett counters that the test is "plenty strong enough as a test of thinking."

In contrast to the Turing test, the frame problem has a briefer, rather less prominent history. While there is a fair amount of sentiment, especially among philosophers, that the frame problem is an old problem freshly disguised in trendy computational attire, other writers argue that the frame problem is essentially a new problem. Speaking for the "it's not as new as it seems" crowd, for example, Clark Glymour (1987, p. 65) argues that the frame problem is closely related to "problems that are old friends to philosophy." While he concedes there are some new twists on this old problem in AI discussions, he insists the problems have a long history in Western epistemology. On the other hand, Dennett and John Haugeland agree that the frame problem does not substantially predate the AI era. Haugeland (1987, p. 77) observes, "As if epistemology hadn't enough troubles, artificial intelligence has generously provided another, called the 'frame' problem." Dennett (1987, p. 42) concludes that the frame problem is "a new, deep epistemological problem — accessible in principle but unnoticed by generations of philosophers — brought to light by the novel methods of AI, and still far from being solved."

The *frame problem* as a recognized problem with this specific name is only about half the age of the Turing test, since it dates to 1969. And while the Turing test is reasonably well defined and understood — even if there is little agreement about the significance of what passage of the test would mean — the term *frame problem*, in its shorter life, has been subject to a greater variety of interpretations. The writers who called attention to the problem for (mainly) technical readers, John McCarthy and Patrick Hayes, perhaps owing to their technical backgrounds, understand the term *frame problem* to name a difficulty associated with axiom revision in an AI system, given new data. Not surprisingly, philosophers such as Jerry Fodor (1987) have understood it in more epistemological terms. The frame problem, for Fodor, should be understood in terms of how a computer system would ascertain which of the "beliefs" about the world it has require updating and which do not, given its interaction with the world. Haugeland (1987, p. 82) interprets it as the problem of revising our beliefs about the world as we change it with our actions. Pylyshyn's (1987) volume, and to a lesser extent, Brown's (1987) volume, underscore how issues associated with the frame problem have assumed a larger role in philosophically oriented discussions of AI.

The frame problem parallels the Turing test in the sense that it occasions some of the same disciplinary skirmishing. As we have just seen, philosophers have analyzed the term *frame problem*, sometimes construing it in different ways from its original understandings. Hayes (1987, p. 82) in particular has been roundly irritated by the ways it has purportedly been misinterpreted. Making explicit reference to Dennett, Fodor, and Haugeland, Hayes has written in an attempt to correct some of what he views as the "sillier misunderstandings" of the frame problem by such philosophers.[1] As might be expected, many

---

[1] At the Computers and Philosophy Conference at Stanford University in August 1990, Hayes told me that he regrets some of the caustic tone of his paper.

scientists see in such problems research agendas that can be pursued profitably if the waters are not too muddied by the philosophers. On the other hand, philosophers sometimes conclude that scientists precipitously construe venerable philosophical problems as technical problems that are, in principle at least, amenable to engineering solutions.

In light of these remarks, it seems fair to conclude that the Turing test and the frame problem count as two major issues in philosophical discussions of AI as we approach the middle of the 1990s. The principal contribution I hope to make in this essay, however, is not primarily new insights about the frame problem or an amplification of more or less conventional arguments for the Turing test. While I think some new clarity can be achieved by carefully defining the frame problem, and while I will attempt to explain why some objections to the Turing test are not convincing, my primary goal is to distill some of the implications of the frame problem for the ongoing discussion of the Turing test. Little has been written on this relationship, and new discussions of the Turing test continue largely to ignore the frame problem. For example, David Anderson (1989) takes up many of the topics considered here: Turing's Imitation Game, simulation, the Dreyfus critique of AI, Searle's Chinese Room experiment, and Dennett's defense of the test. But there is no direct discussion of the frame problem.

I believe that two remarkable results follow if we interpret the Turing test in light of the frame problem. First, considerations attaching to the frame problem significantly reinforce the claim that the Turing test is a formidable test indeed — sufficiently difficult, in fact, that I believe that the probability of a digital computer ever passing it is remote. Second, should it turn out that there is agreement that a computer has passed the test (ignoring the technical details of how such a feat is possible), our confidence that it serves as a reasonably convincing indicator of intelligence is strengthened considerably, since the nature and scope of the frame problem's difficulty make it unlikely that it is amenable to solution by nonthinking algorithmic systems. In fact, a central claim of this essay is that the frame problem, if it is defined in something like the way I do, namely, as a two-sided problem with a common epistemological center, provides a clear demarcation between nonthinking and thinking in a formal system or, to use the finer-grained terms I will introduce later in the essay, between epistemologically simple thinking and epistemologically complex thinking. In sum, the literature I have seen has not adequately explored the implications of the frame problem for the Turing test and the resulting taxonomy of thinking that we are going to need to describe the several types of thinking and nonthinking behavior of computing machines. Such a taxonomy is essential if we are to understand better, for instance, the meaning of claims such as "Cray Research has developed a machine that can pass the test" and "It may be possible to program a Cray computer to pass the test without it thinking at all." This essay is designed to redress this oversight.

Given the interpretation of the relation of the frame problem to the Turing test that I will advance, a theme that will play a large role in this essay is the importance of learning for systems designed to pass the test. Questions associated with learning will prove to be important, since I claim that the frame problem obstructs the kind of learning that is necessary to pass the Turing test. Admittedly, there is considerable disagreement in the literature about the relative importance of learning to the AI enterprise in general. Haugeland (1985), for example, takes learning less seriously than I do, since he claims that "it does not appear that learning is the most basic problem, let alone a shortcut or a natural starting point" (p. 11). At the other end of the spectrum of opinion about the importance of learning, Waltz (1988) argues that future AI models will involve more look-up and less search. I take this to mean that, to an extent that has usually not been appreciated in classical AI, intelligent behavior in problem-solving contexts more often has to do with rather straightforward, algorithmically simple look-up — identifying, for example, a question as quite similar to an earlier, answered question — than it does with algorithmically based search through a large search space.[2] That which is looked up, assuming that we cannot begin to program into a computer all that it will need to cope with the complexity of a real world, would have to have been learned in large part.

The point is that at least some discussions of the Turing test have

---

[2]I don't wish to suggest that biological brains are algorithmically based, since it may turn out that the idea drawn from computing — specifically, that problem solving involves algorithmic search space reduction until a solution is found — may not describe neural processes well at all. *Algorithmically simple* here could include no algorithmic processing at all.

not noticed that there are different kinds of learning that are needed for different kinds of conversational capacities; my claim is that there is a fundamental epistemological distinction that should be drawn between two different kinds of conversation. I claim that this point's importance becomes apparent if we correctly identify how the frame problem bears on the attempt to build computers or, in Haugeland's terms, automatic formal systems, which play the machine's part in Turing's Imitation Game test.

I have not yet attempted to define the term *artificial intelligence*. As would likely be expected, there is nothing approximating a universal agreement on how it should be interpreted. Boden (Gregory, 1987) defines it as "the use of computer programs and programming techniques to cast light on the principles of intelligence in general and human thought in particular." I think this is a respectable first pass — though more aggressive, less philosophically timid, writers would insist that it is the attempt to generate intelligence. What is striking in various definitions of AI is that one example of intelligence that is frequently mentioned almost immediately is conversational ability. Haugeland (1985), for example, discusses conversation and the Turing test in the first few pages of his book. To cite Boden again (Gregory, 1987), the kinds of things AI attempts to get machines to do "include holding a conversation" and "answering questions sensibly on the basis of incomplete knowledge." These examples illustrate that definitions of *artificial intelligence* often make reference to activities that we do that we assume require intelligence. As this essay will argue later, a pivotal question in philosophic discussions of AI is whether it follows that, if we require intelligence to do some activity, such as converse maturely about some subject, it follows necessarily that any computer doing that activity would also require intelligence. While I agree that conversation is just such a computer activity that requires intelligence, I do not argue that this result follows from the general principle that, if, when a human does it, it requires intelligence, it follows that a computer also would require intelligence to do it. I concede that the path to the conclusion that computers require intelligence to engage in mature conversations, for reasons supplied by Searle and Gunderson, is significantly more complicated.

Coming to some clarity about the possibilities and limits of AI presupposes coming to some understanding of what a computer is. This means exploring what it means to compute a function algorithmically. I argue that the concept of algorithm is more important than the concept of computer or program. I have found, nevertheless, that abstract characterizations of the properties of algorithms should be supplemented by more concrete illustrations of what computers do in practice if we want an intuitive sense of what computation can do. As a result, I illustrate computer activity with a small simulation of basic computer operations which I call *AugsAsm*. I also press into service Haugeland's (1985) helpful discussion of a central property of digital computers, namely, the requirement of a set of unambiguous read/ write techniques. I find his discussion of read/write techniques helpful when attempting to make sense of what John Searle is capable of computing in his much discussed Chinese Room experiment.

Parenthetically, I must confess that I attempt to reach some clarity about what a computer "is" with some trepidation. One of the problems of attempting to spell out what a computer is can be compared to being handed a length of black pipe and asked, "What is this?" The question of what something "is," if asked in the context of human convention and practice, cannot be answered without considering the purposes for which that item is employed; a length of black pipe could be used as conduit for natural gas burned to stave off a cold Minnesota winter or as a weapon to murder an obnoxious spouse. Hence, what it "is" depends significantly on how people use it. A computer manipulates bits, given its program, and the question of what it "is" cannot be completely disassociated, in the view I develop here, from the human purposes that generated the program. Admittedly, this view begs a question, for it assumes that there is a significant analogy to be drawn between a length of pipe and a computer. Much AI discussion, in fact, revolves around the question of whether a computer can possess something that has more in common with a thinking, understanding person than a nonthinking, nonunderstanding length of black pipe.

I also will spend some time with issues associated with computer simulation. I argue that the computer's simulation capacities are sufficiently significant that one good way to understand a computer is that it is a simulation machine. The specific reason for doing this, of course, is that, if we are to reach a clear understanding of the significance of a computer passing Turing's test, we need to possess some sensitivities with respect to how a computer can generate a simulation of some phenomenon without actually generating the phenomenon in question. As Searle (1984) points out, there remains a distinct difference between simulation and duplication. I press into service Alan Kay's (1984) provocative suggestion that a computer is a "metamedium" such that which machine it is at any given point is a function of which set of programs is driving it. Kay also speaks of "user illusions" and reminds us that computers are especially adept at generating user illusions. I take this to be a warning that we must especially be on our philosophic guard when it comes to assessing the Turing test since we are so susceptible to being taken in by a conversational user illusion.

I mentioned above the centrality of computer learning for the Turing test. Dealing with computer learning requires a distinction that I believe is pivotal if we are to interpret issues associated with the Turing test perceptively. The relationship of what we call *learning* to what a computer does when it processes information is treacherous for a number of reasons. One reason is that current computer programs cope quickly and effectively with certain kinds of input in a way that often could be understood as a kind of learning, and not at all well with some of the kinds of input we handle well when we are said to be learning. Another reason is that it is not clear whether rapid data assimilation and manipulation that result in programmatic behavioral modification should count as *learning*. I provide an illustration of a computer program that plays the Coin Toss game, which, by some philosophic lights at least, learns but, as I see it, learns in certain strictly circumscribed ways. There is a long history, both in philosophical discussions and in popular perception, of posing the larger AI question in terms of thinking versus nonthinking and learning versus nonlearning rather than developing a finer-grained taxonomy. Nevertheless, I believe that certain kinds of computer behavior, such as that exemplified by the Coin Toss game, which I discuss in Chapter 2, justify the claim that the computer is thinking and learning but that this sense of *learn* should not be taken to be identical with all uses of the term *learn*. My claim is that learning occurs as a computer plays the Coin Toss game but it is a specific, limited kind of learning that should not be confounded with the kind of learning we do, for example, when we correctly see that two things are similar when the common understanding is that they are not. In an attempt to name this difference, I will distinguish *epistemologically simple* from *epistemologically complex* learning. The former has to do with atomic, storage-based, constrained-domain revision and the latter has to do with system-wide, memory-based, unconstrained-domain revision. I argue that this distinction has conceptual correlates, conversationally speaking, namely, epistemologically simple and epistemologically complex conversation, which are helpful in attempting to determine which kinds of conversational ability are computable by a digital computer, which kinds of conversational ability are requisite to passing the Turing test, and, pivotally, whether these turn out to overlap sufficiently such that we can say that it is possible for a digital computer to pass the Turing test. From time to time, as well, I will speak of epistemologically simple and epistemologically complex thinking. I will not consistently distinguish the terms *learning* and *thinking* since I assume that the two terms overlap significantly.

Additionally, I will chronicle some of the AI history leading to the more considered understanding of the frame problem that emerged in the late 1980s. Any such chronicle is obliged to pay some attention to Hubert and Stuart Dreyfus. I will argue that the Dreyfus critique of AI anticipated a good part of the problem that the term *frame problem* names, at least as understood by philosophers. Hubert Dreyfus contends that the attempt to analyze human intelligent behavior in terms of rules, in the hope that we can generate a set of rules that captures the intelligence, presupposes a "certain *ceteris paribus* clause" — that things will go as they usually do when an attempt is made to use the rules to solve a problem. The problem is that it is not possible, according to Dreyfus, to spell out what the clause means axiomatically and it is difficult to determine how to program a system to recognize that a problem situation is at variance with this clause. Dreyfus claims it is impossible, to put it in the parlance of computer programming, to program a computer to deal effectively with the programmatically unanticipatable.

As I said above, there is considerable disagreement about the meaning of the term *frame problem*. Specifically, there is a disagreement between philosophically and technically inclined writers. McCarthy and Hayes, to whom goes the credit for coining the term *frame problem*, construe it more technically in terms of how it is possible to build an axiom-based system that incorporates a "principled" way to make changes in a representational system, given changes in the represented world, without falling prey to a computational paralysis resulting from the need to examine all axioms individually each time one axiom requires change. Brown (1987) defines the problem as one of "describing in a computationally reasonable manner what properties persist and what properties change as actions are performed" (p. v). As Brown sees it, this means "we cannot expect to be able to exhaustively list for every possible action and for every possible state of the world how that action changes the truth or falsity of each individual fact" (p. v). The more philosophically inclined, such as Owen Flanagan (1991), understand the problem to be related to common sense and which criteria a system could use so that it is unnecessary for it to examine exhaustively all it knows, in the attempt to find what might prove to be relevant, when it attempts to solve a problem. It is not a matter of attempting to constrain the *search space* of a problem, which has usually been thought to be the principal problem in AI, but rather it is what this essay will call the problem of constraining the *relevance space* of its own set of representations, given the initial problem to be solved. On this view, it is the problem of the relevance of all that is represented in the attempt to solve problems as they occur in a robot's interaction with the real—as opposed to a "toy"— world. I claim that the two senses of the frame problem have a common core, because as soon as we attempt to find Hayes's "principled" way to avoid the specific frame problem, we get entangled in the epistemological complexities of the general frame problem.

Daniel Dennett has been conspicuous over the years for his spirited defense of the Turing test. Dennett's work, along with recent studies in complexity theory and evolution, I will argue at length, support the claim that we will have to rely heavily on I/O tests in our assessment of purported computer intelligence. The central point that Turing makes, which is not fully appreciated by detractors of the test, which Dennett wants to underscore, is that the test sanctions questions about virtually any of the activities and issues that people find interesting. This doesn't mean that the computer has to be expert in all of these fields any more than we expect a person who is a good conversationalist to be expert in all of them. The expectation is more modest and reasonable—it is that a good conversationalist ought to be able to discuss a reasonable sampling of these areas of human interest and activity well. Not only should a conversationalist be able to discuss many of them reasonably well, he or she or it should be able to make inferences across areas of interest such as being able to say something sensible, to anticipate the example I will use, about the implications of the political demise of Gorbachev for balancing the American federal budget. While I will express some qualms about Dennett's defense of the test, I will second Dennett's suggestion that demanding queries asked of a computer system programmed to pass the Turing test are, indeed, good "quick probes" for an intelligence such that, if a computer were able to pass the test, it would be reasonable to conclude that it possesses a general faculty that is at least roughly equivalent to human intelligence.

Moreover, there are other results that reinforce the need to rely significantly upon input/output tests such as Turing's. Specifically, Christopher Cherniak (1988) argues that a computer program with the approximate powers of the human mind would be so complex that it would be well beyond our ability to comprehend. In a similar vein, Howard Margolis argues that the brain is based on nonprogrammed pattern-recognition processes that developed in natural history. His claim is that evolution works in such a way, namely, generating novel function while using conserved biological structure, that it inhibits investigation into how the conserved structure generates the novel function. The upshot of Cherniak's and Margolis's limitative work is that the prospects are poor for achieving an understanding of the brain and a mindlike program that would be good enough so that we could, in light of investigations, justifiably say things such as "Yes, the brain's *abc* function parallels the program's *xyz* procedure." If they are right, the point is that we are forced largely to rely upon input/output tests such as Turing's more than many writers suppose.

The larger claim I wish to make is that the complexity of the brain and mindlike programs force us toward consideration of input/output assessments of machine intelligence and that the Turing test turns out, even when considered in isolation from the frame problem, to be a good I/O-based "quick probe" for intelligence. More specifically, considerations attaching to the frame problem significantly enhance the traditional argument that passage of the Turing test would be an adequate indication of intelligence but that, even without such considerations, the case for the Turing test is substantial. This is to say that I believe Turing has been right all along about what it would mean if a computer passed his test. But what follows from this positive assessment of the Turing test is not, as Turing supposed, that at some point we will agree that a computer thinks, but that computers are unlikely to pass the test at all. As a result, my view is at odds both with that held by AI proponents, namely, that we will eventually have a computer that can pass the test and therefore we will be able to conclude that computers can think, and the view held by a number of AI opponents, usually philosophers, that passing the Turing test would not by itself warrant such a conclusion.

In fact, I take two such philosophers, specifically, John Searle and Keith Gunderson, to task for arguing that passing the Turing test would not be sufficient to warrant the conclusion that a computer can think. As I read their objections, they have not fully understood how demanding the Turing test is. Instead, they typically assume such passage is probably inevitable and they concentrate on explaining why passage of the test would not mean what AI proponents have usually supposed, namely, that such a computer must be thinking as it converses. I claim that they fail, as many have failed, to see that an unsolved frame problem precludes a computer from having sufficient command of natural language that it could pass the test.

Parenthetically, if I am right that an unsolved frame problem stands in the way of a computer passing the test, it means that the *poor substitute* criticism of AI, which claims that a computer is not likely to pass the test, gets a boost, while the *hollow shell* criticism of AI, which claims that any computer passing the test would still be lacking something necessary for genuine thinking, becomes less plausible. This way of naming two ways of objecting to artificial intelligence dates to Haugeland (1985). The critiques of AI offered independently by Searle and Gunderson are of the hollow shell variety; my objection, as well as those of writers such as Hubert Dreyfus and Hilary Putnam, are of the poor substitute variety.

A central claim of this essay is that the frame problem bears on the Turing test in such a way that several major results follow.

First, I claim that computer systems, which possess no solution to the frame problem, are capable of epistemologically simple learning but are not capable of epistemologically complex learning. An unsolved frame problem, I argue, blocks the kind of epistemologically complex learning that is requisite to the epistemologically complex conversational abilities that are needed to play the Imitation Game successfully. As a result, Searle will not be able to converse in his Chinese room in such a way that his responses are indistinguishable from those of a native Chinese speaker. This is to say that I claim that his much discussed Chinese Room experiment is implausible, because he cannot handle a full-ranging conversation in Chinese the way he claims he can. The result is that his conversational abilities are not indistinguishable from those of a mature, natural speaker of Chinese; therefore, Searle conversing in Chinese in his Room does not, as he claims, constitute passage of the Turing test.

Second, I argue that the relation of the frame problem to the Turing test is sufficiently singular that normally germane cautions about the dangers of drawing inferences from I/O descriptions to intervening process ascriptions, such as those raised by Gunderson, do not apply. Usually, I agree that it is philosophically treacherous to make an inference from such and such I/O descriptions to such and such characterizations about the processes generating the I/O. But I contend that the implications of the frame problem for the Turing test are such that the price we would have to pay for denying thought to a machine passing the test is higher than the one we pay for ascribing thought to the machine. Specifically, I argue that the alternative to agreeing that a computer passing the test is thinking is claiming that a nonthinking, algorithmic machine is capable of solving the frame problem. I believe this is sufficiently unlikely that it is more reasonable to ascribe thinking to the machine passing the test. If we are willing to ascribe thought to persons on the basis of the right I/O and some kind of argument by analogy, I argue, we ought to be willing to ascribe thought to a machine on the basis of the right I/O and considerations stemming from the compelling relation of the frame problem to the Turing test.

Derivatively, and also contra Gunderson, I conclude that the necessity of epistemologically complex conversational ability for passing the test counts against claims that ELIZA or ELIZA-like programs are capable of passing the test. While Gunderson has some distinguished company, such as Arno Penzias (1989, whose position is cited in some detail at the beginning of Chapter 5), in supposing that an ELIZA-like program can pass the Turing test, I argue that such a program, as an epistemologically simple program, cannot respond adequately to queries that presuppose an ability to appropriate and integrate epistemologically complex information. I illustrate this claim by including a "conversation" I had with ELIZA that is much less flattering than the widely (and tiresomely) cited "Men are all alike" example quoted by Gunderson.

Allow me to summarize my general position. While I will have a good deal to say about both, the primary topic of this essay is neither learning nor artificial intelligence, generally understood. Neither is it about the philosophy of language in general or human conversation in particular, although I will offer some observations about the rooted-ness of human language in tradition and convention and how this rootedness bears on the attempt to build an intelligent machine. Instead, it defends the claim that mature conversational ability turns out to be a compelling indicator of the presence of intelligence in machines, because, as Turing supposed, such ability presupposes the capacity to learn and integrate concepts and information at a sophis-ticated level. To the point, an unsolved frame problem, while it does not block a number of techniques that can and might be used to produce some useful kinds of computer learning, does preclude the specific kind of sophisticated learning that is a necessary condition for mature conversational ability. Expressed simply, conversationally fluid, intelligent systems do not suffer from a frame problem; the kinds of computational systems we currently build suffer from a frame problem that we do not know how to solve. My general position, then, is twofold. First, considerations stemming from the frame problem strongly support Turing's intuition that a general conversational ability is more than an adequate test of intelligence. A full appreciation of the frame problem makes it difficult to imagine how a nonthinking system could converse in the fluid, adaptable way Turing had in mind. Second—and this result would surprise and distress Turing—the frame problem likely demarcates the upper boundary of a computer's ability to learn and hence do many things that AI proponents have supposed would be just a matter of time and hard work. While I will concede Kay's (1984) point that we still have only a limited under-standing of the limits of computation, the frame problem is emerging as a profound limitation that we can profitably discuss. As I will argue in the final chapter, if it turns out that the frame problem is not solvable, then such unsolvability counts decisively against AI's under-standing of intelligence.

I should note, in closing this introduction, that I will say relatively little about how massively parallel computing bears or does not bear on the prospects for generating mature language competency in ma-chines. I have limited my task to digital computers, because the relationship of the frame problem to parallel computing is unclear at this point. I have therefore limited my discussion almost exclusively to the attempt to generate intelligence on conventional digital computers and to classical AI's assumption that intelligence is manipulation of symbols under the control of a program. I must confess that I am skeptical that massively parallel computing will significantly overturn the limitative results defended here, but attempting to buttress that skepticism with an argument must wait for another occasion.

CHAPTER 2

Algorithmic Machines and Computer Learning

To simulate all the neurons in a human brain in real time would take thousands of computers. To simulate all the arithmetic operations occurring in a Cray would take billions of people.

—Geoffrey Hinton (Ladd, 1986)

In this chapter, I take up questions associated with what it means for a computer to execute an algorithm and what it means to claim, after the execution of the algorithm, that "it learns." Since we use computers to simulate many kinds of phenomena, a related issue is finding a way to distinguish clever computer simulations from computer activity that warrant ascriptions such as "it learns" and "it thinks." The next chapter takes up issues related to simulation. In the first section of this chapter, I spend some time attempting to reach an understanding of what a digital computer, or what I will call an *algorithmic machine*, is able and not able to do. In the last section, I use the example of a Coin Toss game program to illustrate the major set of distinctions drawn in this essay, namely, that between *epistemologically simple* (ES) and *epistemologically complex* (EC) learning.

More specifically, in the first section, I argue that the operations of a digital computer at the most basic level are surprisingly simple, including operations such as adding 12 to the contents of a register, and storing the results, perhaps 28, in a location in "memory." These simple operations, as is well known, are performed at astonishingly fast speeds, so that computers are able to manipulate large amounts of numeric data rapidly. The chapter uses a simulated simple computer, which I call AugsAsm, to illustrate what a computer does at the assembly language level.

There are two reasons for this brief tour of basic computer operations. First, while most people are aware that machine-level operations are this simple, discussions of issues related to artificial intelligence, in the midst of considerations of such abstract concepts as recursion and backtracking, often lose sight of the fact that AI programming still generates operations that are this simple. Programs using advanced data structures and elegant algorithmic structures, after compilation, still consist of such simple operations. Second, an adequate understanding of the frame problem presupposes a sufficient command of the operations of a computer at this level.

Since the major question of this essay is the relation of the frame problem to the Turing test and how that relationship bears on the attempt to generate intelligence on a digital computer, I attempt to delineate what kind of learning is possible on computers and what kind of learning is required to pass the Turing test. I believe that the distinction I draw between epistemologically simple (ES) and epistemologically complex (EC) learning will shed some light on whether the kind of learning which is feasible on a digital computer is the kind of learning it needs to pass the Turing test.

1. Algorithmic Machines

In this section, I explore what it means to compute something algorithmically. First, I will try to develop an adequate definition of the concept of algorithm. As we will see, the concept of algorithm is more important to questions related to computability than is the concept of a computer. Second, to get a concrete sense of digital computing, I offer a simulation of a simple computer, which I call AugsAsm. At this level of description, there is a simplicity to computer operations that helps illumine why computers suffer from a frame problem.

Algorithms and Programs

The concept of algorithm has long been implicit in mathematics, but the word *algorithm* evidently came into use only during the middle ages. The Muslim mathematician Al-Khwarizm (died ca. 850 A.D.) wrote a book which summarized some Greek and Hindu contributions to elementary mathematics that came to be influential. The Hindu-Arabic numeric system came to be identified with his name and the Latin form of his name, *Algorismus*, became associated with the type of elementary, step-by-step mathematical work used by his book.

The concepts of *algorithm* and *program* are closely related but are not identical. Nicklaus Wirth (1984, p. 60) observes that "data structures and algorithms are the materials out of which programs are constructed." Close up, the ultimate and only data structure of digital computers is the 1s and 0s (or the presence or absence of electrical current) stored in memory cells. From this vantage point, the ultimate data structure of a computer is its 1s and 0s, and its ultimate algorithms are the CPU's instruction set. Data structures—to cite one example, two-dimensional arrays—constitute maps of how information is stored in a computer's main storage, while an algorithm—for example a "quick-sort" algorithm—is the complementary, yet equally essential, procedural element in computing, the "recipe for computation." Hence an algorithm is a necessary component of a program but is not by itself sufficient, since programs are comprised of both data structures and algorithms.

Particularly if we wish to reach some understanding of why algorithmic machines suffer from a possibly insoluble frame problem, we need a more precise definition of *algorithm*. It would also be helpful if we had some idea of how the concepts of algorithm, program, and computer are related. One pass at the idea is that an algorithm is an unambiguous, finite series of steps which will eventually terminate. Given this definition, a program is a convenient way to express an algorithm, and a digital computer is a convenient device on which to execute a program that expresses an algorithm.

As a result, algorithms are theoretically more important than both computers and programs for computing, since computers execute programs that express algorithms. The theoretical significance resides more in the algorithm than in the program or in the computer. Without algorithms, there would be no programs, and, since computers are those systems that execute programs, it follows that, without algorithms, there would be no computers. To put it another way, only problems with algorithmic solutions can be solved by computers. This obtains whether the task is the computation of the next prime number or the simulation of human recognition of faces.

Solving a problem with a computer requires the design of an algorithm. To draw a parallel with another discipline, while the theory of evolution is the unifying concept in biology, without which "nothing in biology makes sense," as the evolutionist Theodosius Dobzhansky used to put it, the concept of algorithm is the unifying concept for the theory of computability, without which little or nothing makes sense. In order to ascertain more clearly what is and is not to count as an algorithm, in addition to saying that an algorithm is an unambiguous, finite series of steps which eventually terminates, the following criteria should be added:

1. zero or more quantities are supplied as input;
2. zero or more quantities are produced as output;
3. every instruction must, in principle, be sufficiently simple that it could be carried out by a reasonably literate person using only pencil and paper.

The first two qualifications are designed to make allowance for algorithms which take as few as zero inputs and produce as few as zero outputs. Here are four program fragments which could easily be made into complete programs. The first takes no input and produces no output, the second has output only, the third takes input and produces no output, and the fourth takes input and produces output:

1) no I/O	2) output only	3) input only	4) input and output
if $0=0$ then do;	write;	read(value);	read(value);
:	:	:	:
if $0 < > 0$ then do;	write('Hello!');	if value $=0$ then do;	write(value);

This taxonomy exhaustively enumerates the different possibilities in terms of algorithmic machine input/output. However, programs that express what might be called *interactively impoverished* algorithms, represented here by fragments 1–3, are of less interest to the theory of computability, since what is most interesting, I take it for obvious reasons, is the following: given input x, is it possible algorithmically to compute output y—that is, given x, is it possible to follow an unambiguous, finite series of simple steps (steps that any reasonably literate person could perform using only pencil and paper, given sufficient time) in such a way that the steps come to an end after a finite amount of time and we have y as an output? That is, what interests us most are the possibilities and limitations inherent in such a step-by-step algorithmic method that attempts to produce y, given x.

Kinds of Algorithm Structure and the Significance of Recursion

While there are many different kinds of algorithm structure, it turns out that no more than three are necessary for the construction of any algorithm. They are *sequence, selection,* and *repetition.* In sequence, the steps are executed one at a time, each step is executed exactly once, and the order of execution is the same as order of appearance of the instructions in the algorithm. Consider the following program fragment example:

```
write('In the sequence construct, steps are executed one at a time.');
write('Each step is executed exactly once.');
write('The order of execution is the same as the order in the algorithm.')
```

In *selection,* the second structure, choice between two or more alternate paths is presented and conditions external to the algorithm determine which path is chosen. The general pattern is: if some condition, then take one action; otherwise, take an alternate action; otherwise. . . . Consider this selection structure from Pascal:

```
if (counter < 5) then
      write('yes')
else
      write('no')
```

Sequence and selection are not sufficient to express algorithms whose execution (in contrast with expressed) length depends on intermediate results. We need some way to make the execution duration depend on the intermediate results. *Iteration* supplies this need. Consider the following examples, again in Pascal:

```
repeat                          while counter > 0 do begin
      counter: = counter -1;          counter: = counter-1;
      write(counter);                 write(counter);
until counter < 0;              end;
```

As these **repeat** and **while** "loop" examples illustrate, iteration allows a process of indeterminate duration to be described by an algorithm of finite length. In each case the number of times the loop executes is a function of the value of the Boolean expression "counter > 0". In the first instance, so long as the Boolean expression evaluates as false, the loop continues; upon evaluating true, the loop terminates. Just the reverse is true in the case of the while loop. These two loop structures are prominent examples of iterative structures in a contemporary high level language.

One last algorithm structure, which is pivotal to AI programming, is the recursive structure. One illustration of the importance of recursion for AI is the relationship between LISP and recursion. As Allen B. Tucker (1986, p. 317) puts it, LISP "emerged as the *lingua franca* of the artificial intelligence community . . . LISP is unparalleled in its ability for expressing recursive algorithms which manipulate dynamic data structures." While recursion is often computationally inefficient, its elegance as a structure sometimes more than compensates for its inefficiency. A recursive algorithm contains a copy of itself (or at least its name as an invoking call of itself) within one of its instructions and hence can be said to "call itself" as a way of accomplishing its task. Wayne Amsbury (1985, p. 169) cites the everyday example of recursion: "a natural and effective definition of the word descendant is: . . . A descendant of a person is an offspring or the descendant of an offspring of a person. The definition is said to be recursive because it is in terms of itself." Here is a Pascal fragment which illustrates recursion:

```
procedure Reverse_Word;
    if (length(word) > = 1) then
        begin
            delete(word, 1, 1);
            Reverse_Word
    end;
```

Since citing the name of the procedure, "Reverse_Word," constitutes a call of the procedure in Pascal, including the name inside the procedure definition constitutes a recursive call. There has to be a terminating condition so that the procedure does not keep calling itself in an infinite loop. In this case, the if clause must be supplied an instance in which the terminating condition, the Boolean expression "(length(word) > = 1)", is satisfied so that the algorithm recursively calls itself at most a finite number of times. And there has to be what Amsbury calls a *refresh clause*, so that the execution is continued at some more restricted level if the terminating condition is not found — in such a way that the "refreshment" will result in the terminating condition in a finite number of steps. In this case, the delete procedure ensures that the procedure operates on a shorter and shorter string, thus guaranteeing, in a finite amount of time, termination.

Recursion is often algorithmically elegant as expressed in a high level language such as LISP or Pascal but is computationally inefficient when actually executed at the instruction level; recursion trades off computational efficiency for elegance in algorithmic expression. But the pertinent point is that recursion is superfluous — any recursive algorithm can be cashed in for an algorithm consisting, at most, of sequence, selection, and repetition. The result will often be less elegant and frequently much more difficult to understand, but it can nevertheless exhaustively capture the recursive algorithm. In principle, if not in human practice, AI programming can be done equally well in assembly language using a simple computer as it can using LISP running on a Cray Research Y-MP C90 supercomputer. Nothing necessarily new is generated at the machine level, in other words, simply by using more elaborate structures.

The general philosophical moral is that, while programmatic structures can be quite elaborate if viewed abstractly "from above," the algorithmic structures that are sufficient for the expression of any algorithmic task, namely, sequence, selection, and repetition, are themselves conceptually simple. Recursion is conceptually more computationally complex but it is used (and sometimes abused) largely for its decompositional economies ("keep doin' it until it's done," as every army private knows, is an economical way to order a great deal of repetitive work); it is finally extraneous. One theme I will push aggressively later is that large programs are inaccessible to human understanding to any simultaneous breadth and depth. This stems, not from the complexity of algorithm structure per se, but from the layering and sheer size of the programs involved. We can find the conceptually simple wholly inaccessible if there is enough of it organized in an elaborate structure.

Pencil-and-Paper Computability

I would like to emphasize the surprising simplicity of each step in an algorithmic process. We often hear that computers "simply add and subtract." While this oversimplifies the matter, since computers, among other things, also depend on logical operations such as complementing, ANDing, and ORing, there is a measure of truth in the claim that elementary computer operations are this simple.

Above, in defining the concept of algorithm, I claimed that "every instruction must, in principle, be sufficiently simple that it could be carried out by a literate person using only pencil and paper." To underscore that this is the case in current algorithmic machines, consider the AugsAsm simulated computer and instruction set that I developed and that is illustrated in Figure 2-1.

There are three principal components to the AugsAsm computer. The Accumulator is the register in which all arithmetic activity takes place. For data to be manipulated, it must be moved to the Accumulator first. Storage is usually called *memory* but I call it *storage* here to be consistent with claims made elsewhere in this essay that *memory*, when used in reference to computer storage, is an unfortunate misnomer. Last, the Program Counter points to the location in storage to be accessed during run time.

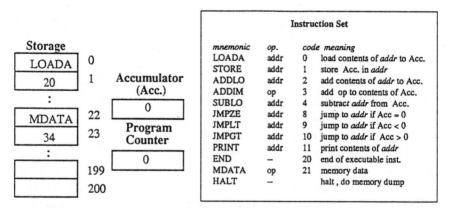

Figure 2-1. The AugsAsm Simulated Computer.   The AugsAsm computer consists of three parts: storage, consisting of consecutively numbered storage (memory) locations, an Accumulator in which all arithmetic activity takes place, and a Program Counter, which determines what locations in storage are accessed. The instruction set is listed at the right.

To be sure, real computers contain components not simulated in AugsAsm. Most real computers contain additional registers, buses, clocks, various auxiliary mechanisms and assisting hardware — all of which are irrelevant to computing conceptually. The AugsAsm simulated computer contains all the components conceptually required by a digital computer.

Figure 2–2 contains a program written in AugsAsm that does two subtractions inside a loop, controlled by a counter. Of course, this example program is trivial. But consider the execution run that

```
TOP  LOADA FIR
     SUBLO SEC
     STORE FIR
     LOADA CNT
     SUBLO FIN
     STORE CNT
     JMPGT TOP
     PRINT FIR
     END
FIR  MDATA 20
SEC  MDATA 08
CNT  MDATA 02
FIN  MDATA 01
     HALT
```

```
============================
       Storage Snapshot
============================
Address:  Opcode:  Operand:
  00        0        18
  02        4        20
  04        1        18
  06        0        22
  08        4        24
  10        1        22
  12       10         0
  14       11        18
  16       20         0
  18       21        20
  20       21         8
  22       21         2
  24       21         1
  26       22         0
============================
       Program Execution
============================
Accumulator = 0
Address: 0
Opcode: 0
Operand: 18
Accumulator = 20
```

```
Address: 2
Opcode: 4
Operand: 20
Accumulator = 12
Address: 4
Opcode: 1
Operand: 18
Accumulator = 12
Address: 6
Opcode: 0
Operand: 22
Accumulator = 2
Address: 8
Opcode: 4
Operand: 24
Accumulator = 1
Address: 10
Opcode: 1
Operand: 22
Accumulator = 1
Address: 12
Opcode: 10
Operand: 0
Accumulator = 1
Address: 0
Opcode: 0
Operand: 18
Accumulator = 12
Address: 2
Opcode: 4
Operand: 20
Accumulator = 4
Address: 4
Opcode: 1
Operand: 18
```

```
Accumulator = 4
Address: 6
Opcode: 0
Operand: 22
Accumulator = 1
Address: 8
Opcode: 4
Operand: 24
Accumulator = 0
Address: 10
Opcode: 1
Operand: 22
Accumulator = 0
Address: 12
Opcode: 10
Operand: 0
Accumulator = 0
Address: 14
Opcode: 11
Operand: 18

4

============================
       Storage Snapshot
============================
Address: Opcode:  Operand:
  00       0        18
  02       4        20
  04       1        18
  06       0        22
  08       4        24
  10       1        22
  12      10         0
  14      11        18
  16      20         0
  18      21         4
  20      21         8
  22      21         0
  24      21         1
  26      22         0
```

Figure 2-2. The AugsAsm Computer Executing a Program. Here the program in the upper left corner has been assembled and executed. As the trace illustrates, each operation is arithmetically so simple it could be done with pencil and paper by a grade school student.

contains a program trace. First, storage is displayed before and after the actual execution. Notice how little of the storage changes as a result of the program's activity. In serial digital computers, very little in the computer's storage changes as a result of the execution of the program; the overwhelming majority of the storage contents remains unchanged. The passivity of most of the digital computer's "memory" is an obvious point of criticism for proponents of the connectionist or massively parallel processing school. It is also a point that I will return to later when I speak of the problems inherent in attempting to use such storage to model a dynamic world that is both complex and sometimes characterized by rapid change.

Second, the trace illustrates how the Accumulator is the center of activity, and that each operation is arithmetically or logically simple. For example, the second operation in the listed program, SUBLO SEC, is simply a subtraction operation. The value 8 is subtracted from the value 20 that is stored in the accumulator, leaving 12, which is then stored in the location named "FIR." Computer operations at the assembly language level are just this simple. The program accesses data in storage, both to get the program and the data to be operated on. At any given instant, only one operation is occurring. In a serial digital computer, which AugsAsm simulates, that is all that happens. Each one of these basic operations, with the exception of the PRINT, is a very simple task that could easily be done mechanically with pencil and paper. While more complicated operations can be defined even at the assembly language level, the fact remains that computational operations for the most part are just this simple at nearly the most basic level of description.

I am not claiming that the complex cannot be constituted by the simple. The claim is not that the simplicity of the operations of a computer at the assembly language level directly entails the result that computers cannot do marvelously complex operations. I take it as an axiom of modern scientific method that complexity routinely is decomposable and is constituted by that which, at least at some level of description, is relatively simple. Rather, the claim is more subtle. My argument is that the kind of simplicity that characterizes computation on a digital computer has distinct implications for the likelihood that the frame problem is amenable to algorithmic solution on a computer.

Notice also that the three kinds of algorithm structure discussed above, those which are essential to an algorithmic machine if it is to be capable of computing all computable functions, are present in the program displayed in Figure 2-2. There is sequence since there is a series of instructions executed sequentially; selection occurs when the computer executes the JMPGT instruction; and repetition occurs since the "loop" of the program executes twice — the number of loops is determined by the value stored in CNT. Since AugsAsm supports the three kinds of algorithm structure necessary for the construction of any algorithm, it is capable, assuming that storage is adequate and that there is enough time, of executing any finite algorithm. That is to say, it is capable of computing any computable function.

This little program exemplifies well my principal claims about what constitutes an algorithm: an unambiguous, step-by-step process, using simple operations, which determines an output given an input and terminates operation under its own control after a finite amount of time. AugsAsm possesses, in sum, exactly the computational capabilities of any other digital computer.

I should spell out a little more clearly what the word *digital* means, especially since I assume that the kind of "computer" at issue in whether a computer can pass the Turing test is a digital computer. In the AugsAsm machine, there must be a way to read what is stored in memory without the material out of which the memory is made playing a pivotal role. It could be made from silicon or toilet paper, provided that the machine can distinguish one mark from another with extraordinary reliability. As Haugeland (1985, p. 54) puts it, "Digital techniques are write/read techniques" which have "the possibility of succeeding *perfectly*." The point is that the minute differences which distinguish equivalent tokens, such as this 1 from this 1 (the first is in Times font, the second in Courier), wash out in digital systems. To provide a further example, a dollar bill is digital in this sense: if a small part of the corner were missing, a bank teller would not insist that the dollar bill was worth only 97 cents.

Haugeland (1985) underscores the importance of digitalness to formal systems.

> The digitalness of formal systems is profoundly relevant to Artificial Intelligence. Not only does it make enormous complexity practical and reliable, but it also underlies another fundamental property of formal

systems: their independence of any particular material medium. Intelligence, too, must have this property if there are ever to be smart robots. (pp. 57–58)

In other words, fundamental to the AI program is the claim that intelligence emerges when the architecture and program are right; it does not have to be embodied in any particular kind of matter. The digitality of a digital computer means the physical medium it is made from is theoretically insignificant so long as one mark can be distinguished from another. As a result, not only can digital computers be made of different kinds of material, as classical AI sees it, intelligence can be embodied in different kinds of material. Since formal operations can occur in any system that can distinguish one mark from another, and since intelligence consists of the manipulation of formally defined constituents under the control of a program, intelligence in principle can be embodied in a wide variety of materials.

Let me explain why this extended discussion of digital computers is pertinent to the major questions of this essay. Notice what computation means in a classical digital computer. Whether the machine is AugsAsm, or a much larger digital computer, one simple operation occurs at a time, with the operations occurring separately from all the passive data stored in storage with the exception of the data being manipulated in the current operation. While such operations occur at tremendous speeds in contemporary computers such as a Sun, with millions of these simple operations occurring during the span of 1 second, the fact remains that there is a kind of atomic, epistemologically monastic isolation between the current operation in the central processing unit and all other data stored in storage in the rest of the computer. In other words, the random access "memory" in a Macintosh Quadra or the storage in the AugsAsm computer are equally epistemologically inert. One surprisingly simple step, such as adding the contents of memory location 5 to the contents of register A, occurs at any given instant in a classical von Neumann computer — and that's it.

Parenthetically, I should emphasize what I hope is obvious: many computer-related terms are philosophically tendentious. *Artificial intelligence* is the obvious case in point. Moreover, *memory* should be called *storage*, which was Turing's practice. My point in this discussion of

AugsAsm is that computer "memory" is storage, and such storage, I will claim throughout this essay, should be carefully distinguished from biological memory. The fact that computers possess storage but not memory, I will claim, is intimately bound up with the frame problem.

While there are significant advantages for traditional computing tasks to this serial computer *architecture*, I will argue in later chapters that there is a steep price to be paid for this computational simple-mindedness. Specifically, I believe that the evidence related to the frame problem supports the conclusion that intelligence on the scale possessed by people cannot be generated in classical von Neumann computers — no matter what improvements occur technologically.

Moreover, notice that it is the prodigious speed of computational operations in a digital computer that makes wrongheaded character-izations about the cognitive significance of these operations likely. Because of the great speeds, it is tempting to imagine that a computer program, and its accompanying data, intermediate data, and so on, should be understood as some kind of cognitive whole that somehow significantly parallels, at least functionally, what occurs in animal cognitive systems. The speed of the atomic interactions (*one* piece of data is changed, *one* register changes, etc., at any specific instant) in some situations (I will argue later that Turing-level conversation is an exception) generates an appearance of simultaneous whole system interaction, such that it appears to have some cognitive parallels to biological systems such as brains, when, in fact, no such simultaneous, whole system interaction occurs. It is this atomicity, if I can call it that, of digital computers that accounts for both their stunning capacities and their striking limitations. The philosophical task, of course, which will occupy the balance of this essay, is distinguishing the former from the latter, especially as they pertain to the Turing test.

2. Epistemologically Simple and Epistemologically Complex Computer Learning

In this second section of the chapter, I will develop a set of distinctions that will be pivotal to this essay. I argue that there is a basic limitation to what a digital computer is able to learn in terms of assimilating new "data" as a program executes. Chapter 6 will argue that the frame problem provides the demarcation between epistemologically simple (ES) and epistemologically complex (EC) learning, thinking, and conversation. This section sets up the first of these three, namely, the distinction between ES and EC learning.

Few would question the computer's singular power to perform simulations well. The next chapter takes up issues related to simulation in depth. A serious question, related to the principal question of this essay, is whether simulation can include aspects of human mentality, especially intelligence roughly approximating human intelligence, and how we should interpret such simulations. In particular, the question which needs addressing is whether some simulations can become good enough to be counted as (functional) duplications.

I would like to consider for a moment the kind of learning that occurs in a computer simulation of the Coin Toss game. I got the idea for developing the program from Fischler and Firschein (1987), who claim that the game is a good illustration of how a computer, using a mechanical record keeping system, can at least appear to be "learning." The game serves to illustrate some of the points I wish to make in this section of the chapter.

Many children play the Coin Toss or "matching coins" game. The idea, depending on the convention adopted, is either to get or avoid a match. In the computer version of the game, which I present here, the computer attempts to avoid a match with the human player. So, for instance, if the computer concludes, as it were, that the person is likely to choose tails, the computer chooses heads, in order to avoid a match. The computer's programmed goal is to win more often than it loses. Up to this point, it sounds merely like a game of rank chance. It becomes more interesting, however, when the computer is programmed to keep a record of how the human chooses. The computer can then be informed that there will be enough of a pattern to the choices made by the person that — in the longer term — "learning" from the pattern will enable it to win more often than it loses.

Consider an example of the program running. I wrote the program with three options: a repeated pattern that would presumably result in more "learning"; a machine-generated random pattern that should be resistant to learning; and last, a user-entered string of 51 characters that likely would have a pattern amenable to learning but not one that would assist the computer as much as the repeated pattern. In the following example run, the user selects the predictable, or third, option.

Please indicate the kind of string to generate:
1) predictable pattern: THTHHTHHHTHHHHTHHHHHT
2) machine-generated random pattern
3) user-input pattern of 51 characters

Please enter choice: 1, 2 , or 3:3

Please enter at least 51 characters:
THTHHHTTHTHTHTHTHHTHTTTTHHHTTHTTHTHTTHHHTTTHHTT-
TTHHHTTTHTHTHTHTTHTTHTHTTTHHTTTHHTTHT

Computer Wins: 5	Person Wins: 5	Percent: 50.0000
Computer Wins: 10	Person Wins: 10	Percent: 50.0000
Computer Wins: 14	Person Wins: 16	Percent: 46.6667
Computer Wins: 19	Person Wins: 21	Percent: 47.5000
Computer Wins: 26	Person Wins: 24	Percent: 52.0000
:		
Computer Wins: 41	Person Wins: 29	Percent: 58.5714
:		
Computer Wins: 62	Person Wins: 38	Percent: 62.0000
Computer Wins: 70	Person Wins: 40	Percent: 63.6364
Computer Wins: 75	Person Wins: 45	Percent: 62.5000
Computer Wins: 84	Person Wins: 46	Percent: 64.6154
Computer Wins: 88	Person Wins: 52	Percent: 62.8571
Computer Wins: 95	Person Wins: 55	Percent: 63.3333
Computer Wins: 103	Person Wins: 57	Percent: 64.3750
Computer Wins: 109	Person Wins: 61	Percent: 64.1176
Computer Wins: 117	Person Wins: 63	Percent: 65.0000
Computer Wins: 122	Person Wins: 68	Percent: 64.2105
Computer Wins: 129	Person Wins: 71	Percent: 64.5000
Computer Wins: 138	Person Wins: 72	Percent: 65.7143
Computer Wins: 144	Person Wins: 76	Percent: 65.4545
Computer Wins: 151	Person Wins: 79	Percent: 65.6522
Computer Wins: 157	Person Wins: 83	Percent: 65.4167
Computer Wins: 163	Person Wins: 87	Percent: 65.2000

The series of tosses used for this learning experiment was:
THTHHHTTHTHTHTHTHHTHTTTTHHHTTHTTHTHTTHHHTTTHHT-
TTTHHHTTHTHHHTTHTHTHTHHTHTTTTHHHTTHTTHTHTTHH-

HTTTHHTTTTHHHTTHTHHHTTHTHTHTHHTHTTTTHHHTTHTTH-
THTTHHHTTTTHHTTTTHHHTTHTHHHTTHTHTHTHHTHTTTTHH-
HTTHTTHTHTTHHHTTTHHTTTTHHHHTTHTHHHTTHTHTHTHHT-
HTTTTHHHTTHTTHTHTTHHHTTTHHTTTTHHHT

Here are the learning tables:

Table	Number of Heads	Number of Tails
HHHH	0	0
HHHT	14	5
HHTH	0	5
HHTT	5	19
HTHH	5	5
HTHT	10	10
HTTH	19	5
HTTT	15	0
THHH	0	19
THHT	0	10
THTH	15	10
THTT	5	10
TTHH	0	20
TTHT	9	10
TTTH	10	5
TTTT	10	0

After ten rounds of play, with little record to go on, the computer resorts to random guessing, with the predictable result of a standoff in terms of wins and losses. As play progresses, however, the computer gets better at the game. For example, after round 20, with a record of 10 and 10, the win/loss percentage is still a desultory .500. Between round 20 and round 60, when the record is 21 wins and 19 losses (.525), and rounds 190 and 240, when the record is 35 wins and 15 losses (.700), there is significant progress in terms of the win/loss percentage. Major league baseball managers, to cite a prosaic parallel, would be ecstatic over such an improvement in their teams during the "September stretch" preceding the playoffs. To claim that a baseball team that had improved that much was "learning to play the game" would scarcely get a rebuttal.

The pressing philosophic question is the significance of the improvement and what kinds of characterizations are warranted. If Herbert Simon's (1983) definition of *learning* is pressed into service, then it looks as though the Coin Toss program learns:

> Learning denotes changes in the system that are adaptive in the sense that they enable the system to do the same task or tasks drawn from the same population more efficiently and more effectively the next time.

As the play progresses in the Coin Toss game, there is adaptation, so that the machine performs more effectively. So it could be argued, using Simon's definition, that there is a measure of learning that takes place. Morris Firebaugh (1988) distinguishes a number of different levels of learning, from learning by rote to learning by induction, with learning by deduction listed as third of the five levels. He suggests that, in learning by deduction, "the learner draws deductive inferences from the knowledge and reformulates it in the form of useful conclusions which preserve the information content of the original data" (p. 586).

The principal mechanism of the Coin Toss program is a small deductive structure, an if/then/else statement, which makes deductions but it does so based on the programmatic assumption that past patterns will persist into the next round of play, so that there is a mix of induction and deduction in the program. As a result, it appears that the program satisfies several of Firebaugh's categories at once and, to the extent that his taxonomy has grasped some of the aspects of learning, it follows that this little program does something reasonably like learning.

Indeed, the heart of the Coin Toss program's *inference engine*, to invoke the tendentious language often used in AI contexts for a moment, is not unimpressive:

```
if length(person_string) < 4 then
    computer_choice {not enough information — call a separate procedure to guess}
else {is enough information to guess intelligently}
    begin
        if number_heads[index] > number_tails[index] then
            computer_guess : = 'T' {guess opposite}
        else if number_tails[index] > number_heads[index] then
```

```
      computer_guess : = 'H'
   else computer_choice; {do random guess}
   :
end; {else}
```

There are two conditions on which the computer simply guesses: when the game string is less than four characters, so there is no information in the table on which to base an informed guess, and when the number of heads and tails for a given four-character string is equal — in which case a random guess is all the database will support. Otherwise, it uses the table, assisted by the implicit assumption that past patterns will hold in the current round, implemented in an if/then/else structure, to draw inferences about likely behavior on the part of the person.

But it should be remembered that the moderately complicated if/then/else structure is cashed out at compilation time for the simple algorithmic structures we saw earlier, expressed abstractly as sequence, selection, and repetition. Or to get closer still to what happens in the machine, the Pascal program is a high level abstraction for a long series of machine level operations such as: move the contents of location 5 to register A, compare the contents of A with B to see which is larger, and so on. The computer is still trafficking in bit manipulation, with bits stored in a vast number of epistemologically passive storage locations. "Dynamic" data structures can be used, the algorithmic "recipe for computation" can employ the most advanced techniques, such as AI's favored recursion, but the operations at the machine level remain just as simple. The pivotal question is whether such simple operations can simulate phenomena as intricate as human intelligence in such a way that the simulation significantly becomes that which it simulates.

To begin tackling this complicated question, I need a distinction that I have said is central in this essay. The Coin Toss game program supports what I call *epistemologically simple learning*, which I distinguish from *epistemologically complex learning*. A number of authors distinguish between two fundamentally different kinds of learning. For example, Forsyth and Rada (1986) distinguish between *knowledge-sparse* and *knowledge-rich* learning. The former are those situations "which take little advantage of the complexity in knowledge"; the latter, by contrast, "show many facets to representation and reasoning." Fischler and Firschein (1987) contrast *autonomous* learning with *non-autonomous* learning. Most striking about the former, they argue, is the ability to recognize one situation or problem as similar to another; most typical of the latter is that supplied information assists the learner to solve a task more quickly or effectively.

Both sets of authors seem to be on to something but, unfortunately, neither set offers a sustained discussion of the distinctions they offer. There's a fundamental distinction to be drawn but, as I see it, there is a better way to do it. The difference between epistemologically simple and epistemologically complex (I'll sometimes use "ES learning" to designate the former and "EC learning" for the latter) turns on limitations inherent in storage-based processing systems, particularly as contrasted with memory-based biological systems. My contention is not that storage-based processing systems are not capable of EC learning, in principle, although that may turn out to be the case. At this point, that is a stronger claim than I wish to defend. My more modest claim is that, barring a solution to the frame problem, the evidence favors the conclusion that they are not capable of EC learning.

Consider the learning tables in the Coin Toss game simulation. Each time a new piece of data is encountered on the game string, an H or a T, the learning table is updated. As the table accumulates information, the computer learns in an epistemologically simple sense. To be sure, the computer's performance improves, but only in a drastically constrained domain, namely, the Coin Toss game. A relatively simple look-up table, linked to a set of production rules, enables the computer to perform in a significant — yet still epistemologically simple — way. Specifically, there is no larger cognitive system that integrates the learning, distilling the implications of the learning for the rest of something like a set of cognitive beliefs.

In epistemologically complex learning, on the other hand, learning involves just this kind of system-wide revision and integration, given new information or experience. I will discuss Howard Margolis' work in greater detail in Chapter 5, but his suggestion that all of biological cognition is based on pattern-recognition and not computation is relevant in this sense: EC learning involves whole system revision and change of the sort one would expect if Margolis is something like right. The *web of belief*, to invoke Quine and Ullian's term (1978), is dynamic and directly sensitive to belief revisions that occur to any part of the web. EC learning is memory based rather than storage based; this means that beliefs are not compartmentalized in storage cells or identifiable with specific production rules; in a profound sense, like a holograph, to grab, as it were, a part of a memory-based system is to grab a microcosm of the whole. Fischler and Firschein (1987) point out:

> except for very short-term sensory storage, the memory function is a complex activity that involves distinct modes of information partitioning, selection and abstraction. It has all the attributes of perception, and in fact, memory recall can be viewed as a form of internal perception. We do not generally retrieve a unique "token" in the exact form in which it was stored, but rather synthesize a "mental construct" (possibly from many different brain storage modalities) that is relevant to some purpose or ongoing process. (p. 37)

If human learning is about the modification of memory, which is a kind of internal perception, then learning is the modification of how we perceive the world. This captures a good deal of what I mean by EC learning. In ES learning, no such modification of how the world is perceived takes place.

While there is surely some localization of brain function such that certain brain functions are more tied to certain locations than others, we smile at 19th-century maps of various mental functions because they are too specific, too localized. Were such maps correct, of course, poststroke therapy would be much less successful today than it often is. Were such maps correct, to press the point, we would be more like computers. The limit point of such localization is a digital computer that stores binary numbers in sequenced, inert storage locations that are referenced serially under the control of an automatically incrementing program counter.

It might be argued that I have it backwards, that, even though there is some distance between brain function and brain tissue, there is enormous distance between a program, which is a conceptual/logical structure, and hardware. Programs can be loaded many different places in storage; procedures can be rearranged, algorithms can be self-modifying (although this is problematic, since any significantly self-modifying program would eventually founder on a programmatic version of the frame problem), and so on. That is, brain function is much more localized and tied to specific areas of the brain than program is to hardware. But my point is not about the relation of software to hardware so much as program to its own constituent parts: programs embody algorithms that happen to be executed on a digital computer. The data on which programs operate are functionally, parochially, tied to software structures. There is no interaction between data with data, or data with structure, except under epistemologically simple software control. There is no true dynamic, parallel interaction of the sort that evidently characterizes the brain.

Epistemologically complex learning is complex epistemologically in at least two major senses. First, in EC learning, it is some part of the real world about which something is learned, not a constricted domain or "toy world." The generation and maintenance of a model of the real world, I take it as uncontroversial, is complex epistemologically when compared to the generation and maintenance of a model of a "toy world" such as the Coin Toss game or even chess. For instance, the relations between the individual pieces of data represented in the Coin Toss game are simple; each is an ASCII character comprising a string. Operations over the pieces of data are straightforward; the data and operations fully represent the game that is modeled.

How much "data" are needed adequately to represent the actual world in a formal system designed to interact with the actual world? Not surprisingly, this is one of the perennial problems of AI. Difficulties abound. One major difficulty is that, when a person learns something new, this often means that his or her ability to interact with the world is improved in some way. In such situations, learning something new improves performance or understanding. By contrast, it often happens that adding new data to a computer system — let's let such data acquisition pass for learning for the moment — results in performance degradation. Consequently, support for epistemologically complex learning involves more than adding more data about the world and even adding structures that can use that data. As we will see when I discuss the frame problem, moreover, we don't know how to construct operations over a database or a program/database that will enable the system to cope with the complexity of the world over a significant amount of time. It is well known that the distinction between "data" and "program" is not a durable one — indeed, since programs and data are similarly stored in storage locations, the computer has to be instructed which bit strings are data and which are instructions. In terms of the history of programming languages, the movement towards "very high level" languages such as PROLOG embodies the attempt to eliminate any distinction between data and program. The result I draw from these considerations is that epistemologically complex learning differs in kind from epistemologically simple learning.

Second, it is complex epistemologically in the sense that it involves the task of generating and revising a large representational system. I will spend much more time later detailing some of the ramifications of the fact that, in modeling the actual world, epistemological complexity is encountered. That which is represented is complex, and so is that which does the representing.

I don't wish to suggest that epistemologically simple programs can be neither algorithmically complex nor large in terms of assembled size. Algorithmic complexity generally is increasing as programs get larger (although, of course, it is not simply the fact that they are getting larger which entails that they are becoming more algorithmically complex) in programming tasks as epistemologically simple as page composition software and operating systems. Assuming for a moment that it is possible to support humanlike intelligence on a digital computer, it might even be that some epistemologically simple programming turns out to be larger, in terms of number of lines of assembled code, than programming that supports humanlike intelligence. It is not algorithmic complexity or the size of programs, per se, that distinguishes the epistemologically simple from the epistemologically complex. Rather, the distinction turns on whether the programming and hardware are capable of supporting intelligence that, positively, is capable of representing the world in an adequate way and supports more or less intelligent real-time interaction with the world and, negatively, doesn't founder on the frame problem.

Moreover, I don't wish to suggest that there is no overlap between epistemologically simple learning and epistemologically complex learning. For example, epistemologically complex learning might well make use of epistemologically simple procedures as subroutines. In fact, perhaps most of whatever it is that comprises EC learning capacity is itself capable only of epistemologically simple learning. I take these to be open, empirical questions that my distinction need not, at this point in the essay, address.

There appears to be no way at present, however, to extend the programming techniques that support ES learning so that they support EC learning. EC learning differs from ES learning qualitatively, not simply quantitatively. My suspicion is that adult persons still know more facts about the world than computers do; however, I take it as an empirical question whether current computers can recall more "facts" than people do. Some writers think they can, some do not. My point is that little turns on this quantitative question. ES learning, as I have defined it, is not extendible into EC learning by means of adding prodigious quantities of facts or production rules.

It might be objected that we don't know whether we can take computer systems capable currently of epistemologically simple learning such as the Coin Toss game and, by extending the techniques we find there, enhancing the techniques, increasing the speed, and so on, that we might encounter an emergent property much as we do in biological systems. In some respects, for example, there is striking functional dissimilarity, presumably, in terms of mental capacities, between the Adapis, of the lemur family, which the theory of evolution takes as our distant ancestor, and Homo sapiens. Yet, the physical dissimilarities seem to be dissimilarities of degree, not kind; the brains of the two species have a good deal in common physically. According to some interpreters of the theory of evolution, such as Margolis (see my discussion in Chapter 5), small genetic and structural differences, under selective pressures, have given rise to stunning functional differences. If we can understand the rich mental life of human beings as an emergent property in natural history, which is supported by functional differentiation over largely conserved physical structure, so the objection would go, we might similarly expect that epistemologically complex learning might emerge when we arrange programs and data correctly, and get enough of it focused in just the right way for the task. Evolution took thousands of millions of years, it is often pointed out; give computer science a few more before drawing such strong conclusions.

I have no telling rebuttal to this variation on the classic "give us a few more years" objection, but I claim that the evidence currently does not favor such a view. Specifically, and I will offer a more developed argument later, the frame problem counts decisively against the hope that programs and hardware supporting epistemologically simple learning can be extended (faster and more CPUs, bigger programs, more efficient algorithms, better look-up mechanisms, etc.) such that support for epistemologically complex learning emerges. It is the frame problem that demarcates epistemologically simple learning from epistemologically complex learning, and it is the evident intractability of the frame problem that makes it difficult to imagine how current programming and hardware can be improved to solve the problem.

CHAPTER 3

Computer Simulation and User Illusions

During the course of teaching computer science for a number of years, I have found that students have difficulty fully grasping that programming involves mapping the problems we want solved onto the resources of a computer. Computers don't intrinsically know anything, of course, about interest rates, derivatives, or thunderstorms, but we can map solutions to such problem classes onto the data structures and instruction sets of computers, and, assuming the programming gets the mapping right, computers can then solve problems that belong to those problem classes. Constructing the map successfully means reaching an understanding of the problem class, the resources available in the computing environment, and how the former can be functionally defined in terms of the latter.

Some problems are computationally irreducible; that is to say, no computationally definable map can be constructed to solve them directly. As a result, it is necessary to attack them indirectly by means of simulations. For example, it is known (see Toffoli & Margolus, 1988) that cellular automata can simulate any possible physical system. Such simulations, however, raise some particularly slippery philosophical issues. For example, since a simulation is designed to get us to see what (with arguably few exceptions) is literally not there, what kinds of philosophical caveats are in order when we characterize the properties of such simulations? In other words, in what sense does a simulation capture the properties of the system it is simulating? Additionally, when the behavior of a simulation, for the purposes at hand, becomes difficult to distinguish from the behavior of the system being simulated, what, if anything, justifies a distinction between the two—at what point does a steadily improving simulation become a functional duplication?

In this chapter, I would like to explore some of what it means for a digital computer to simulate a natural phenomenon. This chapter will look at some common simulations and attempt to understand why they are effective. I will make some comments about simulation in general and advance some philosophical cautions about characterizing the "user illusion" (Kay, 1984) that defines our use of a simulation. I hope that one additional distinction I will develop, namely, that between I/O descriptions and process descriptions, will help illumine aspects of what kinds of inferences we can justifiably draw about computer processes, given certain kinds of simulation I/O. The goal is to begin developing the philosophic resources needed to address questions associated with the Turing test. More concretely, the distinction should help in determining what kinds of process descriptions are warranted by I/O evaluations such as "GreatTalker 5.1 is able to converse about a number of subjects in the kinds of ways we would expect a well-informed, native speaker of the language to converse ."

The Computer as Simulation Machine

Figure 3–1 illustrates convincingly, I think, that the skilled manipulation of binary strings can generate some extraordinary simulations. In Figure 3–1's Graphic 1, for example, we see the binary information that encodes the image in Graphic 2—which is to say that images can be encoded by means of ordering bits on a string, using a computer program. While the image in Graphic 2 does not seem obviously to be part of a recognizable image, with some effort, it becomes apparent that it is a simulation of the lower center part of Graphic 4. All four graphics are simulations, to be sure, but Graphic 2 is a simulation of Graphic 4 because it is a scaled portion of it—each pixel in Graphic 2 is expanded to a 7 × 7 pixel grid.

In Graphic 3, which is a scaled simulation of the extreme lower right of Graphic 4, a distinctive property emerges, namely, three-dimensionality. The short lesson seems to be that, if a computer gets the bits ordered just so, the image stimulates us visually in such a way

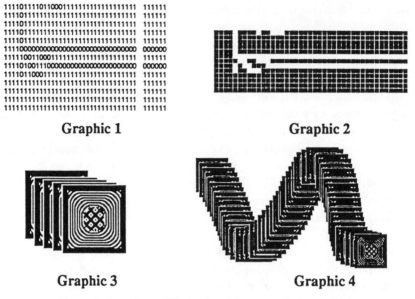

Graphic 1

Graphic 2

Graphic 3

Graphic 4

Figure 3-1. Three Dimensional Image as Information

that we perceive a three-dimensional image. In other words, skilled manipulation of the bits is capable of generating in certain kinds of perceivers an experience that one might not expect bit manipulation to be capable of producing. Graphic 4 gives us the complete three-dimensional image. While it would require a long string of bits, many times longer than the one we see in Graphic 1, Graphic 4 is encoded as one more string of bits in the computer storage. Manipulated the correct way, by a computer program and some reasonably competent "mouse-strokes," the bit string, or *stream*, as the hackers like to put it, yields a stimulating three-dimensional image.

Phenomena of the most diverse sorts can be simulated on a computer. The reason is that one way to understand a computer is that it is a simulation machine. People sometimes think of computers as large calculators, as giant electronic machines woodenly grinding out answers. But this view is shortsighted. Early in computing history, we used a variety of nonnumerical techniques to accomplish mathematical tasks, such as compiling the statistics for the national census. But the tables are turning. Increasingly, we use sophisticated mathematical techniques to accomplish nonnumerical tasks.

What's most remarkable about computers is that, from a blindingly fast ability to "crunch numbers" at their most basic level, a stunning ability to do a host of things emerges at the level at which we usually interact with them. Even in the 19th century, Augusta Ada anticipated that the computer would be the first general purpose machine in which the program determines what specific machine it will be at any particular moment. As we saw in the last chapter, the power of the computer lies in the fact that the simple can generate the complex, provided there are a useful representation, enough time, and the right program to manipulate the representation in the requisite way.

It turns out that a machine which can add and subtract numbers, which can perform logical operations such as ANDing and ORing, can process ideas and manipulate images and, therefore, can also simulate many kinds of phenomena. As Alan Kay (1984, p. 59) observes, the computer is a dynamic metamedium that can simulate any other medium:

> The protean nature of the computer is such that it can act like a machine or like a language to be shaped and exploited. It is a medium that can dynamically simulate the details of any other medium, including media that cannot exist physically. . . . It is the first metamedium, and as such it has degrees of freedom for representation and expression never before encountered and as yet barely investigated.

The freedom of representation and expression is signal. A medium which can dynamically simulate the details of any other medium is a medium made to order for analytical activity. For every analysis of a problem is at once, at some level or levels deep, a simulation of it — a reproduction, an abstraction, a shorthand description of it, so that we can attend to salient mechanisms, pertinent causal relationships and so on in our attempt to understand and predict.

Extending Kay's term, I want to characterize the computer as an *analytical metamedium*. I call it this since the simulation capacity of the computer lends itself so well to conceptual analysis. The computer's simulation of the phenomena we find interesting, if the simulation takes robust advantage of the computer's capacities, occurs at speeds that allow us to attend to the content of the problem's analysis rather than the mechanisms of its representation. In analyzing problems, the human mind often works in flashes and stops; it surges with insight and gets bogged down in quagmires. Since a computer can often simulate faster than we can imagine, it doesn't get in the way when we are "on a roll." And when we get bogged down in the quagmires, it helps us break free by challenging us with alternate construals and what if? games.

Computers are theaters of the mind in which the user plays a significant part in the production on the screen. They enable the theater we create on screen, in Alan Kay's provocative term, the "user illusion," which mirrors what we have in mind as we attempt to conceptualize and analyze the problems we find interesting. Turkle (1984, p. 14) even suggests that the computer is "like a Rorschach inkblot test," a characterization nicely compatible with Winograd and Flores's characterizations of perception that I discuss later in the chapter.

A computer simulates something when it represents, in one or more respects, that thing's behavior or characteristics. The representation need not be exact, nor must it be done at the same speed as the original. The most commonly used simulations on computers today are spreadsheets and word processors. While we might not usually think of a word processing document on a computer screen as a simulation, a moment's reflection reveals that is what it is. As illustrated in Figure 3-2, a word processor simulates how documents would appear if printed. The tiny picture elements on screen, called "pixels," are used to simulate both the text of the working document and the word processing environment that allows the user to manipulate the text.

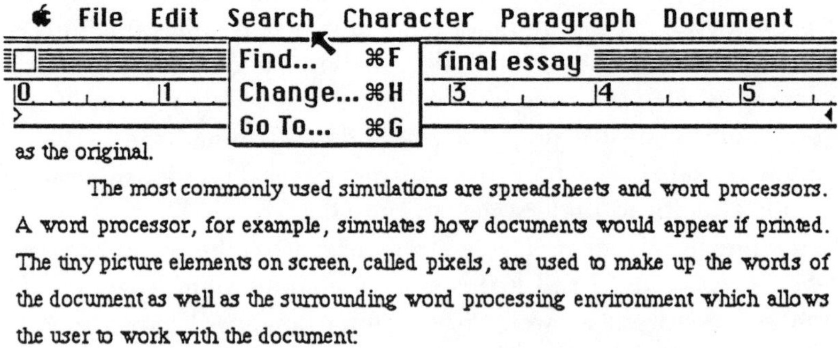

 File   Edit   Search   Character   Paragraph   Document

Find... ⌘F   final essay
Change... ⌘H
Go To... ⌘G

as the original.

The most commonly used simulations are spreadsheets and word processors. A word processor, for example, simulates how documents would appear if printed. The tiny picture elements on screen, called pixels, are used to make up the words of the document as well as the surrounding word processing environment which allows the user to work with the document.

Figure 3-2. A Word Processor Simulated How a Page Would Appear If Printed. Since the screen is made of thousands of tiny picture elements or pixels, text and graphics on a computer screen are comprised of pixels which are arranged in the necessary manner. Since the number of pixels per inch is limited, in this case 72 per inch, the resolution or clarity of the text image is not as good as that which is printed by some printers which print at 300 dpi.

The low resolution of the graphic in Figure 3–2, particularly when compared with the rest of the page, illustrates that characters on a computer screen are comprised of tiny pixels. What is on screen looks much like a part of a page from this essay but closer inspection reveals that it is a clever simulation of a page, which uses thousands of tiny pixels to simulate a sheet of paper with typing on it (the acronym is WYSIWYG — or "What You See Is What You Get"). The simulation is powerful because we can manipulate the simulated document in a wide variety of ways at computer speeds. We can try different approaches, alternate wordings, and variant expressions with only a modest investment of time. As a result, the user can attend more to the analysis and expression of words and ideas and less to the impeding mechanics of the medium.

By virtue of being an analytical metamedium, the computer can serve as a word processor one moment, an art historian illustrating Florentine linear perspective the next, a biologist illustrating the double helix structure of DNA the next. In each case, the analytical freedom that characterizes the composition of words attends the illustration of art and the manipulation of biological structure. As demonstrated in Figure 3–3, which is a three-dimensional exploration of Uccello's chalice study that I developed using a 3-D graphics package, a computer is an analytical metamedium that amplifies our understanding and enables us to make connections, to see things that we almost certainly would miss otherwise. We can look at things from different angles, in varying lights, against different backgrounds, and thereby generate new insight into even what is very old. As Figure 3–3 illustrates, a simulation such as a graphical representation of a medieval chalice can be quite a convincing simulation, but none of us supposes, since we can bring to bear the insight that pixels and gold have different properties, that the chalice can actually hold wine. It gets more difficult when the simulation is something as difficult to characterize adequately as thinking.

The simulation of physical systems has usually been done on conventional serial computers with partial differential equations. In the future, by means of using massively parallel systems, simulations will become more sophisticated and realistic. Massively parallel systems are now beginning to be used to simulate complex adaptive systems that are computationally irreducible. The striking output from serial-based cellular automata, which can simulate evolving systems

Figure 3-3. I did this simulation of Paolo Uccello's (1397–1475) perspective analysis of a chalice using a three-dimensional graphics package. I owe the idea of attempting to do such a simulation study to Jacob Bronowski (1973). It illustrates both the power of computer simulation and some of the history of science this century. As this series illustrates, the principal paradigm in the physical sciences is shifting from mass/energy towards information/program. In the extreme left, the chalice appears substantial; the structural, informational component is hidden. In the middle left, the structural component has emerged but still seems less important than the matter it informs. In the middle right, the structural has submerged the material. In the extreme right, we view the chalice from above; structure has triumphed completely and the dominant motif is geometrical symmetry. I should emphasize that these are not four different graphics but the same graphic viewed from three different angles and two distinct lighting backdrops. As an analytical metamedium, the digital computer excels at this sort of simulation.

whose outcomes cannot be computed directly, hints at some of what will be possible in the future on massively parallel computers.

So far in this chapter I have been extolling the virtues of computer simulation. However, as opponents of the Turing test have emphasized, there is cause for concern in terms of how to understand what appears on screen in a skilled simulation. WYSIWYG is achievable in word processors; the worry in terms of natural language simulations is whether we won't get what we think we are seeing. That is, we will falsely conclude that we see something when, in fact, it is not there. After making several remarks about perception, I'd like to consider the graphics in Figure 3–1 one more time.

The classical assumption in Western tradition, at least, has been that, for the person not hallucinating or otherwise experiencing visual impairment, there is something approximating a one-to-one correspondence between optic nerve activity and retinal stimulation. Classical Western empiricists such as Locke and Hume emphasized and extended what was to become the dominant empiricist outlook in English-speaking countries: all knowledge grows out of what is presented in sensory experience. Some evolutionary studies in the last 30 years, however, have concluded that the survival needs of the perceiving organism play a decisive role in the construction of that which is perceived. One of the things that Fischler and Firschein (1987) remind us of is that vision developed to support survival and that the brain developed to support vision. The obvious inference is that the brain developed to support survival. For example, visual acuity at some distance would only be useful to an organism that could develop a course of action, by some kind of planning or instinctive behavior richer than limited tropisms, that would assist its survival needs. This would explain why grasshoppers, for instance, are evidently quite near-sighted. As Fischler and Firschein wrote, "it would appear that physical, perceptual, and intellectual competence are interdependent and must evolve as a coherent whole, rather than as independent entities" (1987, p. 210).

These sorts of considerations convince me that we have not taken selective pressures seriously enough in attempting to understand the conditions necessary for the generation of intelligence. Evidently agreeing, Winograd and Flores (1986, p. 42) argued that "Perception . . . must be studied from the inside rather than the outside — looking at properties of the nervous system as a generator of phenomena, rather than as a filter on the mapping of reality." Winograd and Flores's claim may be a tad strong, shaped as it is by a Continental philosophical agenda, but it serves as a corrective to the epistemologically naive assumption, partly generated by and embodied in Western empiricism, that we can simply see what is there. But I believe we should accept at least this much: perception is a biological phenomenon as well as an object of epistemological investigation and the plausible story some evolutionists tell us is that it is shaped significantly by the survival needs of the perceiver: what we see is conditioned in part by what we need to find. Appealing to the work of the Chilean biologist Maturana, they add the following considerations:

> Maturana argues that all activity of the nervous system is best understood in this way. The focus should be on the interactions within the system as a whole, not on the structure of the perturbations. The perturbations do not determine what happens in the nervous system, but merely trigger changes of state. It is the structure of the perturbed system that determines, or better, *specifies* what structural configurations of the medium can perturb it. (pp. 43–44)

To cite the obvious, visible light constitutes only about an octave of the "keyboard" of the electromagnetic spectrum. In other words, I am physically able to attend to only a small part of the electromagnetic spectrum that floods this room. I cannot see, unaided, the FM radio waves that I believe surround me at this moment, because the "structure of the perturbed system" (me) is not directly amenable to FM radio-wave perturbation. Even the best researchers, to cite a different example, have a propensity to see that which confirms their theories and to ignore putatively disconfirming evidence. In some cases, they even see, sometimes fraudulently but sometimes not, what others are not able to see, and we conclude that their experimental results have not been replicated.

It is almost a commonplace now that we do not visually perceive with our eyes. The eyes act as sensors and pass along sensory data to the visual cortex of the brain, which is our principal organ of vision. The entire brain is charged with the task of constructing an interpretation of the screened data. Fischler and Firschein (1987) point out that primitive eyes, at "lower" levels in the evolutionary scale, are more like "goal-oriented detectors" than cameras. Memory and "hard-wired" pattern-recognition processes likely have as much bearing on what is perceived as what is sensed by the eyes.

In Graphic 4 of Figure 3–1, we see an image that we interpret three-dimensionally. By contrast, the image in Graphic 2 seems flat and not at all three-dimensional. The arrangement of the dots in Graphic 4, at approximately 300 dots per inch resolution, stimulates the human brain in such a way that we attribute three-dimensionality to Graphic 4 but not Graphic 2. I would guess that lower animals and persons with certain kinds of parieto-occipital damage would not perceive three dimensions upon viewing Graphic 2.

The point I wish to make is that simulations are designed to get us to see or experience something that is literally not there. As Searle (1984) points out, no one imagines that a simulation of a storm will drench the persons witnessing the simulated downpour. Simulation is designed to present a manipulatable image, portrayal, or representation, so that we can manipulate it and hopefully learn more about the phenomenon simulated. Here is the larger philosophic point: because the computer is so ideally suited to such simulations, we have to be careful not to mistake a computer simulation for that which is simulated. It takes some philosophical discipline, in short, to resist specious blurrings of differences between simulations and the phenomena they simulate.

It should particularly be noticed that we have a proclivity to see, at least in some senses, what is not there and to advance ascriptions about a simulation that, upon closer inspection, will often prove difficult to justify. As Hume argued, we are given to making inferences based more upon habituation than any relationships necessarily intrinsic to the phenomena we are considering. To the point, we habitually ascribe intelligence to a skilled conversationalist. It could be argued that to conclude that a machine that passes the Turing test is thinking is to make a mistake parallel to the mistake of concluding that serpentine three-dimensionality is one of Graphic 4's intrinsic properties. The graphical moral is that we have to exercise even more philosophic caution than usual when interpreting computer simulations. It is because the computer is so deft at generating "user illusions" that we have to be particularly careful about the ascriptions we make about what is "there."

I/O Descriptions and Process Descriptions/Ascriptions

This essay has looked at several kinds of simulation. The first, namely, AugsAsm, simulates a primitive assembler. Such a primitive assembler is no conceptual puzzler, since the formal operations were defined exhaustively by the table shown. By contrast, in the Coin Toss game, there is an attempt to simulate a much more formidable phenomenon, namely, learning. To state the obvious, learning is a much more involved, problematic phenomenon to simulate, both because it presumably has many aspects to it and because it is much less well understood. The contrasting levels of difficulty of these two problem domains suggest to me that it would be helpful to draw a distinction between what I will call *I/O-simulation* and *P-simulation* or, as I will sometimes put it, since a primary interest of this essay will be what kinds of descriptions of I/O-simulations warrant which kinds of descriptions of the processes supporting the input/output, between *I/O descriptions* and *process descriptions* or *ascriptions*.

In I/O-simulation (IOS), what we attempt to simulate is output as compared to input, relative to the system being simulated, in the context in which the simulation is taking place. For example, all of the chess programs with which I am familiar should be described as I/O-simulations. There is little or no effort to simulate human chess playing in terms of the *process* that people presumably use to play chess. While we don't know a great deal about how people play games like chess, it seems obvious that they don't play it the way that current chess programs play it. (My guess is that a significant component of human chess playing, as in any game, is deeply pattern-recognition based, rather than rule-based.) As a result, the level of simulation is only input/output deep. In fact, much of what currently passes as "AI" is only IOS, and, to be sure, often such I/O-simulation is perfectly suitable for the task at hand.

In the Coin Toss program discussed in the previous chapter, to choose the obvious example, there is no attempt to write the program so that it simulates the processes that people presumably use to play the game. The programmatic mechanisms are designed to create effective output, given the input of the game string. If the mechanisms are such that the term *learning* should be applied to how they work, at least on some views of what constitutes "learning," it is on the basis of the relation of the output to the input, and the fact that the programmatic mechanisms produce improvement in the play. There is no attempt to simulate the processes supporting how people play the game.

In *process* or *P-simulation*, on the other hand, not only do we attempt to simulate output as compared to input, in a way that parallels that which is being simulated, we attempt to simulate the process, to some level of depth, by which the output is gotten from the input as well, relative to the system being simulated. For example, if we were to write chess-playing programs with an eye to simulating the *way* human chess champions play, this would count as an attempt at P-simulation. We could distinguish a number of levels of P-simulation: a less deep level of chess P-simulation might simply incorporate a number of rules of thumb that specific chess players reputedly employ. A much deeper P-simulation might attempt to simulate the way that one person plays chess, taking into account his or her favored strategies, personal idiosyncrasies, perhaps even taking into account this or that psychological or biological profile of the person. The point is that P-simulation can be taken to many different levels deep. The more deeply a simulation emulates that which is simulated, obviously, the more must be known about the system which is simulated.

In the case of the AugsAsm computer, the simulation formally captures the processes involved — there is nothing left that might be investigated and programmed. Computer simulations of other computers, which are admittedly complex, are nevertheless comparatively straightforward since there is no in-principle or in-practice (for the skilled) inaccessibility in that being simulated. While the limits of what may be computed remain rather poorly understood, there is no in-principle impairment to understanding what a computer does, since Turing machines exhaustively define computability.

As a corollary, it follows that, if little is known about a system that we want to simulate, any P-simulation will necessarily be quite shallow or may not be possible at all; in such a case we may be limited to an I/O simulation. The obvious example is simulation of human mentality, especially intelligence. The larger claim of this essay is that our poor understanding of human intelligence has limitative consequences for our attempt to construct machines that attempt significantly to simulate or duplicate the processes that generate intelligence.

It may be, as is often the case in research in artificial intelligence, that what we are interested in is descriptions of input/output simulations and what we can infer about the processes that are used to generate the simulation. In this case, the processes supporting the input/output simulation are probably not best considered simulations themselves but are simply the mechanisms used to support the simulation. As a result, to be more accurate, it is best to refer to characterizations of the processes that support the I/O simulation as "process descriptions." In terms of the Coin Toss game, for example, a string array was used in a look-up table to support the simulated playing of the game. As the game progressed, what was visible on screen was a simulation of game playing. Talk of "arrays" and "look-up tables" is a process description. In building a program to simulate something, we think in terms of what processes will be needed to support what simulations. But occasionally, we may want to go the reverse direction and attempt to determine if the simulation, along with some general computer science knowledge and some related philosophical considerations, would justify characterizations about the processes supporting the simulation—without specific knowledge of the programming supporting the simulation. Namely, can we justifiably make some process ascriptions on the basis—either principally or exclusively—of I/O descriptions? It is the defensibility of this kind of I/O-based inferences about supporting process, when applied to the relationship of thinking and mature conversational ability, that will occupy much of the rest of this essay.

CHAPTER 4

The Dreyfus Critique and the Frame Problem

In this chapter, I attempt three tasks. First, I undertake an exposition of Hubert Dreyfus's critique of artificial intelligence; second, I attempt to reach an understanding of the frame problem; and, last, and somewhat less importantly, I try to distill some of the relationship of the Dreyfus critique with the frame problem.[1] It is my claim that some of the Dreyfus critique historically anticipated current discussions of the frame problem, and that the frame problem, because it lends itself to a philosophically clearer analysis than much of the Dreyfus critique of AI, is a good way to articulate some of what Dreyfus evidently has been attempting to say for so long. In terms of the principal task of this essay, which is to distill some of the implications of the frame problem for the Turing test, a clear understanding of the frame problem, of course, is essential.

In terms of the Dreyfus exposition, I will attempt to articulate the Dreyfus claim that AI is predicated on a mistaken view of human problem solving and reasoning that is endemic in Western philosophical and scientific traditions. Although I will offer occasional kind and critical words about the Dreyfus program, my principal goal will not be to assay the Dreyfus critique of AI. Rather, my principal goal in the

---

[1]Unless there is a good reason to do so, I will not distinguish between Hubert and Stuart Dreyfus. As a result, I will often use locutions such as "Dreyfus and Dreyfus" or "the Dreyfus critique" to refer to the work of both Hubert and Stuart Dreyfus.

first part of the chapter is an exposition of the critique, particularly as it anticipates the frame problem.

The Dreyfus critique has been widely criticized by both philosophers and cognitive scientists — and, to be sure, I find myself agreeing with many of the criticisms. As chronicled in McCorduck (1979), some writers have questioned Hubert Dreyfus's philosophic ability; others dismiss his Continental philosophy-based work as a "ball of fluff," while still others claim that he understands little technical AI and therefore doesn't warrant serious rebuttal. As a result, it might be asked why the Dreyfus critique warrants investigation in this essay. The answer is that while *What Computers Can't Do* (1979) is showing its age, and while I readily concede that there are numerous problems with its argument, some of the points it makes — as illustrated, I believe, by the increasing interest in the frame problem — are demonstrating significant staying power. With the publication of *Mind Over Machine* (1986), which Hubert Dreyfus wrote in collaboration with his brother Stuart, and with former AI proponents such as Terry Winograd (Winograd & Flores, 1986) now offering criticisms of AI that parallel the Dreyfus critique, it now seems likely that much of the philosophic criticism of artificial intelligence will consist of the "poor substitute" strategy. According to this objection to AI, aside from a preliminary successful first step here or there and some occasional, narrowly defined successes, AI will prove to be a poor substitute for human intelligence. Winograd and Flores (1986), for example, observe that "Dreyfus and Dreyfus, in *Mind Over Machine* (1986, p. 99), argue along lines very similar to ours that expertise cannot be captured in any collection of formal rules."

In terms of the Turing test, AI will not get good enough, according to the poor substitute strategy, that we will have to assess the philosophical significance of the claim that an intelligent computer has passed the test. In other words, we will need to concern ourselves less with what Haugeland calls the "hollow shell" strategy, exemplified perhaps most notably by Searle's "Chinese Room" counterexample, because computers will not get good enough to fool us significantly in the first place. Against Searle, Haugeland (1981b) argues that the poor substitute strategy "is much more likely to succeed" (pp. 33–34). With this type of criticism of AI becoming more widespread, and with Dreyfus offering amplifications of it, as a result, I believe that his work warrants a fresh look.

The Dreyfus exposition is designed to set the stage for the central task of the chapter, which is to reach a clear articulation of the frame problem. As I said at the outset, there are two distinct reasons why an understanding of the frame problem is essential.

First, reaching a crisp understanding of the frame problem is an effective way to explicate in a clearer way what Dreyfus has been claiming for a quarter century. As Dennett (1987, p. 43) remarks, in reference to *What Computers Can't Do*, "Dreyfus sought to show that AI was a fundamentally mistaken method for studying the mind, and in fact many of his declared insights into their intrinsic limitations can be seen to hover quite systematically in the neighborhood of the frame problem." It is my claim that there is a significant relationship between the Dreyfus critique and the frame problem that warrants investigation, and that an understanding of the frame problem is not only pivotal in assessing the Turing test but is also useful in interpreting the Dreyfus critique.

Second, since the primary goal of this essay is to reach an understanding of the relationship of the frame problem to the Turing test, it is obvious that a clarification of the meaning of "the frame problem" is necessary. As stated in Chapter 1, I hope to reach an understanding of the frame problem in order to determine whether or not its solution is necessarily presupposed by a computer system that (in some significant sense) passed the Turing test and, in general, to determine some of the implications of the frame problem for the Turing test. This is not to say that I wish to claim that how I define the *frame problem* is the only way it can be defined. Other interpretations are certainly possible and the frame problem, on those alternate understandings, would presumably bear different relationships to the Turing test.

Another reason to explore the frame problem is the growing interest in it; I'll cite only four of many examples in contemporary literature. Fischler and Firschein (1987), for instance, cite the frame problem as one of the enduring philosophical questions associated with AI. Winograd and Flores's *Understanding Computers and Cognition* (1986) involves many issues related to the frame problem. Flanagan (1991, p. 235) cites it as one of the 10 problems facing AI. Last, and most significant, Pylyshyn's (1987) anthology is entirely devoted to the frame problem. As a result, it seems fair to conclude that the frame problem has achieved the status of an important problem in current philosophical discussions of AI.

1. The Dreyfus Critique

Better than a quarter century ago, Hubert Dreyfus launched his contentious critique of artificial intelligence with RAND Corporation's reportedly reluctant publication of "Alchemy and Artificial Intelligence." Seven years later, in 1972, a book-length expansion of this paper, *What Computers Can't Do: A Critique of Artificial Reason* (Dreyfus, 1979), was published. A central claim of both the paper and the book is that artificial intelligence is predicated on an understanding of human intelligence as rule-based manipulation of formal constituents that goes back at least to the time of Plato.

> Since the Greeks invented logic and geometry, the idea that all reasoning might be reduced to some kind of calculation — so that all arguments could be settled once and for all — has fascinated most of the Western tradition's most rigorous thinkers. . . . The story of artificial intelligence might well begin around 450 B.C. . . . Socrates is asking Euthyphro for what modern computer theorists would call an "effective procedure," "a set of rules which tells us, from moment to moment, precisely how to behave." (1979, p. 67)

Dreyfus disdains what he takes to be the anachronistic attribution of AI claims to Plato by arguing that Plato understood the reasoning brain to manipulate its contents in terms of semantically — rather than syntactically — based rules, since "His [Plato's] rules presupposed that the person understood the meanings of the constitutive terms" (1979, p. 68). As a result, according to Dreyfus, Plato never supposed that reasoning is amenable to formalization; meanings play an indispensable role in the cognitive manipulations.

Dreyfus cursorily traces what he claims is the inexorable movement in Western tradition towards the belief that thought and knowledge are, in principle, completely formalizable. As many others have, he observes that Hobbes claimed that "'REASON . . . is nothing but reckoning'" (1979, p. 69). He attributes to Leibniz, the inventor of the base two number system on which most modern computers are based, the goal of inventing the formal language necessary to realize the purportedly long-held Western goal of an unambiguous formal language capable of manipulating symbols purely formally, according to a clearly defined set of rules.

After surveying familiar 19th-century figures such as George Boole and Charles Babbage, Dreyfus moves the discussion to Turing and the Turing test. Anticipating part of the subsequent discussion in AI, Dreyfus argues that "Philosophers may doubt whether merely behavioral similarity could ever give adequate ground for the attribution of intelligence, but as a goal for those actually trying to construct thinking machines, and as a criterion for critics to use in evaluating their work, Turing's test was just what was needed" (p. 73). Over the last 25 years, philosophers have indeed repeatedly questioned whether attribution of intelligence is justifiable on the basis of externally observable behavior alone, and the Turing test did, in fact, serve as the most important measure for what should count as intelligence for many working in AI. Recall that I called the Turing test a "fountainhead" in Chapter 1 for this reason. As a result, it seems fair to conclude that Dreyfus presciently anticipated much subsequent AI history.

On the other hand, there are some arguments in *What Computers Can't Do* that I find unconvincing. Among other problems, there is a polemical, sarcastic tone to the Introduction to the original version which the older Dreyfus largely avoids in *Mind Over Machine*. I'll cite just one example. Dreyfus calls our attention to the fact that "Of course, no digital computer immediately volunteered or was drafted for Turing's game" (p. 73). While such remarks should be evaluated with at least some reference to the heated context in which they were written (as chronicled by McCorduck, 1979), the fact remains that such comments serve more to inflame passions than enlighten perspectives and, consequently, they diminish the book's value.

More seriously, he reaches many of his conclusions with too little justification. For instance, he suggests that, "if reason can be programmed into a computer, this will confirm an understanding of man as an object, which Western thinkers have been groping toward for two thousand years but which they only now have the tools to express" (p. 78). There are several elementary philosophical objections here: for example, what are we to understand by *reason* in this sentence? *Reason* has many usages and senses, and distinguishing carefully between them is the philosopher's task. In one (perhaps narrow) sense, computers reason when they take one course of action rather than another, given the magnitude of intermediate data. Dreyfus surely means more than this, but at least the immediate context doesn't spell out what we are to understand by his use of *reason*. Much the same objection can be lodged about the word *confirm* in this sentence.

Moreover, he has not spelled out what we are to make of the perplexing notion of "man as object." Two possibilities for why he did not spell out the notion come to mind. First, Dreyfus operates largely from a Continental philosophic perspective, and perhaps he would claim that such a background provides the tacit hermeneutical context for interpreting this passage. If so, since philosophic work in the Continental tradition is especially subject to such varying interpretations and assessments, I don't find this possible assumption reasonable. Second, he might take the phrase "man as object" to be sufficiently obvious in meaning that no special definition is necessary. But I find this even less plausible than the first alternative. As a result, we have ill-defined terms playing pivotal roles in a sentence whose claim cannot therefore be adequately supported. I take this example to be a typical illustration of Dreyfus at his least convincing. Generally speaking, here and there the reader gets glimpses of what he has in mind, but he doesn't take adequate time to spell out unclear notions and contentious use of words that are subject to different interpretations. He moves too quickly, takes scanty evidence to entail more than it does, and takes quick references to prominent philosophers to support disputatious conclusions.

In sum, I take it as established that there are soft spots in *What Computers Can't Do*. But there is something of distinct value here nonetheless. While in the 1960s and even 1970s much of the discussion turned on the expected rapid advances of AI, and many essays tackled the thorny issues involved in Turing's imitation game, presumably on the assumption that a computer would eventually likely do well in the Imitation Game and hence force the big question of whether to attribute intelligence, Dreyfus correctly anticipated that progress in AI would be slower than was widely anticipated, and that some efforts would come to a dead end after an initial period of well-publicized success. Later, in *Mind Over Machine*, The Drefuses call this the "fallacy of the first successful step": success in the first stages does not mean that subsequent efforts will be successful. In other words, there is something to be said for the claim that Dreyfus saw a problem in the raft of audacious claims and expectations surrounding AI when many others did not: AI has, in fact, progressed more slowly than most proponents supposed it would, and, consequently, the prospects of a machine passing the Turing test in the near term now appear much lower than many would have guessed 10 and 20 years ago. To put it another way, as the years have passed, the poor substitute critique of AI, which was initially espoused by Dreyfus and not many others, has come to rival the hollow shell argument as a compelling way to criticize AI.

Much more recently remarks published by S. R. Graubard in the Preface to the *Daedalus* issue (Winter, 1988) devoted to AI provide at least some vindication for Dreyfus's early objections:

> AI is something of a myth. Had the name not existed, certain consequences might have been averted — for example, in the early AI community a tendency to exaggerate what might be impending, showing — however unwittingly — a kind of hubris that, in retrospect, seems both unbecoming and unnecessary. In suggesting that a machine with vast intellectual capability was in the offing and that this new intelligence might quickly be attained, these advocates made themselves hostage to critics, who, increasingly aware of the limitations of certain of the theories being advanced, insisted on their inadequacies. The critics resented the exaggeration implicit in the claims of those who saw only the promise of quick results and the epistemological assumptions implicit in the name the field had given itself. (p. V)

It is interesting that this passage shares some themes with the early Dreyfus, yet it was published in 1988. Conspicuous among such early "critics" would, of course, have been Dreyfus. As a result, I think it is fair to conclude that at least some of the objections articulated by the early Dreyfus have found wider acceptance than many Dreyfus critics would have supposed in the late 1960s and early 1970s.

Moreover, he correctly surmised that there is an acute problem in the general vicinity of what we now call the *frame problem*. The specific argument that most clearly anticipates the frame problem appears in the introduction to the revised edition of *What Computers Can't Do*, which was published seven years after the first edition, in 1979. Here Dreyfus claims that the importance of common sense, of background knowledge, became increasingly evident in the years following the publication of the first edition. Not only common sense, generally understood, but what is to count as relevant, is claimed by Dreyfus (1979) to be overlooked in the AI account of intelligence:

> Work during the first five years (1967–1972) demonstrated the futility of trying to evade the importance of everyday context by creating artificial gamelike contexts preanalyzed in terms of a list of fixed-relevance features. More recent work has thus been forced to deal directly with the background of commonsense know-how which guides our changing sense of what counts as the relevant facts. (p. 56)

As I will attempt to argue, the question of what "counts as the relevant facts" in a changing situation is integral to the general frame problem. Of course, Dreyfus is quite correct in reminding us that the move from artificial contexts such as game playing, which are examples of *microworlds*, to the real or *macroworld* context is the move that generates the need for an AI system to have something like common sense so that the problem of what is to count as relevant can be solved. Dreyfus appeals to Wittgenstein's discussion of rules and rule following to point out that the attempt to base behavior on rules has to make a troublesome assumption:

> My thesis, which owes a lot to Wittgenstein, is that whenever human behavior is analyzed in terms of rules, these rules must always contain a *ceteris paribus* condition, i.e., they apply "everything else being equal," and what "everything else" and "equal" means in any specific situation can never be fully spelled out without a regress . . . [since] the *ceteris paribus* condition points to a background of practices which are the condition of the possibility of all rulelike activity. (pp. 56–57)

I believe this is the part of the early Dreyfus critique to which Dennett (1987, p. 43) would point to substantiate his claim that "Dreyfus never explicitly mentions the frame problem, but is it perhaps the smoking pistol he was looking for but didn't quite know how to describe?" The problem, then, is that we have to assume, if we are basing behavior on a rule-governed system, that everything else will be equal; but this is an undifferentiated way to point to the general frame problem, as I will describe it below. Cashing this out into more concrete terms, a rule-based system such as an AI-based robot, according to Dreyfus, has to assume that everything else will be equal. For example, if it takes a step up an illuminated flight of stairs, it has to assume that this step will not result in the stairway light being switched off—it has to assume that things go as they usually do. In this example, "as they usually do" includes not encountering a first step of a stairway which is a toggle for the stairway lighting. Generally, as we will see, it is quite difficult, perhaps impossible, for a rule-based system to determine what the *ceteris paribus* clause means. This is the part of Dreyfus that I think most clearly anticipates the frame problem.

Dreyfus above acknowledges a debt to Wittgenstein. There is an interesting relation, which I haven't adequately assessed, between the frame problem and Wittgenstein's skeptic as developed by Saul Kripke (1982) in *Wittgenstein on Rules and Private Language*. My suspicion is that we can understand Kripke's skeptic as pretending that he is a machine that contains the rules and definitions that we attach to language, and yet we suppose (erroneously, according to the skeptic) that the rules and definitions are adequate to generate answers to questions we ask him. The skeptic points out they are not. The skeptic effectively seems to feign a frame problem with respect to language usage.

I should emphasize the point that the earlier work anticipated the later work in *Mind Over Machine*. As I will attempt to substantiate below, one of the primary themes of the later work is the claim that human skill acquisition moves from rule-governed *knowing-that* to intuitive *knowing-how*. This theme is present in *What Computers Can't Do*, in nascent form:

> Generally, in acquiring a skill—in learning to drive, dance or pro-
> nounce a foreign language, for example—at first we must slowly,
> awkwardly, and consciously follow the rules. But then there comes a
> moment when we can finally perform automatically. At this point we do
> not seem to be simply dropping these same rigid rules into unconscious-
> ness; rather we seem to have picked up the muscular gestalt which gives
> our behavior a new flexibility and smoothness. (Dreyfus, 1979, pp.
> 248-249)

This claim, that rule following is pronounced early in skill acquisition but is gradually supplanted by a less discrete, more intuitive "gestalt," is articulated in greater detail in *Mind Over Machine*. The Dreyfus claim in this later work is that human skill acquisition involves advancing, progressively, from knowing-that to knowing-how:

> You probably know how to ride a bicycle. Does that mean you can formulate specific rules that would successfully teach someone else how to do it? How would you explain the difference between the feeling of falling over and the perfectly normal sense of being slightly off balance when turning? . . . No you don't. You can ride a bicycle because you possess something called "know-how," which you acquired from practice and sometimes painful experience. The fact that you can't put what you have learned into words means that know-how is not accessible to you in the form of facts and rules. If it were, we would say that you "know that" certain rules produce proficient bicycle riding. (Dreyfus & Dreyfus, 1986, p. 16)

Dreyfus and Dreyfus agree that rule following is necessarily an early ingredient in the skill acquisition process but argue that it progressively fades in importance as the practitioner moves from early, novice states to later, more expert stages. In support of this argument, a five-stage skill-acquisition scheme is advanced.

Before I survey this scheme, however, I would like to identify what I believe is a confusion in their discussion of the relation of human to machine intelligence. In the context of their discussion of the five stages of skill acquisition, they comment, "Once we adequately appreciate the full development of human skilled behavior, we can ask how far along this path the digital computer can reasonably be expected to progress" (p. 20). I assume here that *human skilled behavior* is sufficiently synonymous with *intelligence* that I can use the terms interchangeably in the discussion of what I claim is a confusion on the part of Dreyfus and Dreyfus. This is somewhat unfortunate, since *skilled* human behavior often includes bodily components whose relationship to intelligence is at once fascinating and mysterious. I think Searle (1984, p. 62) is correct that, in the Western analytical tradition, too little attention has been paid to the philosophy of action. He writes, "until recently the philosophy of action was a somewhat neglected subjection. The Western tradition has persistently emphasized knowing as more important than doing." It might be the case that machine intelligence would have to take the same "path" as human intelligence, for reasons ingredient in the nature of intelligence itself, but this auxiliary claim requires the benefit of some evidence or argument.

There might well be *empirical* constraints such that the only path to intelligence is the one followed by protohumans and humans over the eons of natural history—but I fail to see that there are logical constraints forcing artificial intelligence along the same path. Hilary Putnam's (1988) argument, which I discuss below, provides precisely the argument that *Mind Over Machine* needs but does not present. In fact, for reasons discussed later in the chapter, I am sympathetic to this view. My complaint here is that it should not be simply assumed but needs to be acknowledged as an assumption or, alternately, some support should be advanced. I see neither. Support for this auxiliary claim might be found implicitly elsewhere in the text, but I see no support for it in this context and I have not been able to find support for it elsewhere. As a result, coming to a better understanding of human skill acquisition would not, by itself, necessarily shed any light on the prospects for imparting similar skills to machines and it might turn out to be an impediment.

There is a sense, moreover, in which this confusion pervades the entire book. If the goal of AI is to duplicate human intelligence in the sense of replicating intelligence as humans have it, then the Dreyfus criticisms are more compelling. But if the goal is to produce intelligence in machines by whatever means that seem to work—and one powerful insight of functionalism is that the same function (at the I/O level) can be implemented many different ways at the process level—then the Dreyfus critique stands in need of defending the assumption I just mentioned, namely, that we would expect that machine intelligence would develop in ways pioneered by human intelligence.

This caveat noted, consider the claim that, "once we adequately appreciate the full development of human skilled behavior, we can ask how far along this path the digital computer can reasonably be expected to progress" (Dreyfus & Dreyfus, 1986, p. 19). If this is the case, and if we also appeal to Putnam's argument that building an artificial device that can learn in the human community is the most likely or perhaps the only promising avenue for AI, then we are in a position to continue with the Dreyfus program that, by understanding human skill acquisition, we will be in a better position to understand what the prospects are for developing intelligent AI systems.

But let's assess the significance of the five stages. The first stage, according to Dreyfus & Dreyfus, is the *novice* stage. The principal task facing the novice is the acquisition of facts and rules pertinent to the skill in question. According to them, the novice lacks the insight which experience provides, and so judges how well he or she does by how well the rules are followed, given the relevant facts. The point to be noticed, according to them, is that facts and rules dominate the skill acquisition of the novice.

The second stage is the *advanced beginner*. Experience begins to shape the interpretation of the rules and facts that characterized the first stage. Comparisons with earlier examples raise the issue of how the current situation is similar to earlier situations. Even at this early stage, the learner begins to traffic in "perceived similarity" that is not simply a matter of rules ranging over facts, according to Dreyfus and Dreyfus.

The third stage is that of *competence*. This stage is characterized by mastery of the rules and facts, and the learner is a good problem solver in the sense of using the rules and facts, and recognizing that certain "constellations" of rules and facts mean that certain conclusions should be drawn. This stage is important for at least two reasons. First, the Dreyfus claim is that this stage is what cognitive scientists have in mind when they advance the CS understanding of problem solving. At this stage, the learner/problem solver is good at decomposing problem situations into constituent parts, analyzing the parts, and applying pertinent rules and facts to reach a solution to the problem. Second, Dreyfus and Dreyfus argue that expert systems are really competent systems, that what are called "expert systems" have expertise at the level of competence only.

The first three stages exhaust, according to Dreyfus and Dreyfus, what cognitive science understands by possessing a skill and, in fact, intelligence generally. A skill, according to the cognitive science or information-processing model, is the ability to decompose a problem and apply rules, given facts pertinent to the problem, and deduce a solution. The Dreyfus claim is that the cognitive science research program supposes that all intelligent behavior is explainable in these terms.

Simon has written that the entire cognitive research enterprise "rests implicitly on the physical symbol hypothesis: possession of the basic resources of a physical symbol system is both the necessary and sufficient condition for intelligent behavior." (1986, p. 27)

The claim, then, is that the cognitive science program in general and AI in particular have got hold of only part of what skilled intelligence is about, and the most rudimentary, uninteresting part at that. The first three stages comprise what the Dreyfuses understand by the term *knowing-that*. The principal goal of *Mind Over Machine* is to convince us that know-how is not reducible to knowing-that, that knowing-that is what computers are capable of capturing, and that know-how is what human expertise and skill involve. Dreyfus and Dreyfus take it that following from this set of propositions is the conclusion that computers cannot (even functionally) equal human intelligence and skill.

By way of contrast, in their widely cited essay, "Computer Science as Empirical Inquiry," Newell and Simon (Haugeland, 1981) advance the classic AI claim that a physical symbol system is both a necessary and a sufficient condition for intelligence:

> The twenty years of work since then has seen a continuous accumulation of empirical evidence of two main varieties. The first addresses itself to the *sufficiency* of physical symbol systems for producing intelligence, attempting to construct and test specific systems that have such a capability. The second kind of evidence addresses itself to the *necessity* of having a physical symbol system wherever intelligence is exhibited. (pp. 46–47; emphasis in original)

To say that a set of circumstances is sufficient to cause x, of course, is an ambitious claim. To say that it is necessary for x, that x cannot occur without the set, is also a strong claim. To say that it is at once sufficient and necessary is to make the strongest claim possible. It is to say that a physical symbol system is sufficient for intelligence and that, where intelligence exists, there also exists a physical symbol system. It is tantamount to equating intelligence with a physical symbol system. On their view, and diametrically against the Dreyfus brothers, know-how, at least in principle, is reducible to—can be expressed functionally in terms of—knowing-that.

Stages 4 and 5 represent a difference of degree that has become a difference of kind. Proficiency and expertise, for Dreyfus and Dreyfus, are not to be understood in terms of following rules and applying relevant facts in the attempt to solve problems. Instead the analytical increasingly gives way to the intuitive, the decomposable to the holistic.

What they call *holistic similarity recognition* is the claimed ability to recognize patterns as similar to earlier, experienced patterns without having to decompose them into constituent parts. *Know-how* refers to the ability to recognize, without the rule-based effort required at earlier stages, a situation as similar to an earlier situation. What was a piece-meal, mechanical effort earlier becomes a skill characterized by a sense of being effortless and fluid. The graininess of discrete steps, which results from the application of rules, given facts, is replaced by quick recognition of what needs to be done. The skilled expert does not need to modify a "knowledge-base" consisting of representations, because whatever representations and rules he or she possesses are incidental to the intuitive know-how.

Stage five, expertise, means that the skill is so integral to the person that the expert does it as readily as he or she breathes. The know-how of the expert is, at its best, nonanalytical and can be applied at great speed. Dreyfus and Dreyfus point to the fact that expert chess players can play several games simultaneously, with moves every few seconds, without the kind of degradation in the quality of play that one would expect if the prodigious search spaces involved were analyzed according to the rules and heuristics that constitute chess-playing programs.

> Excellent chess players can play at the rate of five to ten seconds a move and even faster without serious degradation in performance. At that speed they must depend almost entirely on intuition and hardly at all on analysis and comparing alternatives. (1986, p. 33)

The result, according to Dreyfus and Dreyfus, is that the assumption that expertise consists of increasing mastery of rules, of increasingly abstract skills, is the wrong way about; increasing expertise typically means the progressive abandonment of rules and abstract reasoning for intuitive recognition of concrete cases as similar to earlier, experienced cases.

> What should stand out is the progression from the analytic behavior of a detached subject consciously decomposing his environment into recognizable elements, and following abstract rules, to involved skilled behavior based on an accumulation of concrete experiences and the unconscious recognition of new situations as similar to whole remem-

bered ones. The evolution from the abstract toward the concrete reverses what one observes in small children dealing with intellectual tasks. (p. 35)

Dreyfus and Dreyfus thus challenge the AI supposition that expertise is formal manipulation of discrete symbols. Know-how finally resists the Western, analytic desire to decompose into constituent parts.

> Thus according to our description of skill acquisition the novice and advanced beginner exercise no judgment, the competent performer judges by means of conscious deliberation, and those who are proficient or expert make judgments based upon their prior concrete experiences in a manner that defies explanation. . . . The moral of the five-stage model is: there is more to intelligence than calculative rationality. . . . A vast area exists between irrational and rational that might be called arational. . . . arational behavior, then, refers to action without conscious analytic decomposition and recombination. *Competent performance is rational; proficiency is transitional; experts act arationally.* (p. 36; emphasis in original)

Moreover, Dreyfus and Dreyfus claim that conscious use of rules by an expert often produces regression in expert behavior. They take this to indicate that conscious use of rules constitutes a regression to earlier stages of the acquisition of the skill in question.

As I stated earlier, my principal task in this chapter is to establish a relationship between the Dreyfus critique of AI and the frame problem. As a result, I will not criticize the Dreyfus critique as much as I would otherwise. Nevertheless, there is so much here claimed so relatively quickly that a few criticisms seem in order.

It is frequently said that we are poor observers of our own psychological states and processes. Pointedly, the fact that an expert is not conscious of using rules and heuristics while applying his or her expertise certainly doesn't entail the claim that rules and heuristics are not being used. It is a truism by now in computer science that the workings of subroutines are usually not known to the calling routine; subroutines are treated as black boxes to which parameters are passed and values returned. It is possible, as AI is wont to claim, that the self is an executive master program that invokes subroutines, which, in turn, invoke subroutines, and so on, until the task is done. The master program need not concern itself, in everyday psychology, attend to, or even be aware of the workings of the subroutines called.

As a result, from the fact that we are not aware of using routines, of using rules ranging over databases, or suchlike structures, without the assistance of additional support, it doesn't follow that expertise does not typically involve the use of rules, facts and heuristics. That is, this fact alone doesn't particularly count against the physical symbol hypothesis which informs AI's understanding of intelligence.

Additionally, there are some claims in *Mind Over Machine* that are overstated. In discussing expertise, for example, Dreyfus and Dreyfus claim that, "when things are proceeding normally, experts don't solve problems and don't make decisions; they do what normally works" (1986, p. 30). This claim is related to the last comment in the displayed quotation above that "experts act arationally." I think what they have in mind is the following kind of situation. I would guess that, in an emergency room, life-saving activities happen so quickly that it is questionable whether the word *decision* is the most appropriate way to describe what happens, if by *decision* is meant a pensive consideration of the range of possible alternatives. The expertise is presumably deeply enough ingrained that the activity has more in common with a professional tennis player's split-second forehand response to a serve than it does with a new home buyer's belabored choice. In their defense, moreover, Dreyfus and Dreyfus might point to Sherry Turkle's (1984) work and suggest that the word *decision* itself has been so conditioned by the "computer science revolution" that, increasingly, what we usually understand by *decision* is analytic decomposition and recombination of symbolic elements that represent the world. But, all these considerations notwithstanding, to say that "experts don't solve problems and don't make decisions" is surely gratuitous hyperbole. It may be, as Turkle argues, that the computer paradigm is changing our understanding of words such as *decision*, but I don't see that saying "the doctor decided not to operate," even given the semantic "drift" of words such as *decision*, commits me to the view that the doctor's behavior is to be understood in physical symbol system terms. All it commits me to is the folk-psychology understanding that the doctor looked at a situation and, doing whatever health experts do in choosing one course over another, quickly concluded against surgery. To use the word *decide* in this context, therefore, is an apt use of the word.

In closing this section, I would like to summarize the Dreyfus critique of AI, casting it in terms that will be helpful in looking at the frame problem. Consider this remark:

> It is no wonder that among philosophers of science one finds an assumption that machines can do everything people can do, followed by an attempt to interpret what this bodes for the philosophy of mind. . . . Thinkers . . . have failed to ask the preliminary question whether machines can in fact exhibit even elementary skills like playing games, solving simple problems, reading simple sentences and recognizing patterns, presumably because they are under the impression, fostered by the press and artificial-intelligence researchers such as Minsky, that the simple tasks and even some of the most difficult ones have already been or are about to be accomplished. (1986, p. 81)

Dreyfus probably overstates his case some—the polemic is still here—but he is right in this regard. It is simply unfounded to talk as though computers have matched human competencies in game playing, reading, pattern recognition, speech, and so on. This needs some qualification. Of course, there are some quite good chess and checkers programs today, and these can defeat most human players. The Dreyfuses discuss some recent good chess programs and argue that the best human players still defeat them—especially if the human players are privy to the strategies programmed in the computer. Scottish International Champion David Levy's commentary (Dreyfus and Dreyfus, 1986, pp. 111-115) on the potential of chess programs, is insightful. Levy's observations sum to the claim that, if a human chess player has a good grasp of how a chess-playing program has been written, it becomes significantly easier for the human to defeat the machine. Additionally, a qualification that should be noted is that games that incorporate a significant amount of chance, such as backgammon, may produce occasional significant (really insignificant) computer successes.

In fact, the evidence is that philosophers over the last 25 years have too often concluded that the progress has been or would be rapid when, for the most part, it has been painfully slow. Dreyfus has been arguing that it would be either slow or nonexistent for more than 25 years, and he deserves a measure of credit for the prescient intuition if not the actual argument. The reason for the dearth of progress, according to the Dreyfuses, is that human expertise does not consist of skilled manipulation of formal symbols, of rules that range over facts and issue in deductions; instead, it consists of the holistic recognition of a new situation as similar to a previously experienced situation. The expert acts, making the necessary adjustments, based on her or his experience. *Holographic correlations* are made quickly, without the problem decomposition, accumulation of facts, and application of rules, step by step, which classical AI supposes characterizes intelligence. Dreyfus and Dreyfus quote, with approval, Stanford neurologist Karl Pribam's claim that "decisions fall out as the holographic correlations are performed. One doesn't have to think things through a step at a time. One takes the whole constellation of a situation, correlates it, and out of that correlation emerges the correct response" (1986, p. 108). This comment evidently targets the classical AI paradigm, of course, but I don't see that the classical AI paradigm will be radically overthrown soon by, for example, connectionist models.[2] According to Dreyfus and Dreyfus, to sum up the case that Hubert Dreyfus has been making for so long, at least classical AI profoundly misunderstands the nature of intelligence.

Finally, AI proponent David L. Waltz (1988, p. 197), perhaps surprisingly, is not as far from the Dreyfus position as one might suppose. He writes, "Craig Stanfill and I have argued at length elsewhere that humans may well solve problems by a process much more like *look-up* than *search*, and that the items looked up may be much more like representations of specific or stereotyped episodes and objects than like rules and facts." I take this to be surprisingly close to the view I find most compelling, namely, that cognition is likely based on some kind of noncomputational pattern recognition. Conversely, Dreyfus and Dreyfus (1987) have some rather complimentary things to say about AI work with parallel distributed processing, which is not rule-based as is conventional AI, and, purportedly, is amenable to some forms of "instruction." The limits and possibilities of massively parallel computing are less well known than those of classical serial

---

[2]At the AI Conference at Carleton College in February 1989, the consensus of the presenters, who included Michael Arbib and Paul Thagard, was that traditional AI models will be supplemented by the new connectionist models but not outright replaced.

computing, in part because of its complexity and because we have had less experience with it, but as a model of learning and the brain, it appears to be somewhat more promising.

2. The Frame Problem

In the first part of the chapter, I attempted to outline the Dreyfus critique of artificial intelligence. I argued that there are numerous problems with the critique, but that it has turned out more accurate than many detractors would have supposed in terms of the seriousness of the difficulties facing AI at the "I/O" level. Dreyfus claimed that the scope of these difficulties was not understood by either proponents of AI or those philosophers who were otherwise critical of AI but were too uncritical in terms of how successful AI would prove in the last 20 years at the I/O level; much philosophical criticism of AI historically has been of the hollow shell variety, namely, "given successful I/O, what does it signify?" Increasingly, perhaps in part due to the Dreyfus critique, the debate has evolved to focus more on how much should be expected at the "I/O" level. Increasing interest in the frame problem, I believe, exemplifies just this evolution.

In this section, I try to show that getting a clear understanding of the frame problem does two things. First, it typifies a good part of what Dreyfus has attempted to argue, but, interpreted carefully, does so in a less ambiguous, more philosophically adequate, way. Second, and most importantly for the purposes of this essay, it shows that the frame problem is a formidable problem which obstructs the epistemologically complex learning, which I claim is essential to the passage of the Turing test.

The term *frame problem* dates back about 20 years, specifically to the work of Hayes and McCarthy. Since that time, there have been two fundamental approaches to how the term should be used. First, when used by computer scientists and cognitive scientists, it has often been understood in a narrower, more technical, less philosophical way. Second, when used by philosophers and those with more philosophical interests, it has usually been understood in a broader, less technical, more epistemological way. Hayes in particular, as I will attempt to explain later, believes that the two senses are quite different and that

the former is correct and the latter represents a deplorable metamor-
phosis of the term.

But the task of reaching a clear interpretation of what the problem
is, it turns out, is more complicated than just distinguishing between
the technical and philosophical senses. Even a quick reading of the
literature reveals that there is considerable difference of opinion over
what the frame problem is, whether it is one problem or many, and
whether it is a new problem, as Dennett, for instance, claims, or a
classical problem, recently retrofitted with digital attire, as others such
as Glymour argue. Dennett (1987, p. 42) claims that the frame
problem is a new, quite serious, epistemological puzzle, since it "is a
new, deep epistemological problem — accessible in principle but unnoticed by generations of philosophers — brought to light by the novel
methods of AI, and still far from being solved." Because AI involves
new research done with a "novel" approach, Dennett seems to be
saying, it has uncovered this new philosophical puzzle we call the
frame problem. The frame problem is discovered, I think Dennett
(1978) wants to say, because AI consists of thought experiments "about
whether or not one can obtain certain sorts of information processing — recognition, inference, control of various sorts . . . from
certain sorts of designs." Dennett defines AI as a variation on a
classical epistemological question: how is knowledge possible in a
system? When the question is posed in terms of an automatic formal
system, instead of being asked from a human perspective as it has been
historically by philosophers, the frame problem develops.

Clark Glymour (1987, p. 65) takes exception to Dennett's claim and
argues that AI, effectively exposing its own philosophical naïveté, has
simply stumbled onto a perennial problem that philosophers have
known and argued about for centuries:

> I think it is more accurate to say that there is no novel problem at all,
> only a novel and powerful constraint on problems that are old friends to
> philosophy. . . . I think the "frame problem" is not one problem, but an
> endless hodgepodge of problems concerned with how to characterize
> what is relevant in knowledge, action, planning, etc.

Haugeland (1987), more sympathetic with Dennett's position than
Glymour's, suggests that, "as if epistemology hadn't enough troubles,
artificial intelligence has generously provided another, called the

'frame' problem." These claims alone make it clear that there is considerable difference of opinion over whether the frame problem is a new problem or an old problem rediscovered by a new academic pursuit.

To compound matters further, the frame problem is one of several imbricated problems. Related, possibly overlapping problems include the *prediction* problem, the *bookkeeping* problem, the *qualification* problem, the *installation* problem, and, perhaps most important of all, the general problem of induction and how they differ, assuming they do, from the frame problem. Given this epistemological imbroglio, the task which I undertake is to find a definition of the frame problem, argue why this definition is preferable to rival definitions, and then argue how the frame problem is distinguishable from the problem of induction and the several "related" problems just cited. The goal of the discussion, of course, is to achieve a clear enough characterization of the frame problem that I will be in a position to determine its relation to the Turing test.

In turn, I will discuss the general frame problem, the specific frame problem, several problems related to the frame problem, and, last, I will attempt to show why there is a space problem generated by the frame problem, which I will call the *relevance space problem*. I will close the chapter with a summary of how I understand the frame problem and a summary statement of how the general frame problem is related to the specific frame problem.

The General Frame Problem

In this section I want to relay the general frame problem, that is, the frame problem as philosophers, for the most part, have understood the frame problem, and I wish to trace some history of various interpretations of the frame problem.

In *Brainstorms*, which was published in 1978, Dennett devoted two pages to expanding this brief depiction of the frame problem:

> The frame problem is an abstract *epistemological* problem that was in effect discovered by AI thought-experimentation. When a cognitive creature, an entity with many beliefs about the world, performs an act, the world changes and many of the creature's beliefs must be revised or updated. How? It cannot be that we perceive and notice *all* the

changes . . . and hence it cannot be that we rely entirely on perceptual input to revise our beliefs. So we must have internal ways of up-dating our beliefs that will fill in the gaps and keep our internal model, the totality of our beliefs, roughly faithful to the world. (p. 125)

According to this relatively early, philosophical understanding, the frame problem is one of updating the beliefs that a "cognitive creature" has about the world, since an act performed by the creature presumably changes that world in some way. An act that results in change in the world requires a change in the belief system if that system is — in some sense or other — to be a "faithful" (I'd be happy to settle for "useful") representation of the world. More to the point, the question is *how* such updating should be done.

Writing perhaps 8 years later, Dennett (1987) suggests that Hubert Dreyfus and John Searle are "ideological foes" of AI and employ the frame problem as grounds for opposing it.

the ideological foes of AI such as Hubert Dreyfus and John Searle are tempted to compose obituaries for the field, citing the frame problem as the cause of death. In *What Computers Can't Do* . . . Dreyfus sought to show that AI was a fundamentally mistaken method for studying the mind, and in fact many of his somewhat impressionistic complaints about AI models and many of his declared insights into their intrinsic limitations can be seen to hover quite systematically in the neighborhood of the frame problem. Dreyfus never explicitly mentions the frame problem, but is it perhaps the smoking pistol he was looking for but didn't quite know how to describe? (p. 43)

The association of Dreyfus with the frame problem, of course, is not surprising, but suggesting that Searle's opposition to AI rests on the frame problem is more tantalizing than helpful, since, quite contrary to usual classification, Dennett associates Searle more with the poor substitute strategy than with the hollow shell strategy. I wish that Dennett had developed this purported connection between Searle's view and the frame problem, since Searle has not done so.

In his 1983 *Modularity of Mind*, Jerry Fodor casts the frame problem in terms of a robot's activity. Fodor is interested in the question of how the robot could determine which beliefs need updating in light of some of its behavior, and which do not. Using a helpful example that dates to Hayes and McCarthy, Fodor asks how a robot, once it has begun to dial a telephone number, should know that the number itself will not be altered by the action of beginning to place the call. Since nothing in its belief complex averts the possibility of this kind of causal relationship, the robot rechecks the number, begins the call, rechecks the number, and so on, effectively disabled by a real-time, frame-problem-based, infinite loop. As Fodor suggests, "Unless the robot can be assured that some of its beliefs are invariant under some of its actions, it will never get to *do* anything" (p. 113).

Fodor identifies three corollaries stemming from the frame problem. I'll interpret these corollaries in my terms:

1. there is nothing like a rule which would enable a robot to know which set of beliefs require updating for any given action;
2. newly acquired beliefs do not contain explicitly their implications for other beliefs;
3. there seems to be no relation between which beliefs require revision, given an action, and when they were acquired or what the semantic relations happen to be between the beliefs and descriptions of related actions.

These three corollaries of the frame problem, according to Fodor, can be understood in light of the question, "What, in general, is the optimal adjustment of my beliefs to my experiences?" As he points out, the general frame problem, as I call it, turns on the fact that "cognitive processes" have to be "sensitive to the whole belief system" (p. 114). We don't know, Fodor seems to be saying, how to construct cognitive processes for an automatic formal system that are sensitive to the whole belief complex. He concludes by suggesting that the "seriousness of the frame problem has not been adequately appreciated" (p. 115).

Owen Flanagan (1991) cites the frame problem as one of "Ten Objections to Artificial Intelligence" (pp. 230–247). Flanagan understands the problem to be one of common sense and of the relevance criteria we would have to draw on so that we don't have to examine exhaustively all the beliefs and knowledge we have in attempting to solve the raft of problems we solve routinely and often with little effort.

Fischler and Firschein (1987), somewhat surprisingly, given their technical background as researchers at SRI International, define the frame problem in quite general terms:

> How can an intelligent system, in trying to solve a problem or carry out
> an action, know what information in its database should be ignored, and
> what is relevant to the problem at hand? . . . The big problem is
> knowing what is indeed relevant, since the time constraints will not
> permit examination of the implication of every fact in the database.
> Many AI systems have the unfortunate characteristic that increasing the
> amount of knowledge in their database degrades, rather than improves,
> their performance. (p. 305)

They understand the frame problem to be one of effectively using the
store of information that an "intelligent system" has, of possessing an
ability to distill what is clearly and usably relevant and, conversely,
what is not relevant, in that store to the solution of the problem, and
doing it in a timely fashion. Their comments remind us how unfortunate the term *memory* is when used in reference to the internal *memory*
of the Macintosh SE/30 I am using to write this chapter, which has 5
megabytes of random access *memory*. One of the reasons that the frame
problem arises, I believe the evidence suggests, is that computers
possess storage and not memory; memories organized as ours are, it
appears, do not run into the problem of "relevance" with anything like
the frequency storage-based systems encounter. It would be surprising
indeed if "increasing the amount of knowledge" a human has would,
under most circumstances, result in a degradation of performance. It
is typical, by contrast, in the case of storage-based systems.

In still more general terms, Fischler and Firschein (1987) argue that
the frame problem is "closely related" to the decomposability of
intelligence question. The question is whether all problems are amenable to decomposition in such a way that we can decompose them,
study the parts, and thereby understand their functions in such a way
that we can replicate them artifactually. I take it that they mean that
whether intelligence is a decomposable problem is an empirical
question; it may turn out that intelligence is not a decomposable
problem. With evident approval, they quote Dreyfus' remark that
"Since intelligence must be situated, it cannot be separated from the
rest of human life." Presumably, this means that intelligence necessarily is rooted in life in such a way that taking it to be decomposable,
as AI does, is to misunderstand it profoundly.

Haugeland acknowledges the problem in his 1985 text, *Artificial
Intelligence: The Very Idea*. By this later date, the frame problem is
commanding greater attention. He compares it to the "knowledge

acquisition" problem but claims that there is a distinct difference. Ingredient in the solution of both the knowledge acquisition problem and the frame problem is the essential goal of avoiding deciding, for each piece of information in a database, whether or not it is relevant. This is a generalized way of saying that intelligent systems must constrain the solution space; brute force is ineffective as a search method for significant problems.

Beyond this by now rather pedestrian computer science claim, Haugeland claims that the difference between the two is a matter of time. The problem is a matter of the intelligent system determining how to update its database as events develop. He suggests that any system's knowledge must be of at least two types: that which does not change over time, given some event or act, and that which does. The problem with the latter, of course, is not only knowing *that* some knowledge is time and context dependent, but knowing *how* that knowledge is time and context dependent:

> the frame problem arises with knowledge of the current situation, here and now — especially with keeping such knowledge up to date as events happen and the situation evolves. . . . When things start moving and changing, "knowledge" of the current situation may not stay valid . . . the system's knowledge must be divided into (at least) two categories: *perennial* facts that stay the same and *temporary* facts that are subject to change at any moment and therefore must be actively kept up to date. (pp. 204–205; emphasis in original)

Still later, he observes that AI systems are prone to being "jerky":

> AI systems seem to lack the flexible, even graceful "horse sense" by which people adjust and adapt to unexpected situations and surprising results. So it's tempting to suppose that adding more "clauses" merely postpones the inevitable; like greasing a rusty bearing, it doesn't address the underlying problem, but at best hides it a little longer. In this view, then, graceful and jerky differ not in degree but kind — and never the twain shall meet. (p. 209)

Haugeland offers an analogy: the "jerky" (a relative of the *frame*) problem may turn out to be like the films consisting of frames that, when run too slowly, obviously consist of frames. But when run at the proper speed, graceful, fluid motion results. Initially, this might look like a plausible analogy, but it seems to skirt the frame problem as well as the jerky problem: one could surmise that the frame and jerky problems are a matter of speeding up the processing so that they dissolve. It is not that simple. Speed is not the problem but rather is symptomatic of a deeper problem — the frame problem's solution will require more than speedier CPUs. As a representation problem, the issue is not speed but sufficiency of the representation and the principles of representation maintenance, given that it has to represent a dynamic world with epistemological adequacy.

Pylyshyn (1987, p. viii) suggests that the frame problem is related to the fact that a general purpose reasoning system, in contrast to a special purpose system such as an expert system, has to have the ability to "connect any item of knowledge or belief (i.e., any representation) with any other." Assuming that cognition encompasses inference, since any belief might be related to any other belief in a system that represents the world, "there is no way to exclude any fact in advance as being irrelevant, without considering all the implications of that fact" (p. viii). The vexing problem is to find a way to distinguish between relevant beliefs and irrelevant beliefs; if the irrelevant beliefs cannot be identified and hence ignored, "the cognitive system will become mired in an exponentially expanding range of inferences and will never be able to deal intelligently with domains requiring a potentially unbounded domain of knowledge such as is involved in carrying on the simplest everyday conversation" (p. viii).

The general frame problem, as Janlert understands it, is the epistemological problem of finding a way to represent a complicated world characterized by significant change. On this interpretation, the frame problem should not be understood as a problem of algorithms or data structures. The frame problem is not a traditional computer science problem but one of determining how the world is to be represented — it is a problem in modeling, a problem for epistemology; Janlert (Pylyshyn, 1987) would even say it is a metaphysical problem. The reason that "microworlds" have played an important role histori- cally in AI, this interpretation would point out, is that microworlds significantly obviate the epistemic issues involved in modeling a dynamic system as complicated as the real world. Once we attempt to model the full-bodied real world, in the attempt, for instance, to write a program that would enable a robot to make its way down a sidewalk on a moderately busy street, we've committed ourselves to doing epistemology, according to this view, even metaphysics.

One additional consideration adds to the difficulty of solving the general frame problem. The general frame problem, at least if we let the philosophers have their way, is a problem in epistemology — the theory of knowledge. Epistemology in this century has been preoccupied with science and the foundations of scientific method. One assumption that has dominated Western views of science is that science is virtually immune to fraud. Ingredient in this assumption has been the understanding that experimental results, since replicability is an essential characteristic of science, will eventually, given enough time, be purged of mistaken and fraudulent claims. But John Hardwig (1991) argues that the explosion in research, along with the weakening in the monitoring of experimental results, when added to the fact that research now requires large teams and often large amounts of time and specialized equipment, sum to the conclusion that the replicability of experimental results is no longer as much of a leash on the mistaken and the fraudulent as it once was. Moreover, he claims that surveys have turned up plagiarism or outright fraud in up to 25% of published scientific work. Thus, he concludes, the trustworthiness of experimental results has become a major concern.

> The conclusion that knowledge often is based on certain kinds of relationships between people, on trust, and consequently on the character of other people is an epistemologically odd conclusion. It is odd even for pragmatists, though pragmatists have generally had more room for epistemic community in their theories. To my mind, this oddness is symptomatic of what will be needed to assimilate an acknowledgement of the role of trust into our epistemologies. We have a lot of work to do. (p. 708)

The result, according to Hardwig, is a reversal of the usual view of the relation of ethics to epistemology. The general assumption in the Western tradition is that ethics presupposes epistemology — that ethics is obliged to meet the standards of the conditions for knowledge generated by epistemology. Given the importance of trust in the evaluation of scientific claims, however, it turns out that epistemology significantly presupposes the standards of ethics. The consequence is

that epistemology must now take into account ethical factors—
epistemology is an alloy of evidence, logic, epistemic considerations of
one kind or another, and ethics. Knowing is inexorably conditioned by
ethical judgment—trust, or the "credit of the proposer," to press into
service John Locke's term, is a necessary condition for knowledge
based on experimental results.

If Hardwig is right, and I believe that he makes a convincing case,
then the general frame problem cannot be solved without addressing
the significantly complicating factor of how judgments of the trustworthiness of scientific claims might be decomposed and functionally
defined in terms of a program. When should certain claims be trusted,
and when should they not? On what grounds? Are the skills requisite
to such judgments computationally reducible—amenable to capture in
a program? Even if we could actually generate some kind of programmatic mechanism for such assessments, perhaps employing the probability calculus, we would then be faced with this variation on the
frame problem: when one item in the "knowledge base" is no longer
judged trustworthy, the system is faced with the task of assessing the
trustworthiness of every other item that presupposes the item no longer
judged trustworthy. The system will then have to spend significant
amounts of time confirming that most of what it knows remains
trustworthy, given that some small percentage of what it thought was
trustworthy erroneously earned that evaluation. In sum, the general
frame problem isn't as simple as a tangle of epistemological issues; it
has a treacherous "credit of the proposer" dimension as well.

The Specific Frame Problem

As noted above, the way that computer scientists and many other
cognitive scientists use the term *frame problem* is much more specific
than the more general, epistemological sense in which it is used by
philosophers or those such as Fischler and Firschein, who have a
distinct interest in the philosophical issues associated with AI. In more
recent discussions of the frame problem, Hayes in particular has been
outspokenly critical of the epistemological construal of the term. My
aim in this part of the chapter is to articulate an understanding of what
I call the *specific frame problem*. I'll cast the discussion in terms of what
we would need to keep a robot named SIMON functioning.

The "original frame problem," according to Janlert, had to do with the fact that modeling was understood to be a matter of representing facts in the world modeled with proper axioms. The difficulty was determining what changes in model would be dictated by a change in the world modeled. If no theoretical way can be identified for avoiding the task of examining each proper axiom each time a change occurs in the modeled world, then SIMON would become hopelessly bogged down "in the midst of a sea of axioms representing non-changes, endlessly calculating non-effects" (p. 6).

Axioms that might be put into a program to assist SIMON's movement could take the form of a familiar IF/THEN statement:

IF (object O Isin room R1) or (object O Isin room R2)
AND IF not (object O Isin R2)
THEN LOOKFOR(O,R1).

The point of developing such axioms is that it makes it possible to generate a model that represents states in some world. Of course, the axiom just cited, assuming the truth of the two IF conditions, entails the call LOOKFOR(O,R1). With a system like PROLOG, for example, with a few qualifications, it is (usually) fairly straightforward to generate truth-preserving conclusions, given premises in the data-base. The specific frame problem arises when we attempt to determine noninferences or nonconsequences from an axiom system, given a change or set of changes. Most changes in the world evidently result in few other significant changes — the world, at least in terms of macro-scopic, common sense descriptions that we apparently use to make our way in the world with routine success, is not characterized by massive change from one moment to the next. Chaos theory notwithstanding, a tune-up for my car, for example, presumably would not alter the publication date of John Updike's next novel. Yet the fact that the publication date of Updike's next novel does not depend up my car's tune-up is not a necessary truth, since logic doesn't preclude the possibility that there is such a relationship. As a result, if we wish to model a nontrivial world with an axiom system, we have to find some way of expressing the obvious fact that most changes in the world leave most of the world unchanged. Hayes (1987) put it this way:

One feels that there should be some economical and principled way of succinctly saying what changes an action makes, without having to

explicitly list the things it doesn't change as well; yet there doesn't seem
to be any way to do it. That is the frame problem. (p. 125)

In terms of axioms in SIMON, Hayes claims that there is no
"principled" way to decide which of the axioms *don't* need revision, given an action by SIMON or some change in SIMON's world.
Not only does SIMON have the task of inferring deductions, but also
nondeductions, given an action. That logic is not equivalent to metaphysics is underscored by Hayes's comment that, "in this ontology,
whenever something MIGHT change from one moment to another,
we have to find some way of stating that it DOESN'T change
whenever ANYTHING changes."

Hayes's second characterization of the frame problem warrants a
brief comment. He suggests that we imagine that we had enough facts
about a state that we thought it an adequate characterization—a
snapshot in time, as it were. If we introduce one change, a function
carrying the system from one state or states to another state or states,
the question becomes how large a description will be needed to
characterize the new situation, after the change. Not only will the
model have to specify what changes occurred, it will have to specify
what does *not* change. The description of the change will rival, in terms
of size, the original description. The frame problem, on this characterization, is "to find a more principled, compact, and sensible way to
state or infer these platitudes, or somehow avoid the need to infer them
at all." What Hayes calls the *frame problem*, I wish to call the *specific frame
problem*.

What interests me about this second characterization is a passing
reference that Hayes makes, in a footnote, about the implications for
learning. He suggests that attending to the "litany of reassurance that
this action doesn't change this or that or the other" has many
unacceptable consequences. In the footnote, he suggests "when a new
time-dependent relation is added to the reasoner's repertoire of
concepts, it should not be necessary to update all the action descriptions. This would make learning very difficult" (p. 126). I think this is
too generous. If SIMON has an unsolved frame problem, it appears to
bring learning effectively to a halt because the overhead of attending
to the "litany" of nonconsequences, as the representation of a nontrivial
world becomes more adequate, increasingly crowds out attending to
the efficient and effective modification of the representation of the

world that learning surely requires. A robot that can't learn is a robot that cannot function in a real world. A robot with an unsolved frame problem, I will claim in Chapter 6 of this essay, is a tongue-tied robot that cannot engage in a conversation at an epistemologically complex level.

Several Problems Related to the Frame Problem

The first problem that I wish to consider, which is related to the (general) frame problem, is the *prediction problem*.[3] If a cognitive system is to make its way more or less successfully in the world, it has to have some facility for anticipating what will happen next in its environment. In other words, it has to have something like a common-sense understanding of how currently observable events will affect the future. But there are several difficulties with generating such a prediction capacity. We have nothing like a set of deterministic laws at the macroscopic level that we could use to represent the world a robot will have to make its way in. The second half of Searle (1984), in fact, labors to establish just this point. Even if we had such deterministic laws, moreover, it would be extremely difficult to model the world in sufficient detail that such laws would allow predictions that would be sufficiently reliable. Increasing complexity of representation, other things being equal, tends to degrade performance. The more detailed the map, the more complex the computation, other things being equal, so that, at some point of increased complexity, it appears, the robot would not be able to manipulate the representation fast enough; it would begin to predict, even with a superb representation and deterministic laws, that which has already occurred.

The prediction problem's relation to the frame problem should be apparent, but so are the differences. The prediction problem is the task of adequately representing how the world goes, its physics. How the model is manipulated internally is not part of the prediction problem. The frame problem, by contrast, does concern administration of the representation once formulated. As Janlert puts it, the frame problem is "mainly the problem of representing the metaphysics of the modeled world" (1987, p. 5).

---

[3]Some of the characterizations of problems related to the frame problem are indebted to Janlert (1987).

Another problem involves the qualification of rules or assumptions. In confronting any problem situation, we usually take for granted a raft of assumptions about the situation. For example, if I am asked to open a window on the other side of the room, in taking on the task, I would assume that the window can be opened, that the Persian rug covering the floor in the middle of the room does not conceal a hole into which I would drop while crossing the room, and so on. Janlert calls such assumptions *rules*. An exhaustive listing of such assumptions for any real world problem situation, of course, is generally not possible.

Another way of stating this problem is to point out that idealized understandings of items in the world are often at variance with what we find. Without qualifications, it is reasonable to assume that a styrofoam cup will keep hot coffee from burning a hand. With some frequency, as we know, the assumption proves false. The *qualification problem* is the problem of how to program SIMON so that it can interact in the world without becoming jerky (in Haugeland's sense) in the face of qualifications that characterize so much of our experience.

On the other hand, the *updating problem* has to do with updating the representational system data in the representation changes. For example, if SIMON is moving down the hallway and three chairs are moved by people, the representation of the three chairs in SIMON has to be changed to reflect the new situation in the world. This is different from the frame problem in that SIMON is not faced with determining the consequences and nonconsequences of the chair's new position, but simply changing the the actual representation of the chairs' location.

The Frame Problem, Search Spaces, and Relevance Spaces

According to the classical AI paradigm, an important step in making computers more intelligent is to program them in such a way that the *search space* of a problem the computer is attempting to solve is successively reduced until either an answer is found or an acceptable approximation is reached. The search space is the set of spaces — physically or logically understood — that a person or program is prepared to look in for a solution or an approximation to a solution. It is a truism by now in both artificial intelligence and conventional computer science that brute force, or, as it is sometimes called, a *British*

Museum algorithm (BMA) approach, won't work for very many interesting problems. A BMA algorithm identifies all the possible places that might contain a solution and examines each one, one at a time, until the solution is found. In other words, a BMA algorithm serially searches each element in the problem's search space until a solution is found.

Classical AI as well as conventional computer science have both rightly concerned themselves with the constraint of search spaces, on the ground that the search spaces of most interesting problems are too vast for even the fastest machines to search in an acceptable amount of time. As Raphael (1976, p. 95) puts it, "Search is an important part of most problem-solving processes." If one way to constrain search spaces includes knowledge of some kind, then AI practitioners are inclined to label their programs "intelligent," on the presumed ground that it is the knowledge in the program which enables it to do better than a BMA algorithm. Search spaces of tractable problems such as games are reduced by a variety of techniques. Techniques include "look-ahead" and "minimax." As the improvement in the performance of checkers and chess-playing programs illustrates, such techniques have generated a fair amount of success in coping with problems with large search spaces.

I won't say much more about search spaces. One reason I won't is that I believe, along with Waltz (1988), that look-up is a more promising avenue for AI than search if AI projects are to "scale up" better than they currently do. There's a respectable case to be made that people identify solutions to problems by means of something like look-up and, assuming this is so, an attempt to emulate human practice may prove fruitful. My principal reason for not saying more about search spaces, though, is that the reason for talking about a search space is that I want to contrast it with what I will call the *relevance space* of a system's attempt to solve real-world problems.

An unsolved frame problem means that a computer system possesses no programmatic mechanism for ignoring irrelevant facts, as it takes on a problem, short of attempting to identify the implications of that fact for the other facts it possesses in its "knowledge base." In my terms, it has an enormous relevance space which resists reduction by any technique we currently possess. As a result, not only do we have to be concerned about a problem's search space, which is external to the AI system, as it were, we must be concerned with the system's relevance space, which is internal to the system. We know some ways to reduce search spaces for certain kinds of problems, but we know of no way to reduce relevance spaces for problems requiring what I have called *epistemologically complex learning.*

In fact, not only do we not know a way to reduce relevance spaces; given an initial consideration of a problem and an initial state of a system, relevance spaces exponentially explode as a computer system attempts to assimilate epistemologically complex information. If a new piece of information is encountered, for example, in a conversation, even assuming there is some way to encode the information in a production system, the task is not only to encode the information, but to determine what the implications are of the new information for the rest of the system, both positively in terms of what needs to be changed and negatively in terms of what doesn't need to be changed. That is, it has to examine each element of the representation, attempting to determine if the new information entails a change in old information elements *aaa . . . 999* (however many there are). If *aaa* does not change, the system is left with the task of examining elements *aab . . . 999* in light of the new information. In this case, the relevance space decreases slightly. If *aaa* needs changing, however, not only does the system have the task of examining elements *aab . . . 999* in light of the new information, it must also evaluate elements *aab . . . 999* in light of the fact that *aaa* has been changed. Each time a change occurs, the relevance space increases dramatically in size. If only a tiny percentage of the elements require a change for each pass through the system's representation, the relevance space grows exponentially. The fundamental problem is that there is no known way to develop a general-purpose executive program or production rule that could exclude examination of what we could readily identify as irrelevant elements on grounds of *prima facie* irrelevancy. Most things in the world don't change (significantly) when one thing changes, and most of what we believe does not require alteration when we change some small part of our beliefs about the world. We accept these epistemological truisms; the problem is determining how to encode them in a production system. We don't suffer from exploding relevance spaces as we assimilate information about the world, but automatic formal systems do.

In the terms I developed in the last chapter, epistemologically simple learning does not founder on exploding relevance spaces, while epistemologically complex learning does. In the Coin Toss game, to use the example from Chapter 2, assimilation of data from the game string generated no exploding relevance space, since increasingly successful play of the game did not presuppose examination of each cell of its database each time one cell was changed. While a chess program has to cope with a large search space and, necessarily, must restrict "look-ahead" in order to keep the search space manageable, it has no relevance space problem either, since events that go on in the real world are irrelevant. As a formal game, the only learning that it has to do is epistemologically simple and is therefore representationally manageable.

A brief consideration of some of the reasons why we don't suffer from the frame problem and how Hilary Putnam believes AI might be able to overcome difficulties related to frame problem may be helpful at this point. Putnam (1988) argues that AI, if it is to be more than a "notional" activity, has to produce an intelligence that learns much as children do. Putnam's piece is a reproach of AI as it is currently practiced but it nevertheless offers some constructive advice on what the agenda should be for AI proponents.

Putnam argues that there are two basic approaches that AI researchers could take in the effort to produce machine intelligence. First, AI researchers could attempt to program into a machine all the information that an adult human has at his or her disposal, in the expectation that this would be necessary for intelligence. The problem with this, according to Putnam, is the sheer enormity of the task. The amount of information would "require generations of researchers to formalize the information." As a practical note, software giant Microsoft now breaks up its larger projects such as spreadsheets and high-end word processors into as many as 2,000 tasks. But projects such as spreadsheets and word processors are surely many orders of magnitude, if a number can be attached at all, simpler than all the "information" which would be available in a normal adult. Several years are now required, even for large programming teams, to bring comparatively simple programs such as spreadsheet and word processing programs to market. Even then, of course, they have numerous bugs. Expressed more theoretically, David Waltz (1988, p. 192), an AI proponent, agrees that "It will be extremely difficult to characterize and build into a system the kinds of *a priori* knowledge or structuring principles people have."

If he were being more consistent with what he argues elsewhere in his paper, Putnam would question this alternative even more than he does. He spends a fair amount of time discussing the problem of induction as it pertains to AI and calls our attention to the problem of "conflicting inductions," as Goodman, in part, understands it. The idea is that there is no mechanical way to arbitrate between innumerable conflicting inductions that, short of command of the entire body of background knowledge that mature people take for granted as they make their way in everyday activities, would immobilize a formal system interacting with typical real-world situations. I take this complaint as a rough approximation of the general frame problem.

He cites Goodman's example that it appears true that no one who has entered Emerson Hall at Harvard speaks Inuit (Eskimo). From this we might draw the induction that if a person enters Emerson Hall, the person is not able to speak Inuit. But if an Eskimo were to appear at the doors of Emerson Hall, few of us would subscribe to the induction that the Eskimo would suddenly lose the ability to speak his or her native tongue. We are able to draw on our background knowledge and discount the suggestion that a person would lose the ability to speak Inuit simply by passing through the doors of Emerson Hall, even if we have not had to make such a judgment before. In a word, we readily resolve the conflict of inductions correctly. The issue, for Putnam, is whether this ability, as part of what he calls "human nature," is amenable to capture in formal rules.

> Again, it is not clear that the knowledge that one doesn't lose a language just like that is really the product of induction; perhaps this is something we have an innate propensity to believe. The question that won't go away is *how much of what we call intelligence presupposes the rest of human nature.* (p. 277; emphasis in original)

I take this last statement to be a philosophic pointer to the host of competencies humans possess as linguistically capable animals produced by natural history. The larger problem, then, is a matter of what is ingredient in "human nature." In other words, the relevance spaces (on an AI paradigm) we would otherwise face in all kinds of problems have been vastly shrunk for us by the very natural history which produced us; ineffectual problem solvers did not pass on their genes to succeeding generations. The fact that we are here, can ambulate, and can indulge in philosophic problems associated with AI, means that solutions to many of the large problems facing AI are necessarily ingredient in the natural intelligence we possess.

Ingredient in the "rest of human nature," for Putnam, is an evolution-generated competency that enables us to cope with what would otherwise be an infinitude of conflicting inductions — in terms I have used in this chapter, we normally don't suffer from a relevance space problem. Putnam appeals to the work of evolutionary biologist François Jacob, who compares evolution to a tinker who works, not according to a master design, which is what traditional AI presupposes, according to Putnam, but to meet the exigencies that appear over a long span of time, modifying the design in a piecemeal, serendipitous fashion. The upshot is that "natural intelligence is not the expression of some *one* program but the expression of billions of bits of 'tinkering' " (p. 272). Perhaps a good analogy to the evolutionary development of intelligence as tinkering is the Watts Towers in Los Angeles, built by Simon Rodia. As Bronowski (1973, p. 118) puts it, "He never had anyone to help him because, he said, 'most of the time I didn't know what to do myself." To ask the question, what general principles did Rodia use in building the Towers? then, is to ask the wrong question. There were no general principles, just 30 years of tinkering with wire, glass, concrete, and odds and ends such as plastic saucers and broken sea shells. Analogously, there may be no general principles to intelligence as developed by evolution, just 3 billion years of tinkering with amino acids and suchlike. One way to understand evolution is that it is brute force applied biologically to an enormous search space over a very long time. Perhaps such tinkering is the *only* way to develop intelligence. If this is the case, according to Putnam, then "we may never get very far in terms of simulating human intelligence" (p. 273).

Consequently, the problem with the first alternative, namely, the definition of AI as the effort to encode in a computer all the background information that every mature person has, is not so much the prodigious quantity of information, which is what a reader could take Putnam to be saying at the end of his paper if much of the rest of the paper were ignored. Though this is a daunting problem in its own right, the monumental difficulty is determining what Evolution the Tinker did through the eons of time in developing what we too facilely call *human nature*. Putnam likes the suggestion that AI "is one damned thing after another," because he supposes that AI's unwitting mission, in purportedly aspiring to replicate intelligence, amounts to recapitulating the Promethean saga of natural history. Putnam takes this result to mean, at least practically, and I think he could be coaxed to agree that it is an in-principle limitation, that the first alternative is beyond our collective grasp.

The other alternative Putnam proposes is that "AI practitioners could undertake the more exciting and ambitious task of constructing a device that could learn the background knowledge by interacting with human beings, as a child learns a language and all the cultural information, explicit and implicit, that comes with learning a language by growing up in a human community" (p. 278). Putnam urges this alternative of learning upon us as the best way to understand AI if it is to be more than a "notional" undertaking.

The problem that is not addressed by Putnam, however, is that there are limits to the kinds of learning a computer system can do, if there is no solution to the frame problem and the relevance space problems it creates in a system attempting to learn. If by *learn* Putnam means that AI practitioners should develop programs that can learn at an epistemologically simple level, then, since we are able to do this now, I have no objections. If, on the other hand, by "learn," Putnam means that AI practitioners should attempt to develop programs that can learn at an epistemologically complex level, then my objection is that I don't see how this can be done, barring a solution to the frame problem. Learning may prove to be one way to generate a measure of intelligence in machines, but, until we have a solution to what appears now to be an intractable frame problem, the learning that such systems can do will not get AI to the announced goal of an intelligence that rivals that possessed by people.

3. The General and Specific Frame Problems and Their Principled Link

As noted earlier, historically many AI efforts have centered on microworlds. Winograd in particular, while he was skeptical even early in his career that language is finally neatly divisible into isolatable domains, knew that drastic restrictions in the language domain were necessary, at least at first, if computer-based natural language com-

petency was to make some progress. While sequence may be important
in writing a chess-playing program, for example, time does not play a
role dynamically. Games such as chess lend themselves to computer
simulation, as Haugeland (1986) reminds us, especially because they
are formal:

> The essential point is that nothing in a formal game depends on any
> specific features of its physical medium, as long as the same sequences
> of legal moves and positions are maintained; hence the game itself
> seems less directly tied to material embodiment. (p. 59)

As long as AI restricts itself to such limited, formal domains, problems
such as the frame problem do not arise. When a reasoning system,
however, takes on the task of reasoning about an informal macroworld, such as that faced when a robot walks down a college building
hallway crowded with people and objects, the frame problem develops.

Cashing out the contrast in terms of examples may help make my
point. In a chess game, while the search space is notoriously large,
everything, in principle, is predictable. While there is certainly change
on the board as the game progresses, it is anticipatable, unambiguous,
what I would like to call *metaphysically simple* change. There isn't the host
of epistemological and metaphysical difficulties attending formal
games that there is in the attempt to model a dynamic, real world. By
contrast, in a crowded hallway, people move around, unpredictable
events take place, the knotty task of representing a complex, ambiguous, metaphysically problematic real world is joined.

Any representation of the scene must take into account that, from
moment to moment, the representation must change, accommodating
the changes observable in the hallway as time passes. On the face of it,
perhaps, this seems to be a manageable task. But our robot must
undertake two tasks: (a) making changes in the representation to
reflect dynamic changes in the world, and (b) determining what the
implications are for the rest of the representation, even though only a
small part of the representation was changed to reflect the different
state of the world. The implications include not only what must be
changed in the representation but what must be left unaltered —
determining the difference in a principled, as opposed to an instance-
by-instance, examination is essential if the robot is to function in real
time.

The distinction between the general and specific frame problem is significant; Hayes is correct in insisting that conflating the two can lead to confusion. I want to characterize the general frame problem, contrast it with the specific frame problem, and then say how the two are related.

As we have seen, the general frame problem concerns how a "cognitive system" goes about updating beliefs. The question is how such updating should be done. The robot, for example, acts, or some part of its world changes, and it is obliged, if it is to interact with something like success, to determine which of its beliefs need updating in light of its behavior (or the fact that some part of its world changed significantly) and, importantly, which do not. There is an effective procedure, a finite number of mechanical steps for reaching an answer to a problem, for determining, for instance, whether the black king is in check in a chess game, but there is not one for determining which beliefs need updating and which do not, given a robot attempting to cross a street at a crosswalk, which does not include examining every item in its "database."

The general frame problem concerns reasoning about the "whole belief system" and the implications of actions or newly acquired beliefs for that system. Above, I drew the distinction between memory-based systems and storage-based systems. Storage-based systems, which include digital computers as we now understand them, have to have, effectively, an executive charged with the task of updating; there is no "web of belief" that seems to characterize memory-based cognitive systems such as people. This executive is forced to take on the task, given a problem, of determining what is relevant, what is not, what ought to be changed, what need not be changed, for each item in the database, as the system interacts with a macroworld. The items don't directly, efficiently interact as they evidently do in a memory-based system. Moreover, the general frame problem has, if Hardwig is right, both epistemic and ethical components. Not only must epistemic considerations, whatever they are, be incorporated into the maintenance of a representation of a dynamic world, but considerations of the trustworthiness of claims about the world must be factored into the updating. It means not only identifying and discarding the untrustworthy, it means repeatedly confirming the trustworthiness of the many components that comprise the representation, each time one component is judged untrustworthy.

A solution to the frame problem, which I have not attempted, would be to achieve this goal: how does SIMON avoid having to decide, for each piece of information, that it is or is not relevant? Given an action, such as beginning to place a call, as in Fodor's borrowed example, how does SIMON avoid having to decide, for each piece of information, that it does not change under the impact of the action? Haugeland distinguishes between *temporary* and *perennial* facts. The general frame problem is identifying a "principled" way to distinguish temporary facts from perennial facts, for each moment the robot interacts with its environment, without beginning an examination of its axiom system which would generate a relevance space explosion. SIMON has to avoid considering all facts in his database, and all implications of those facts, in representing its world, given an act or a new belief, on pain of screeching to a halt, frozen, as it were, in frame-problem-induced catatonia.

The specific frame problem involves discussing axioms and how they are organized. The problem is to find some way to express the necessary fact that most changes in the world leave most of the world effectively unchanged. Suppose that Axiom 1 changes. Barring some "principled" way to do it, SIMON has to begin the following task:

Does Axiom 1 entail or require a change in Axiom 2?
Does Axiom 1 entail or require a change in Axiom 3?
:
Does Axiom 1 entail or require a change in Axiom n?

This would be a costly computational endeavor, even assuming that we know what *require* means algorithmically. But SIMON is not done. Suppose that SIMON discovers after doing this exhaustive search, that Axioms g1, h23, . . . , m-3 (just some axioms in its system) need to be changed because Axiom 1 changed. SIMON must now determine, for each and every axiom not in the set (Axioms g1, h23, . . . , m-3), whether the changes in Axioms g1, h23, . . . , m-3 entail (or require) further changes. And so on. I called this problem the problem of an exploding relevance space in the representation, which should be kept distinct from the search space of the problem, that has been the space problem which has interested AI historically. It doesn't take many of these cycles to appreciate fully Janlert's comment that SIMON would become hopelessly bogged down "in the midst of a sea of axioms representing non-changes, endlessly calculating non-effects."

The general and specific frame problems should be distinguished, for at least some purposes, so I am content to defer to Hayes in his insistence that we keep the two senses distinct. However, he misses an important connection. As soon as we attempt to find a "principled" (Hayes's term) way to avoid the specific problem, we get entangled in the general frame problem. The attempt to find a principled way to solve the specific frame problem inexorably entangles one in the general frame problem — which I get the impression Hayes would just as soon avoid as long as possible. The general and specific frame problems are distinct, yet linked decisively and importantly by epistemological "principle."

The importance of the frame problem, general and specific, should now be apparent but let me close with these remarks. It is one of those rare problems that can be made specific enough that some "science" can arguably be brought to bear on it — I am happy to let Hayes have his way and say that some "science" must be part of the agenda. At the same time, interpreted generally, it is one of those rare problems that embodies many new and classical philosophical problems. Positively, as a result, the frame problem seems destined to be one of those important problems about which philosophers and cognitive scientists can — just possibly — have a profitable conversation. Less happily, for AI proponents, it is a problem that those who have opposed AI on "poor substitute" grounds can claim supports their objection with significant justification.

CHAPTER 5

The Turing Test, Dennett's Defense of the Test, and Mindlike Programs

The Turing test is almost singular in its ability to generate both quick dismissals and summary praise. For example, Arno Penzias (1989), the Nobel Laureate physicist, offers the following critique of the Turing test in his *Ideas and Information*:

> The great computing science pioneer Alan Turing once said that he would call a machine "intelligent" when it held up one end of a dialogue well enough to convince him — via typed messages — that he was exchanging thoughts with a human being. In fact, however, it's a lot easier for a dumb machine to converse with a human being than Turing thought. People fill in missing pieces with unconscious ease. (p. 143)

The claim seems to be that ascriptions of intelligence to a conversing machine, should it occur, would owe more to the person's unconscious propensity to gloss over deficiencies in the machine's responses than to the ability of the machine to converse. Following the well-worn path of other writers, Penzias attempts to augment his case by citing a brief example of a "conversation" involving ELIZA, Joseph Weizenbaum's widely discussed "counseling program" that simulates a Rogerian-style psychotherapist "counseling" a client. Two pages later, he draws his conclusion:

> The point is basic. Confronted with isolated acts of "intelligent" behavior in cars — or with any intelligent entity — we must look deep enough to see how that entity functions under changing real-world

conditions. If we don't we cannot evaluate the true intelligence of a system — its ability to acquire and apply knowledge in a variety of contexts. (p. 145)

Penzias's assessment, that the Turing test is too easy because people readily compensate for the "missing pieces" in a conversation, and that, as a result, we must "look deep enough" into a program simulating a mind in order to reach a considered view about whether it is "intelligent," is one of the latest in a long line of similar interpretations. Much could be said in response to this abrupt dismissal of Turing's test, but for now I'll settle for a consideration of the scope of ELIZA's purported linguistic competence. Rogerian-style counseling deliberately traffics in stock responses which, for putative psychotherapeutic reasons, are minimalist by intention. In Rogerian-style counseling classes, students are told to get lots of mileage out of "yes," "um," "I see," "please go on," and even nods of the head. The theory is that, in "client-centered therapy," it is important that the client do most of the talking, and that the principal task of the counselor is to make it clear that he or she is listening — which is why the stock responses are used. During practice counseling sessions, members of such classes often laugh at the use of such stock phrases because of their obviousness. The interesting fact is that, in real counseling, they serve a purpose if the client has not been trained in such techniques.

The larger point, of course, is that such specialized, constrained "conversation" has little to do with the Turing test as Turing advanced it. In fact, ELIZA should be understood as a bantam expert system that deliberately — and I will claim necessarily — constrains the conversational search space. Given such a radical constraint, it is not surprising that ELIZA can seemingly perform well for a few lines. Generally, as Penzias does, the proponents of such a view trot out the few lines and take them to be a clear-cut example of how a program can speciously satisfy Turing's test. As I will argue in greater depth at the end of Chapter 7, the fact of the matter is that lengthier "conversations" with ELIZA, especially if one has some awareness of the strategy used in the program, and one asks the kinds of questions that Turing had in mind, unmask it for the inflexible, narrow program that it is. As a result, ELIZA-like examples, where the conversation is drastically constrained, is not even remotely equivalent to the test Turing had in mind.

On the other side of the philosophical aisle, consider the *Oxford Companion to the Mind's* enthusiastic assessment of Turing's Imitation Game (Gregory, 1987):

> Turing suggested how we could recognize whether a simulation of the human mind had succeeded or failed. His paper, 'Computing machinery and intelligence' (1950) remains the clearest short account of the philosophy of artificial intelligence, as it came to be called, and 'Turing's test' for judging the adequacy of a simulation of mind remains the best criterion for recognizing intelligence in a machine. The 'test' is the Imitation Game . . . It is of course behavioristic; but, as Turing says, we cannot 'get inside' another human being, to know directly whether he or she has conscious experiences, such as sensations of colour and emotional state.

Partially because of its brusqueness, I like this paragraph. It has much the same succinct flavor that Turing's "Computing Machinery and Intelligence" has, it is forthright in the strong claims that it makes, and it captures some of the history of the controversy in just a few words. Whether the test is the "best criterion for recognizing intelligence in a machine," of course, is a conclusion that would need considerably more support to be convincing. While the reader likely can't reasonably expect a lengthy treatment of the issues in such a publication, whether the paper, even though it is deservedly a classic, is the "clearest short account of the philosophy of artificial intelligence" is arguable. It is undeniably provocative, insightful, and I believe it is right on its major points. Alas, it is not particularly well argued in a number of places.

Parenthetically, the striking feature of both of these assessments is that, evidently, their authors assume that relatively few words are sufficient to substantiate remarkably strong claims; the reader gets little sense that the test, as I will attempt to argue, embodies numerous subtle philosophical issues that warrant much more extended treatment.

The Turing test has been subject to a good deal of criticism by philosophers in the four decades since the appearance of Turing's (1950) "Computing Machinery and Intelligence," which advanced the test. Chapter 7 will look at some of the major criticisms of the Turing test that have appeared during that time. The purpose of this chapter is to attempt to make the strongest case for the Turing test that I can, amplifying insights in Turing's essay but augmented by considerations stemming from Daniel Dennett's defense of the test. Since I will do so in the next chapter, I will not make any sustained reference to the frame problem's implications for the Turing test. Instead, I attempt to buttress the importance of "I/O" tests such as Turing's by appealing to recent work, especially by Christopher Cherniak, on rationality, computability, and the difficulty of understanding a mindlike program. Related to the issues that Cherniak raises, but coming at them from the "hardware" side, I press into service Howard Margolis's work on the importance of evolution to assessing how far we are likely to get in understanding the brain.[1] As a result, this chapter represents largely a classical, non-frame-problem-buttressed defense of the test.

Let me summarize my position in this chapter. I claim that parts of Dennett's defense of the Turing test significantly amplify Turing's sketchy articulation, and that Dennett's defense, in turn, can be improved so that a compelling conventional case can be made for the Turing test's difficulty. Moreover, I argue that Cherniak's and Margolis's work goes some distance towards showing that we will have to rely largely on "I/O" tests such as Turing's because of the apparently intractable opacity that both characterizes mindlike programs and retards investigations of the brain and mind. The reason I say *largely* is that I believe considerations associated with the frame problem can be brought to bear on the relation of the Turing test to the question of machine intelligence in such a way that there is an indirect way to get some intervening process considerations that can supplement the I/O case for the Turing test.

I should emphasize that I argue in this chapter that the Turing test is adequate as a test for intelligence. I could distinguish between the *adequacy* of the test and its *difficulty* and claim that the test is difficult but that the test's difficulty does not entail its adequacy. That is, I could argue that, while the adequacy of the test would presumably entail its difficulty, the difficulty of the test does not, by itself, necessarily entail its adequacy. While I worry about the test's anthropocentrism, and while it is admittedly treacherous to advance characterizations about

---

[1]Unless there is good reason to do so, I will sometimes not distinguish between the mind and the brain. I assume that the words *mind* and *brain* point to different aspects of the same entity.

intermediate processes from the relation of input to output, I am going to take on the larger task of arguing that the demands of natural language competency are so comprehensive, and that the capacities of mindless, rule-governed symbol manipulation are sufficiently ill-suited for such a competency, that the best explanation that could be offered for a machine that passed the test is, simply, that it thinks. In short, my position is that Dennett's, Cherniak's, and Margolis' work, suitably clarified and amplified, helps establish both the Turing test's sufficiency and utility, neither of which has been adequately appreciated by its detractors.

Last, I should add that some defenders of the Turing test, impressed by the capacities of computers, have been favorably disposed to the likelihood that a computer or a robot could pass it and this would confirm that it indeed thinks. Dennett is perhaps the most obvious example of this view. On the other hand, some who have attacked the Turing test have been less impressed by the difficulty of the test (and usually by computers as well) and, as a result, have often argued that passage of the test would signify much less than defenders suppose. The most obvious examples are Searle and Gunderson. My view is at odds with both of these historical currents. I am impressed by the capacities of computers and robots—I believe Alan Kay (1984) is correct that we have only begun to appreciate the potential of automated computation—but I am even more impressed by both the difficulty of the test and its anthropocentrism. I think it is unlikely that a computer will pass the test, not because I have a low estimate of the capacities of computers (or AI-based systems), but because I am particularly impressed by the test's difficulty. Passage of the test is unlikely, on my view, not because the capacities of computers are relatively modest, but because the test is more difficult and anthropocentric than even Turing fully appreciated. Should a machine pass the test, however, precisely because I am impressed by the exceptional difficulty of the test, I would readily agree that the machine is a member of the exclusive club of thinkers.

1. Turing's Imitation Game

A few years ago, just outside the lounge door at a swank hotel in the French quarter of New Orleans, an exceptional scene captured my attention. An elegantly attired woman, perhaps in her early sixties, whose flushed face and slurred speech disclosed that she should have declined at least her last cocktail, exclaimed for all in the lobby to hear, "I just can't believe it! I just can't believe it! I just can't believe that that stripper was actually a man!" I surmised that she had just seen the widely publicized French female impersonator the hotel's bar was boldly featuring. It is a testimony to the scope of human creativity, I suppose, that female impersonation has become an exquisitely refined art, especially in Continental Europe. I wish now I had taken in the show to better appreciate how convincing a skilled charade can be.

Alan Turing (1950) was also interested in female impersonation. Perhaps there is a veiled touch of autobiographical allusion in his well-known suggestion, in "Computing Machinery and Intelligence," that we should (temporarily) replace the question "Can machines think?" with his Imitation Game. In the Imitation Game, a man and a woman are separated from an interrogator, whose task is to establish the sexual identity of the two people hidden from view. The job of the man is to convince the interrogator, contrary to fact, that he is the woman; the job of the woman is to convince the interrogator, true to fact, that she is the woman.

Next, Turing proposes a slight variation on the original Imitation Game. Instead of the man playing the role of the female impersonator, Turing asks us to consider the situation in which a computer plays the role of the impersonator. The situation is illustrated graphically in Figure 5–1. Instead of using variable names such as "A", "B", and "C", I use conventional names. Given such a situation, according to Turing, this is the pertinent question: Will Alayna, the interrogator, decide wrongly as often when the game is played like this as she does when the game is played between a man (skilled at impersonation) and a woman? What conclusion should be drawn, Turing effectively asks, if this happens?

Turing believes that he knows the answer. If the machine proves to be so good at imitating Teresa (an adult, native speaker of the language, reasonably well educated, etc.) that Alayna has extended difficulty determining which responses come from Teresa and which from the machine, then we have adequate grounds for concluding that the unnamed machine thinks, which, despite mildly misleading initial suggestions to the contrary, Turing still wishes to take as his question.

Sparing the reader sustained discussion of any one issue, Turing

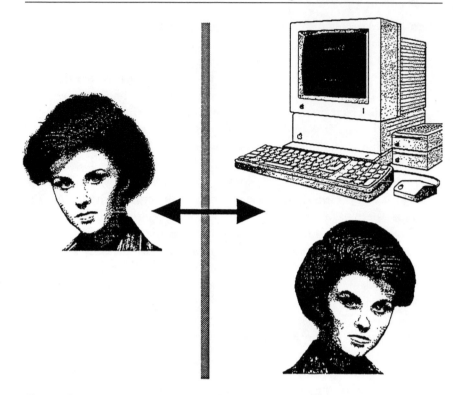

Alayna, the interrogator   *separated by a wall ,*   *Computer, Teresa*
                               communication is by teletype

Figure 5.1.   Turing's "Imitation Game" Test for Computing Thinking

points to a couple of considerations that he believes make the Imitation Game a good test. First, he claims that "the new problem has the advantage of drawing a fairly sharp line between the physical and the intellectual capacities of a man" (Anderson, 1964, p. 4). Thus the test rules out asking the machine to hit a major-league curve ball or asking it to sing an Italian aria. The Imitation Game is to be conducted exclusively by means of conversation, preferably by means of a terminal that serves to mask irrelevant factors.

Second, and central to his case, "the question and answer method seems to be suitable for introducing almost any one of the fields of human endeavor that we wish to include" (Anderson, 1964, p. 5). The test is intended to include a random sampling of the astonishing range of human interests, practices, and passions, which are amenable to linguistic expression, bar none: the constitutionality of flag desecration, the relation of Muslim mysticism to petroleum geopolitics, formal wedding etiquette, and the possible relation of all these to each other, are all fair game. This second consideration surely rules out Penzias's counterexample appeal to ELIZA, with which I began this chapter, with its drastically constrained conversational competence. It is the sheer complexity of this vast interlocking web of "human endeavor," and the concomitant difficulty of conversing adequately about it, that anchors Turing's appeal to human conversation as the best test we have. He supposed, correctly I think, that this complexity means that any successful conversational partner in a full-fledged Imitation Game would have to think—not just mechanically, mindlessly manipulate symbols—in some significant sense. The ability to converse well, to respond adequately to the queries of the interrogator, to ask the informed questions, in turn, which inevitably characterize good conversations, are exclusively the grounds on which the judgment is to be made. I'll return to this second consideration at length later in the chapter.

Turing's long paper covers quite a broad range of issues generally related to the question of machine intelligence. At this point I would like to make one objection to a comment that Turing makes in the paper and call attention to one tantalizing statement that Turing makes but, as usual, does not amplify. One comment in Turing's "Computing Machinery and Intelligence" particularly warrants censure.[2] Specifically, Turing's optimism about "what steps should be taken now if the experiment is to be successful" is at once amusing and preposterous. Consider the following remarks:

> Estimates of the storage capacity of the brain vary from 10^{10} to 10^{15} binary digits. . . . A storage capacity of 10^7 would be a very practicable possibility even by present techniques. . . . Our problem then is to find out how to program these machines to play the [imitation] game. At my present rate of working I produce about a thousand digits of program a day, so that about sixty workers, working steadily through the fifty years might accomplish the job, if nothing went into the wastepaper basket. (Anderson, 1964, p. 26)

---

[2] I use the full version as it appeared in *Mind* and was reprinted in Anderson (1964). Hofstadter and Dennett's (1981) truncated version omits some important remarks, in my opinion.

While the orders of magnitude seem about right, Turing's qualifier "if nothing went into the wastepaper basket" is programmatically equivalent to saying "if God did the programming"—so this idealized qualification is useless. If no mistakes are made, quite a lot that is practically impossible for many theoretically interesting reasons suddenly becomes just a matter of time. Moreover, the tacit assumption that this is fundamentally a quantitative endeavor bespeaks a naïveté that is difficult to understand today. Correctly coordinating the code of 60 workers working through 50 years and producing a thousand digits of code each day is surely distantly beyond the humanly possible. This idealized qualification aside, Turing deserves credit for intuiting something of the scale of such a programming task. I'll return to a discussion of "scale" problems when the chapter takes up issues related to rationality, debuggability, and the problems inherent in attempting to understand a mindlike program.

The tantalizing remark made by Turing in fact anticipated much of what Cherniak has been working on with regard to rationality and undebuggability. In terms of engineering a machine which might be capable (with some education) of passing the Imitation Game, Turing remarks:

> We also wish to allow the possibility that an engineer or team of engineers may construct a machine which works, but whose manner of operation cannot be satisfactorily described by its constructors because they have applied a method which is largely experimental. (Anderson, 1964, p. 7)

Turing raises the possibility here that a machine that "works" (I assume he means one that successfully participates in the Imitation Game) might be so complicated, owing to "experimental" engineering, that it cannot be satisfactorily described. As is usually the case in his paper, he does not expand the point but moves abruptly to another. I take it that he means that the experimental engineering sufficient to produce such a machine would be so complicated that it would preclude our comprehension of it. It might be that the engineering he has in mind has a lot to do with education, since he spends a considerable amount of time discussing the education of a computer in the paper. I suspect, however, that he had another point in mind. Perhaps by accident, he obliquely raises the point I will consider later in this chapter: suppose it turns out that a mindlike program necessarily must be so complicated, with a vast panoply of logical and nonlogical components, that we cannot seriously even entertain the hope of understanding how it works. In an article for which I have lost the reference, a writer some years ago suggested that for people to write a program which successfully duplicated the powers of the mind's program, we'd have to be a lot smarter than we are. But if we were a lot smarter, the program would, of course be more difficult, and so on, so that a mind's program becomes, to use Cherniak's (1988) term, an *impossibility engine*. How would we evaluate a mindlike program? What grounds could we possibly cite to substantiate the claim that it thinks? The answer I wish to sponsor is that an I/O test, specifically Turing's test, is the best recourse we have given our inability to understand well either the brain or programs that significantly emulate the powers of the brain.

2. Dennett's Defense of the Turing Test

In his Nobel talk at Gustavus Aldophus College in St. Peter, Minnesota, several years ago, Dennett (1985) took up the question that Turing, in "Computing Machinery and Intelligence," briefly discarded, namely, "Can machines think?" The announced intention of this talk and the corresponding paper to "show that the Turing test . . . is . . . plenty strong enough as a test of thinking." Dennett's claim is that critics have failed to recognize what the test actually requires and, as a result, have dismissed it unjustifiably. As stated earlier, I believe that Dennett succeeds in amplifying Turing's case but fails to notice the test's unfortunate anthropocentrism and makes no mention of other considerations, to be explored in the last half of this chapter, which count in favor of the claim that using such I/O tests is unavoidable.

Dennett ties what he takes to be Turing's insight, namely, that successful conversation between a machine and a person would necessarily indicate machine intelligence, to a "hunch" dating to Descartes; as we would expect, Dennett readily embraces the insight:

> Descartes's hunch that ordinary conversation would put as severe a strain on artificial intelligence as any other test was shared by Turing. . . . The assumption Turing was prepared to make was this:

Nothing could possibly pass the Turing test by winning the imitation game without being able to perform indefinitely many other clearly intelligent actions. Let us call that assumption the quick probe assumption. . . . success on his chosen test, he thought, would be highly predictive of success on many other intuitively acceptable tests of intelligence. Remember, failure on the Turing test does not predict failure on those others, but success would surely predict success. His test was so severe, he thought, that nothing that could pass it fair and square would disappoint us in other quarters. (1985, p. 124)

Let me attempt to identify two important claims ingredient in this passage:

1. Quick probe assumption: since passing the test is so demanding, any machine that was successful in the Imitation Game would be successful at many other tasks we would associate with intelligence — which is to say that language competency is not, like chess, an "isolatable talent." The assumption is that full language ability, like that which would be required to pass the test, has as a necessary condition a general ability that would not be limited to one or only a few domains. By contrast, chess-playing ability, as current chess-playing programs and "idiot-savant" chess players in Western history both illustrate, does not guarantee much in terms of other abilities. Both Turing and Dennett claim that language competency presupposes a general faculty that could be used in many areas that we associate with thinking.
2. No false-positives: failure at the Imitation Game would not be a predictor of failure at other tasks requiring intelligence; the weaker claim is that, while there might be some false negatives (a machine could fail at the Imitation Game and still be intelligent), there would be no false positives (no machine could succeed at the Imitation Game and not be intelligent).

Dennett begins his discussion of the quick probe assumption by appealing to some work by Terry Winograd, whom he describes as a "leader in artificial intelligence efforts to produce conversational ability in a computer" (p. 125). After citing an example from the early

Winograd,[3] which involves an ambiguous usage of a verb, Dennett argues that such disambiguation ability presupposes quite a lot:

> But mere rules of grammar or vocabulary will not fix the right reading. What fixes the right reading for us is knowledge about the world, about politics, social circumstances, committees and their attitudes, groups that want to parade, how they tend to behave and the like. One must know about the world, in short, to make sense of such a sentence. (p. 125)

Dennett claims that questions that could be a part of an Imitation Game conversation are good quick probes because of the deep, wide range of knowledge, and a faculty capable of skillfully using that knowledge, that are requisite to successful conversation. In fact, he emphasizes the importance of the surprise or unusual question:

> People typically ignore the prospect of having the judge ask off-the-wall questions in the Turing test, and hence they underestimate the competence a computer would have to have to pass the test. But remember, the rules of the imitation game as Turing presented it permit the judge to ask any question that could be asked of a human being—no holds barred. (p. 126)

The point is that the range of questions that could be asked in an Imitation Game, in the effort to unmask the computer and identify the person as really the person, is so large that the problem facing the computer programmers cannot be solved using conventional programming techniques such as stock responses, random guessing, or look-up in a large database. There has to be, in Dennett's terms, a *general ability* to respond to questions that would characterize an engaging conversation. This general ability should not be confused with a narrow, isolatable talent such as chess playing or counseling a client using Rogerian psychotherapy. This general ability to converse across a wide range of subjects, possessing at once breadth and depth, Dennett

---

[3]The example is from *Understanding Natural Language* (Winograd, 1983) which was published in 1972. The Winograd (1986) of *Understanding Computer and Cognition* takes a different view.

seems to suggest, requires nothing less than thinking in every philosophically interesting sense.

Dennett is not obliged to detail what thinking is or is not, nor is he
obligated to spell out, even speculatively, what computer techniques
might provide such a general ability (he is much more sanguine than
I about this). Rather, Dennett's argument is that, whatever thinking is,
and however it might be accomplished on a machine, if a machine
passed the full-fledged Turing test, it would have be able to think in
ways that fulfill the commitments we make, to use terms derived from
Winograd and Flores (1986) when we say "So and so thinks."

To emphasize his point, he proposes that we accept Ned Block's
suggestion that we limit the conversation to the 850 words of "Basic
English" and to short sentences. Even in this extremely limited context,
according to Dennett, the number of possible conversations is prodigious:

> Of course, the number of good, sensible conversations under these
> limits is a tiny fraction, maybe one in a quadrillion, of the number of
> merely grammatically well formed conversations. So let's say, to be very
> conservative, that there are only ten to the fiftieth different smart
> conversations such a computer would have to store. Well, the task
> shouldn't take more than a few trillion years—given generous federal
> support. Finite numbers can be very large. (p. 131)

What Dennett is getting to is that we can't hope to store every
possible conversation in a computer in hopes of enabling it to pass the
Turing test by means of simple look-up. Combinatorial explosion
plagues chess and, *a fortiori*, conversations even as dramatically and
artificially circumscribed as Block's. There is nothing like a detailed
argument here, to be sure, but I don't believe that his reminder that a
conversation between a computer and a person, of the type suggested
by the Imitation Game, would quickly overwhelm a computer not
specifically and imaginatively designed to defeat the resulting combinatorial explosion, is seriously disputed by anyone. He concludes that
"there is considerable plausibility in Newell and Simon's proposal that
avoiding combinatorial explosion (by any means at all) be viewed as
one of the hallmarks of intelligence" (p. 131). The avoidance of
combinatorial explosion is a problem on the view of cognition as
computation assumed by classical AI. Below, I cite Howard Margolis's

promising new work, which takes cognition to be based on pattern recognition and not computation at all; the result arguably is that combinatorial explosion is avoided and problems such as the frame problem do not occur.

As it is, Dennett's defense recognizes only half of the "space" problems facing a computer designed to pass the Turing test. The number of combinations of words in a possible conversation in a search space is so large that nothing like a conventional database is likely going to be able to put together the word combinations that will work in the Imitation Game. He has therefore correctly called attention to this problem effectively, even scaling the claims he could make to quite modest levels. The space problem he does not recognize and press into service in defense of the test is the relevance space problem that results from the frame problem. As I will argue later, not only is there an enormous linguistic search space problem at the I/O level, there is an equally daunting relevance space problem at the process level inside any would-be conversing program.

Dennett's defense resembles Haugeland's (1986) brief defense of the test in the sense that both point to the range of knowledge that a maturely conversing system would have to have. Anticipating what I will expand upon at much greater length in the next chapter, Haugeland observes that "to converse beyond the most superficial level, you have to know what you are talking about" (p. 8). Haugeland's claim is that the competency involved in mature language ability is not just linguistic but involves a "passable understanding" of issues ranging from poetry to Federal Reserve policy. As Haugeland puts it, "That's why the Turing test is so powerful."

I believe that this is generally the right direction to take, although the case that Haugeland and Dennett make, unaided, is partially vulnerable to the kind of argument advanced by Searle and Gunderson, which I look at in the next chapter. If an observer only has input/output in a conversation, and claims, in light only of this fact, that the computer must have a "passable understanding" of the topics covered in the conversation, one might still question whether such a Haugeland-style argument is vulnerable to the criticism that understanding (or thinking) may turn out to be only one of two or more ways to account for the input/output. Understanding and thinking are a sufficient condition for passing the test but it might be questioned whether such high level mental activity is necessary. Impressive input/output may be thought to be *indicative* of understanding and thinking, if it is aided by auxiliary philosophical considerations, so the concern might be expressed, but it is surely not simply *synonymous* with it. What we need from Haugeland, and do not get, is a convincing argument that there cannot be other ways to produce the input/output than that the system understands what it is talking about.

In fact, I think this criticism of Haugeland applies partially to Dennett as well. We get a general "since combinational explosion is solved there must be a general intelligence"-style argument from Dennett, but he doesn't supply a sufficiently specific explanation of why combinatorial explosion cannot be managed by some new algorithmic technique.[4] After all, the game of chess suffers from combinatorial explosion and, especially in the early days of AI, some people were skeptical that that problem would fall to clever programming but, since chess programs play master-rating chess these days, it seems fair to say that at least some problems with enormous search spaces are amenable to respectable algorithmic (or, if it is preferred, "heuristic") management.[5] As I will argue in Chapter 6, however, the better explanation is that it is the frame problem that can be used to show why chess as a problem falls to algorithmic management but mature conversation does not. It is not just that the search space is larger for mature conversation but that, on my view, it differs in epistemological kind from chess. As I see it, then, it is the combination of the good input/output plus considerations stemming from the frame problem that, in tandem, generate a convincing case that a maturely conversing system must be thinking. As a result, Dennett and Haugeland are strong on the input/output side but weak on the indirect, internal considerations side, which can be used to augment the case for the Turing test.

In a claim that sounds as if it could have been written by Dreyfus and Dreyfus, Dennett points out that programs such as expert systems

---

[4]I use the word *manage*, since the problem of combinational explosion is scarcely solved. According to latest characterizations I have read, the best chess programs are capable of only about three turns of "look ahead."

[5]An alleged example of this is Hubert Dreyfus's purported claim in 1965 that computers would never play good chess. Since he was defeated by the chess program Mac Hack in 1968, that was taken as evidence by some, such as the futurist Alvin Toffler, that such advances would be rapid in coming. Dreyfus denies that he made such a prediction. See Dreyfus and Dreyfus (1986, p. 112).

and other AI programs, of necessity, are engineered to manage a narrow range of problems.

> All expert systems, like all other large AI programs, are what you might call Potemkin villages. That is, they are cleverly constructed facades, like cinema sets. The actual filling-in of details of AI programs is time-consuming, costly work, so economy dictates that only those surfaces of the phenomenon that are likely to be probed or observed are represented. (1985, p. 135)

Let's call this quality of expert systems and AI programs the *Potemkin village problem*. The Potemkin village problem is the characteristic problem that plagues computer programs in general and AI programs specifically: within a narrow range, they function well. But in order to be successful, the range must be drastically constricted. Once the user attempts to go outside the bounds, the programs fail spectacularly — recall that Haugeland calls this the *jerky* problem.

Unfortunately following Turing's method too closely, Dennett fails to amplify this point as fully as it deserves. A Dennett-compatible amplification can be obtained by citing some considerations that Dennett (1987) attempted to bring to bear in his discussion of the frame problem:

> artificial agent[s] with a well-stocked compendium of frames or scripts . . . perform creditably when the world co-operates with their stereotypes, and even with anticipated variations on them, [but] when their world turns perverse, such systems typically cannot recover gracefully from the misanalyses they are led into. In fact, their behavior *in extremis* looks for all the world like the preposterously counterproductive activities of insects betrayed by their rigid tropisms and other genetically hard-wired behavioral routines. (p. 57)

Stereotypical behavior is the stock-in-trade of software as it is currently understood and developed. But mature conversation is not stereotypical, so, consequently, stereotyped responses to conversational queries of the type Turing had in mind will also be betrayed, as Dennett puts it, "by their rigid tropisms." In a word, they will fail to pass the Turing test.

Dennett could have reminded us that one goal of software development should be robustness over invalid input data; robust software

should handle inappropriate data entry by identifying the inappropriate data to the user and reprompting so that, using Dennett's terms,
in extremis situations are circumvented at the outset. Software as it is
now produced is engineered to constrict the interaction between user
and computer into the narrow, stereotypical range that software must
be designed, at least so far, to handle. Conversation, by contrast,
possesses the broadest of imaginable ranges; *in extremis* conditions
abound and stereotypical conversation is inept conversation. The mark
of an engaging conversation is the skill and urbanity of the conversational partners coping with the surprising twists and unanticipated
turns of the conversation, with *in extremis* moments in particular
handled skillfully. Consequently, and Dennett should have emphasized this more than he did, *in extremis* conditions are as often the rule
as the exception. To force the user back into the circumscribed
input/output range characteristic of software as we know it now—
which is how ELIZA handles responses that do not fit into its tiny stock
of phrase-matching routines—is pointedly to fail the test. Passing the
test requires a general, flexible facility to handle such extreme
conditions with routine ease in the very short periods of time that are
available during a human conversation. To cope gracefully when the
conversational world turns "perverse," to respond creatively to "off the
wall" questions, is the *sine qua non* of the kind of informed, mature
conversational ability that Turing surely had in mind. Torrance (1986)
seconds this and reminds us of the importance of AI's nemesis,
common sense, by arguing that "any Turing test program must be
extremely robust, versatile and comprehensive . . . and must also have
extensive reserves of common-sense knowledge" (p. 298).

Let me amplify this by appealing to relatively recent work in the
psychology of testing. Sternberg (1986) has pointed out that, while
there is generally less reliance now in the assaying of intelligence on
psychometric tests than was the case some years ago, considerable
consensus remains that vocabulary tests are a good way to measure
intelligence. The reason, according to Sternberg, is that vocabulary
tests represent an indirect measure of the general ability to appropriate
new information and integrate it into old. He writes:

> vocabulary [is] . . . generally considered to be one of the best measures
> of individual differences in intelligence (Matarazzo 1972). Vocabulary
> tests are such good measures of intelligence because they indirectly

measure the ability to acquire meanings of new words from natural contexts and thus reflect the ability to acquire new information.

Mature conversational ability, as I have tried to define it, includes the skilled use of a large vocabulary, both in terms of using it and understanding it when it is used by a conversational partner. Often it is the case, moreover, that an intelligent person can understand a new word, or a new use of a familiar word, by taking the context in which the word is used into consideration and drawing upon "extensive reserves of common sense knowledge." Surely, this is part of what we value in a stimulating conversationalist. Conversely, repeated failure to do this would begin to count against the claim that a specific system can pass the Turing test.

In terms of an automatic formal system, success at handling a rich vocabulary, appropriately integrating and using newly learned words, and disambiguating new words during the course of a conversation is compelling evidence that the frame problem has been solved. As a result, and Dennett misses this pivotal point, the way to understand why skilled use of a large vocabulary is Turing-test significant is because we have successful constraint of two distinct spaces, namely, search and relevance. At the search space level, successful I/O means that words are handled well in the course of the conversation. The number of meaningless combinations of words far exceeds the number of meaningful combinations, especially since the set of meaningful combinations of words in a specific conversation is much smaller than the set of meaningful combinations of words. The result is that there is constraint of the I/O search space, as Dennett underscores. At the relevance space level, it means that the system is able to integrate words used in different senses, as they almost invariably are in engaging conversations, into its own representational system, and, even more significantly, it will often mean that the system is able to surmise the meaning of words used in the conversation which are new to the system, successfully incorporating the new words into an existing vocabulary. Such successful incorporation means the problem of an exploding relevance space has been solved. It is the second constraint that Dennett does not explicitly underscore.

The Newell/Simon suggestion about the relation of intelligence to the problem of combinatorial explosion, therefore, should be amplified to take into account how the frame problem also inhibits intelligence.

An (epistemologically complex) intelligent computer system is not only one which avoids or solves the search space combinatorial explosion at the I/O level, it avoids or solves the relevance space combinatorial explosion problem at the representational level. The combinatorial explosion problem not only occurs "out there" in the problem domain, such as a conversation that can be observed by the interrogator, it exists "in here" in the system of representation that is used to generate the computer's successful output. In fact, solution of the latter is a necessary condition to solution of the former, although solution of the latter is not a sufficient condition to solution of the former. This is the case since, on the assumption that the relevance space problem is soluble, it is conceivable that a system incorporates a solution to the relevance space problem but, owing to other deficiencies in its programming, performs ineffectually at the I/O level. A successfully conversing system, one that converses effectively at an epistemologically complex level, thus has necessarily solved both combinatorial explosion problems — at the same time. The general point is that Dennett has made a good — albeit rather traditional — start toward a full defense of the test, but that he has not adequately taken into account the implications of the frame problem for the test.

There are other problems as well. Later in his paper, for example, he writes, "But all AI programs in one way or another have this facade-like quality, simply for reasons of economy" (1987, p. 137). This comment, taken together with the longer passage appearing before it, seems to suggest that this is Dennett's understanding: AI programs suffer from the Potemkin village problem because the problems that AI, in contrast with conventional computer science, tackles are usually the most difficult problems. Since writing computer programs is time consuming and resources are scarce, programmers have to be very selective in choosing which parts of the facade to build. The problem I have with this characterization is that it makes the problem sound akin to the couple building a new house who have to decide, because they are already at their mortgage limit, between a third stall on the garage, which would be convenient to house the riding mower, and a guest room on the lower level, which would be handy to put up visiting in-laws at a comfortable distance. Both *could* be done, if only the resources were there. But Dennett has given us no good reason to suppose that the problem is as simple as "economy." In fact, it is the claim of this essay that there are severe theoretical problems standing in the way of flushing out the programmatic Potemkin village, so that it more nearly approximates what it feigns. We get dismayingly little indication that Dennett understands that there are formidable problems, such as the frame problem, standing in the way of the production of AI programs that attempt to generate intelligence.

At this point, I would like to raise the question of whether Turing's test is too anthropocentric and hence too narrow to be a good test of thinking, generally understood. I believe the following is the case: passing the Turing test would surely require thinking, as both Turing and Dennett claim. But, by basing the test on human conversation, could it be that they have made the standards too stringent and too predicated on thinking in ways compatible, at least at the I/O level, with human thinking? If the issue is, "Can machines think as people do (at the I/O level, at least)?" then the test is appropriate. As a result, in terms of computer simulation of human intelligence, the test is not too species specific. But if we prefer the much more general question, "Can machines think?" the test is more specific than that. Another way to put this is: if what we are concerned about is computer simulation of human intelligence, then the Turing test, for reasons articulated in this chapter, is quite suitable. But if we are interested in the more general question, "Can machines think?" which both Turing and Dennett profess to be their question, then I am less confident that the test measures this and only this.

Allow me to consider the role of natural language in the Imitation Game so that I can explore the problem of the test's anthropocentrism more fully. Part of the appeal of the Imitation Game, as Dennett correctly underscores, is that the interrogator is precluded from discriminating against the computer on the grounds of appearance, of unfairly concluding that, since the computer doesn't *look* anything like a person or a particularly smart dog, it could not possibly belong to the club of thinkers. Dennett writes that Turing's "point was that we should not be species-chauvinistic, or anthropocentric, about the insides of an intelligent being, for there might be inhuman ways of being intelligent" (1985, p. 132).

It is this claim which occasions my somewhat reluctant appeal to the later work of Terry Winograd and Fernando Flores (1986). It is somewhat reluctant because Winograd, in his post-AI-proponent days, has become a disciple of Continental philosophy. I don't wish to impugn Continental philosophy per se; rather, my concern is that Continental philosophy tends to wrestle with those dimensions of human experience that are far beyond the announced topic of this essay.

The question is this: does the Turing test preclude species chauvinism in the way that Turing and Dennett suppose? It does so only on one view of natural language, namely, that language significantly is a matter of correspondence between that which is represented and the linguistic representation. Winograd and Flores document at some length what they call the *rationalistic* theory of language. Ingredient in this rationalistic theory, according to Winograd and Flores, is a *truth theoretic* characterization of meaning. To put it roughly, natural language is extricable from the context of human tradition and expectation, such that it can, in principle, be expressed in terms amenable to capture by computer program. Such a view of natural language, they argue, denigrates the essential rootedness of language in human tradition and experience.

Appealing to the phenomenological work of Heidegger and the hermeneutical work of Hans-Georg Gadamer, Winograd and Flores argue that human language is grounded in the human situation, with its background of tradition and tacit expectations, in such a way that the meaning of conversation or a piece of writing is necessarily dependent on the "horizon" that the conversationalist or reader brings to the linguistic task. This involves the vast range of cultural conditions and human experiences that largely tacitly condition any human conversation. In this view, it is not possible to isolate human language from its thoroughly human context, thereby seemingly purging it of its chauvinistic qualities.

The question I raise is this: do we obviously escape the problem of species chauvinism by hiding the computer behind a wall and judging its intellectual capacity on the basis of its ability to handle natural language as well as an adult? Is taming the problem of species chauvinism in judging the intellectual capacity of a radically different "cognitive system" this straightforward? The case that Winograd and Flores make is that our language, probably more than any other human phenomenon, embodies who and what we are. The objection I raise is not the difficulty of using the language in such a way that the Imitation Game is successful; rather, the objection is that, in assaying the intelligence of a computer by testing its natural (human) language competence, we have not obviated the species-chauvinism that Turing and Dennett suppose. In fact, Winograd and Flores, whose extended argument has been only briefly alluded to here, would surely claim that just the opposite is the case. In selecting human language as the test medium, Winograd and Flores would surely counter, Turing selected that medium most likely to result in the species-chauvinistic judgments that Dennett praises the test for avoiding. Minimally, I don't see that hiding the computer behind the wall and using a teletype for communication, alone, clearly solve the problem or assist the identification of "inhuman ways of being intelligent."

Admittedly, finding a way to identify and measure intelligence that does not presuppose the species-specific ways we happen to be intelligent will not be easy. If, as the biologists tell us, vision developed to support survival and reproduction, and intelligence developed to support vision, attempting to say something nonchauvinistic about machine intelligence will be even more difficult than attempting to say something nonchauvinistic about grasshopper vision. Classical AI proponents, of course, will not be swayed by this point since, as they see it, intelligence just is the manipulation of logically related constituents under the control of a program — and this can occur, at least in principle, just as readily and measurably in a machine as it does in a person. In a word, biology is finally irrelevant.

3. Cherniak's Critique and the Mind's Program as an Unknowable *Ding an Sich*

Suppose that we were given a program by visiting, extremely smart aliens which, running on our best hardware, duplicated closely the properties of the human mind, whatever they are, and that such a program would be worth academic acclaim and enormous financial return — provided that we could (to a reasonable degree) demonstrate that it closely duplicated the properties of the mind. Coveting distinction and treasure, how could we do this?

Two possibilities come to mind. One would be to study the program until we understood it so well that we could articulate how it had the properties at issue. This first alternative assumes that we understand the properties of the brain/mind. In the last section, I challenge this assumption. As a result, I claim that the first alternative fails on two counts. First, it fails because we don't understand the brain well enough to claim that we could identify a mindlike program. Second, I claim that we cannot understand, because of its complexity and size, a mind-like program. Since we have only the dimmest understanding of both minds and mindlike programs, it follows, on my account, that we cannot say that program x has the properties of a mind. The other possibility would be to test it at the input/output level, which, of course, is what the Turing test does. As a hybrid third alternative, one might argue for a combination of these two methods.

What I propose to do in this section is discuss and amplify some of the limitative claims advanced by Christopher Cherniak, with the goal of advancing a substantial case that the first alternative is not viable. If these are the only two methods of reaching our goal, and it turns out that the first is not viable, then it would follow that our only recourse would be the input/output method.

Cherniak's (1988) principal claim is that a program that thoroughly models the mind will turn out to be a program that differs fundamentally from conventional programs. In other words, it would not be the case that such a program would be similar to the latest expert system except that it would be, to pick a theologically interesting number for lack of a better method, 666 times larger. Instead, it is the unparalleled characteristics of a mindlike program that deserve our attention.

> A complete computational approximation of the mind would be a (1) huge, (2) "branchy" and holistically structured, and (3) quick and dirty (i.e., computationally tractable, but formally incorrect/incomplete) (4) kludge (i.e., a radically inelegant set of procedures). The mind's program thus turns out to be fundamentally dissimilar to more familiar software, and software, in general, to be dissimilar to more familiar types of machines. . . . In this way, the full mind's program appears to be a type of practically unknowable thing-in-itself. (p. 402)

Each of these characterizations complicates our ability to understand such a program. Let me amplify them briefly, in order. First, even with modular structure, huge programs are notoriously difficult to comprehend. By treating subroutines as black boxes, we can have some understanding of large programs in terms of breadth. Or we can get some in-depth understanding of specific routines if we are willing to sacrifice breadth. But simultaneous breadth and depth understanding of large programs, especially those approximating the size of a mindlike program, is not possible. Second, a good part of recent computer science has been devoted to limiting branchy computer structures because they so quickly impair human understanding. However, the singular demands of a mindlike program require the branchiest of program structures. Third, quick and dirty routines, often the brunt of jokes in software engineering contexts, turn out to be, according to Cherniak, necessarily characteristic of a mindlike program; such routines also cloud our ability to fathom how a program works. Last, kludge, or "radically inelegant set[s] of procedures," are far from computer science ideals because they reflect the fact that the needed operation is not well understood, so that we wind up using programmatic structures that we don't understand to solve problems that we understand poorly, crossing our fingers that the kludge will get us past the programmatic crisis.

Cherniak argues that mindlike programs have these four under-standing-limiting characteristics simultaneously. The result, if he is right, is that mindlike programs are monumentally inaccessible to human understanding. This is the reason why Cherniak reaches back into philosophical history for Kant's term, *ding an sich*, which, as Kant understood that German phrase, means that which is beyond human observation or experience, and uses it to emphasize the inaccessibility of a mindlike program. For Cherniak, a mindlike program is a 20th-century instantiation of a Kantian *ding an sich*.

Much of Cherniak's recent work, both in this paper and in his *Minimal Rationality* (1986), has to do with challenging the cognitive science view that mentality is largely cognition, which is largely ratiocination, which, in principle, is amenable to study and under-standing. As Cherniak puts it, "cognitive science seems to presuppose the manageability and feasibility of such a total mind's program" (1988, p. 402).

In fact, the feasibility of understanding a mind's program is what is at issue. Part of the reason why cognitive science has turned to software as an objective cognitive investigation stems from the diffi-culties in analyzing the brain. The hope is that the software will be accessible in ways that the brain has not been, at least up to now. The problem with this assumption, according to Cherniak, is that it does not take into account the extraordinary difficulty of understanding software that even begins to approach the complexity of a mind's program. Software's characteristic "branchy structure" means that a mindlike program has its own unique opacity which stands in the way of understanding either how it works or what causes it to fail:

> The texture of failure for a program differs [from hardware] because of its branchy structure: There are not just many distinct states, but a combinatorially exploding number of ways in which one state can be connected to another. The branching is not just wide, but deeply hierarchical in organization, nested iteratively through many layers as in truth tables. (1988, p. 409)

Cherniak takes the result of this to be that our hope for debugging a program simply by I/O testing alone is illusory. Given that there are a combinatorially exploding number of ways in which one program state can interact with another for even conventional, smaller programs, the result I take from these considerations is that they count against the hope that we can even begin to understand a mindlike program with its size, formally incorrect structures, and inelegantly related procedures.

One of Cherniak's claims is that formally incorrect heuristics, which he believes characterize human mentality, are not irrational but stand reasonably between formal correctness, which yields computational paralysis, on one hand, and random guessing, which generates at best rare success solving problems on the other, both of which are presumably antithetical to successful problem solving. The problem, according to Cherniak, is that many cognitive models fail to recognize the problems inherent in attributing to cognitive agents the "impossibility engine" of a deductive system able to produce usable inferences in the context of finite time and virtually infinite real-world complexity.

> Standard rationality models require the agent to be some sort of perfect logician, in particular, to be able to determine in finite time whether or not any given formal sentence is a first-order logical consequence of a given set of premises. Half a century ago, however, Church's theorem showed that the predicate calculus was undecidable—that is, no algorithm for this task is possible. (p. 403)

The point is that a person cannot begin to determine which propositions follow from a set of premises, even if the set is unrealistically small. Quantifying his claim, he suggests that, given a set of 138 independent propositions, a speedy inference engine could not evaluate the truth table for the set in the time the universe has existed. Put in more qualitative terms, he suggests that such considerations lead to the conclusion that there is a distinct "upper bound on the size of a human cognitive system" (p. 404).

Cherniak accepts the common estimate that the human cognitive system is able to store something on the order of 1 to 10 million different items. The question he wishes to ask is: What is the significance of this magnitude for cognitive science? He juggles quite a few purportedly related numbers and then suggests that, in order for the mind's program to handle such a vast amount of data, it would have to be on the order of one hundred times the projected size of the immense Strategic Defense Initiative (or "Star Wars") battle-management software. He rehearses some of the well-publicized recent history of differences of opinion on the part of software engineers as to the reliability of the proposed SDI software. The point of such controversy, according to Cherniak, is that large programs encounter at least practically intractable problems in terms of reliability; the mind's program, on the plausible assumption that it would be many times larger than the SDI software, would likely be even more riddled with reliability problems, since "a cognitive system's program will tend to act as a failure amplifier because of its intrinsically holistic structure of interconnection" (p. 408).

Cherniak's analysis can be augmented with some of the following considerations from the theory of algorithms. Discussion of program correctness often concentrates on bugs and debugging for the reason that computer scientists, not surprisingly, value the goal of bug-free programs. Generally, program testing turns out to be of two categories, which, given the previous discussion, should not be unexpected. First, programs can be tested against a set of data. As Goldschlager and Lister (1982, p. 107) put it, however, "The important feature of testing is that the effect of the program is discovered only for the particular chosen set of test data." It might be argued that Goldschlager and Lister's comment counts against the Turing test, since it is an I/O test. However, I claim that this comment pertains only to more conventional programs; the branchy quality of a mindlike program acts, as Cherniak noted, as a failure amplifier. That is to say, serious problems in a mindlike program will appear quickly, especially in a conversational context, precisely because a good conversation is an excellent quick probe. As a result, I don't see that Goldschlager and Lister's observation is particularly a problem. The problem with testing over a necessarily finite set of test cases, of course, is that most interesting programs accept a large number of inputs; testing can only verify correctness for a tiny percentage of inputs. The number of valid inputs for a mind's program, obviously, would be prodigious.

Second, we can attempt to prove a program correct. The advantage of proving a program correct is that we can be sure, if in fact the program is correct, that it will work for all valid input data (a program that finds square roots for all numbers less than the maximum representable number for that system will not be able to find a root for a negative number, which is not a valid input). But proving a program correct requires a proof distinct from the program itself. Now, instead of one suspect item, namely, the program, we have two, the program and the proof. But suppose we write a proof for a program. The new worry is whether the proof itself is correct; since proofs can be larger than the programs they prove, the proof becomes more subject to error than the original program. As Cherniak puts it, "To establish adequate confidence in a program by this [proof] methodology, one moves out of the frying pan of questions about the program's correctness and into the fire of an even more real-world unmanageable correctness proof" (1988, p. 407). We now have questions about program correctness *and* proof correctness. We might attempt a proof of the proof, but even the thought suggests we have become entangled in an infinite regress. Unless we can attach complete confidence to the proof, we have inadequate grounds for concluding that either the program or the proof(s) are correct.

One practical point that rarely gets mentioned in these discussions is that programmers rarely write a program directly in machine code — especially in the case of large, ambitious programs like those attempted in AI. Instead, such programs are often written in a language such as LISP or PROLOG. Suppose that we write the mind-program in PROLOG. The PROLOG interpreter or compiler itself would be written in another language, such as a C compiler or LISP, which, in turn, presupposes an operating system, which presupposes both code written in ROM and the hardware's microcode. Each of these levels almost certainly has bugs. As a result, attempting to prove a large PROLOG program correct would be a matter of showing its correctness on all these different levels, not just the PROLOG program itself. Moreover, PROLOG is neither complete nor consistent. My point here is that correctness of the program is only one small part of what might be called *systemic correctness*. Even if proving the correctness of the PROLOG program were remotely possible, it becomes humanly impossible to construct a convincing proof of this magnitude. As Cherniak puts it, "As programs and their verifications get bigger, the proof's power as convincing machines thereby asymptotes" (1988, p. 407). As a result, I conclude that proving a large program, such as a mind program, correct is not feasible.

I also maintain that proving a program correct and understanding it are significantly related. If it is not feasible to prove a program correct, then our justification for claiming that we understand it erodes because we can't claim to understand how it performs in all situations; conversely, if it is not understandable, it is difficult to imagine how a proof would be constructed. As a result, I would rephrase Cherniak's observation this way: as programs get bigger, the feasibility of understanding them decreases. If we can accept Cherniak's claim that the mind's program would be on the order of 100 times the size of the SDI's battle management program, it would seem that, as the mind's program approaches an adequate duplication of the properties of the mind, our ability to understand it radically wanes. In practice, in fact, on large programming projects, in which the program is much smaller than a mind program would be, each programmer typically "understands" at best a tiny percentage of the production process. In sum, the hope that we can understand a mindlike program to any significant simultaneous breadth and depth is a false one.

The picture of a mindlike program that emerges from studies in computability theory is one that is anything but clean, logical, and symmetrical. In taking the computer to be analogically helpful in understanding the mind, we run the risk of mistakenly imposing logical structure on that which was generated out of biological necessity and which had to settle for an inelegant hodgepodge of mechanisms that, according to Cherniak, is the equivalent of a kludge:

It is at least a question of current empirical investigation, and of some controversy, whether the mind is in fact hyper-Euclidean in this way. After all, what is elegant to the eye of the cognitive theoretician may not be obediently implemented by Mother Nature because it may not be efficient for actual processing: Thus, the alternative emerging picture of mind instead as an in-practice anomalous kludge of limited-applicability special-purpose procedures. (1988, p. 409)

Surely an enormous, "anomalous kludge of limited-applicability special-purpose procedures" is not a promising candidate for significant understanding.

The result I take from this section is that we are unable to reach a general understanding of a mind-like program which is sufficiently rich that we could characterize how it works at anything more than an I/O level or, at the most, a level or two down in the process itself.

4. Pattern Recognition, Evolution, and the Mind's Accessibility

In this last section of the chapter, I will call attention to some of the pertinent aspects of Howard Margolis's (1987) account, in his relatively recently published *Patterns, Thinking and Cognition*, of how human mentality, especially cognition and judgment, is based exclusively on a pattern-recognition faculty that developed in natural history. Advanced as an alternative to the computational picture of the mind that is most notably associated with AI and cognitive psychology, Margolis's theory does not attempt to detail how pattern recognition works since, as he points out, pattern recognition is poorly understood. Instead, he attempts to provide an account of how pattern recognition developed in natural history in animals as a way to solve survival problems. The reason his work is relevant to this chapter is that, if he is right, our ability to achieve a deep understanding of human mentality at what I have called the *process level* is likely to remain inconsequential for the foreseeable future.

Before I begin, however, I wish to rehearse briefly the distinction I developed in Chapter 3 between P-simulation and I/O-simulation. In I/O-simulation (IOS), what we attempt to simulate is output as compared to input, relative to the system being simulated, in the context in which the simulation is taking place. For example, all of the chess programs with which I am familiar should be described as I/O-simulations. There is little or no effort to simulate human chess playing in terms of the *process* that people presumably use to play chess.

While we don't know a great deal about how people play games like chess, it seems obvious that they don't play it the way that current chess programs play it. (My guess is that a significant component of human chess playing, as in any game, is deeply pattern recognition based.) As a result, the level of simulation is only input/output deep. In fact, much of what currently passes as "AI" is only IOS and, to be sure, often such I/O-simulation is perfectly suitable for the task at hand.

In process or P-simulation, not only do we attempt to simulate output as compared to input, in a way that parallels that which is being simulated, we attempt to simulate the process, to some level of depth, by which the output is gotten from the input as well, relative to the system being simulated. For example, if we were to write chess playing programs with an eye to simulating the *way* human chess champions play, this would count as an attempt at P-simulation. We could distinguish a number of levels of P-simulation: a less deep level of chess P-simulation might simply incorporate a number of rules of thumb that specific chess players often employ. A much deeper P-simulation might attempt to simulate the way that one person plays chess, taking into account his or her favored strategies, personal idiosyncrasies, perhaps even taking into account this or that psychological or biological profile of the person. The point is that P-simulation, if we know enough about the phenomenon being simulated, can be taken to quite a number of different levels. The more deeply a simulation emulates that which is simulated, obviously, the more must be known about the system that is simulated. As a corollary, it follows that, if little is known about a system that we want to simulate, any P-simulation will necessarily be quite shallow or may not be possible at all; in such a case we may be limited to an I/O simulation.

It should be obvious where I am headed: in simulations limited to shallow P-simulations or especially I/O simulations, I/O-based tests, such as Turing's, become more important. If deep P-simulations are possible, then, other things being equal, I/O-based tests are less important. I believe that Margolis's work counts in favor of the claim that simulations of human mentality, at least in the foreseeable future, are likely to be limited to quite shallow P-simulations at best and, in the worst case, I/O-simulations.

Margolis concedes that he is not the first to advance a theory of cognition based on pattern recognition. He does claim that his is a radical proposal, since he wishes to base cognition exclusively on pattern recognition, and not appeal to computational mechanisms when all else fails:

> So it is essentially universal to concede an essential role to the cuing of patterns and patterned responses; but precise articulation of just what is happening when a pattern is recognized is an unsolved problem. Because so little can be said, the dominant tendency (until very recently, at least) has been to move as quickly as possible from pattern-recognition to some algorithmic, rule-following procedure which can be articulated in a discussion and perhaps instantiated on a computer program. (p. 3)

Fischler and Firschein (1987) make exactly the kind of move that Margolis rejects. They observe that very little is known about the brain. Since so little is known about the brain, they suggest, we should turn to the computer for analogical help.

> there is little hope that the structures we can currently observe and describe will shed much light on how the brain really functions. In a device as complex as the brain, function is too deeply encoded in structure to be deciphered without already knowing the relationships for which we are searching. . . . At present, our best hope for under-standing the brain and the nature of human intelligence appears to be through analogy with the computer and the associated mathematical theory of computation. (pp. 23–24)

Of course, this presupposes that a computer and the brain have enough in common that study of the former can shed some light on the latter. By way of contrast with many cognitive theories, Margolis wishes not to suggest that his theory can be expressed in a computer program:

> Unlike the many students of cognition for whom a viable cognitive theory must be implemented as a computer program, I have disowned trying to build a theory of that sort. Pattern-recognition is all there is to cognition, on the account I will give; but no one can say much yet about what the brain is doing when it recognizes a pattern. (1987, p. 3)

Instead of attempting to build a theory that could be tested by means of simulation on a computer, Margolis attempts to account for what little we know of the brain — and to explain at the same time why so little is known — by tracing some natural history and attempting to tease out some resulting considerations. He particularly focuses on the relation of decision making to evolution. Echoing some of Cherniak's articulation of the cognitive agent's dilemma of computational paralysis versus random guessing, Margolis claims that the two extremes facing the agent making a decision which affects its survival are hesitating too long and jumping too soon:

> For less trivial brains absolute perfection could hardly be approached. So we want to be alert to various properties which, if achieved by a system, would contribute to its ability to perform well despite flaws. . . . it would surely be undesirable to work out the response to every situation from scratch. Rather, we should look for standard responses to various frequently encountered situations. . . . Consequently, there surely will be some tradeoff between what statisticians call errors of the first kind (hesitating too long in seeking the best response) and errors of the second kind (jumping too soon). (p. 27)

While he doesn't use results from the theory of computability, as Cherniak does, there are some clear parallels. Animal survival depends on making good choices a significant percentage of the time; those who do not make good choices perish and sometimes do not pass on their genes to the next generation. Animals who hesitate too long before deciding may perish; likewise with those who decide too quickly. What is needed is some kind of faculty that will enable the animal to avoid the perils of the two extreme poles. That faculty, Margolis claims, is the ability to recognize similarities between current situations and past situations — in a word, pattern recognition.

Margolis attempts to explain why pattern recognition, which, in his view, is all there finally is to cognition, is so poorly understood. He claims that two Darwinian principles, namely, that variation is blind and selection is nearsighted, result in conservative continuity in systemic structure as the generations pass. These two principles, combined, entail that systemic structure will change only as fast as it must to support the function or functions favored by selective pressures. Margolis labels this relationship between the two Darwinian principles, on one hand, and structural conservatism on the other, the *principle of continuity*.

> evolution is creative with respect to function in ways that remain very conservative with respect to structure. . . . Structure tends to be conserved, even while function (in evolutionary time) tends to be marvelously creative, not because that leads to the best of all possible outcomes but because a process that proceeds by nearsighted selection among almost random variations has much better chances to produce new functions out of old structures than to produce new functions and new structures. (p. 36)

To put it simply, evolution had to work with what was, so to speak, at hand, rather than what would have been ideal in terms of our ability to investigate and understand. The principle of continuity provides an account, for instance, of why there is such similarity, in terms of evident physical structure, between a feline brain and a human brain, but significant functional difference.

Margolis observes, as others have, that "the way our brains operate seems quite odd." He argues, however, that it is odd only from the perspective most associated with conventional cognitive science and AI. Logical structure, that which is amenable to computer programming, is what AI wants to see in all cognitive structures, the brain included. Margolis claims that this attempt to attribute logical structure and computational mechanisms to biological structure, which was produced by a natural history that found, as it were, pattern recognition to be the most efficient way to impose new function over slowly changing structure, will mislead us if we wish to understand the brain rather than "cognitive systems" we can build and, to some extent, understand better than we do the brain.

The analogy that Margolis suggests is not the computer, with its logical architecture, but an old city with its architecture dominated by historical events and turns, layer upon layer, new grafted onto old, with little evident long-term planning:

> once we think about the brain as necessarily the latest stage of some Darwinian pathway . . . We must expect that the architecture and functioning of the brain would be more nearly analogous to the structure of an old city like Paris or Rome than to a contemporary,

designed from scratch machine like a spacecraft or a computer. . . .
Under Darwinian evolution, novelties emerge from a process of blind
variation, favored (or not) by near-term advantage. There is nothing in
the process that is more than vaguely analogous to planning ahead. (p.
33)

Since we're reduced, at present, to trafficking in analogies, allow me to
expand Margolis's analogy. An old city strikes me as a good analogy
since, as Fischler and Firschein (1987), who, as we saw, are otherwise
disposed to using the computer analogically, put it, "the evolution of
the human brain has been a process of rearranging and augmenting
the basic parts of the brains of lower vertebrate animals" (p. 35).
Moreover, Penfield's (1975) suggestion that conscious awareness
resides in the brain stem, or old brain, rather than the neocortex, or
new brain, is compatible with the larger claim of radical functional
change developed over conserved physical structure. Given these
considerations, I suggest the modified analogy of an old city seen from
the air in which the underlying layers can scarcely be seen at all and
what we have to do is surmise both underlying structures and how
those structures support the life of the city, by looking, while flying
over the city. The general point is that novel function embodied in
conservative structure is a formidable object of study. While we can
see the outside of the structure, it is extremely difficult to surmise
function from structure alone or how such structure can support such
seemingly different function — which is another way to articulate the
classical mind/body problem.

Margolis also argues that the kind of calculation ability we associate
with computers appeared only very recently in natural history. On his
view, pattern recognition is fundamental; logical and calculative
reasoning, on the other hand, represent something like a functional
overlay.

reasoning appears only at the most recent stage of a very long course of
evolution, [so] that we would hardly expect that a refinement of
reasoning (calculation) — the capability for manipulating abstract rules
of inference — would lie at the root of everything, or anything else. On
the argument here, that puts things exactly backward.

. . .Under this [Margolis's] view, even the most abstract sorts of
reasoning (formal logic and mathematics) must be reducible to pattern-

recognition. The skill human beings exhibit in such matters would be akin to the skills we exhibit (for example) in playing the violin. It is not a natural, inborn, or routinely developed activity of the mind. Cognition (on this view) is intrinsically "a-logical." (pp. 44–45)

According to Margolis, logical and mathematical skills as we have them depend on pattern recognition. The claim is that pattern recognition, as developed in natural history, is the kind of faculty that can support natural language, logic, and mathematical reasoning but not the other way about.

These considerations, it seems to me, support two general conclusions. First, the brain will continue to be resistant to investigation, because the principle of continuity, for all its marvel as an evolutionary mechanism, serves to mask its own workings. The fact that we have made such comparatively modest progress in brain science over quite significant spans of time seems much more compatible with the analogy of the brain as an old city rather than a new computer, and with the basic cognitive process as pattern recognition rather than computation.

Second, and consonant with the major theme of this essay, it calls into radical question the appropriateness of the computer as an analogical object of study at deep P-simulation levels. Margolis surely has not demolished the classical AI view of intelligence, but his approach to the problem, it seems to me, possesses some distinct advantages. It would explain the syndrome of initial success, frustration, and then abandonment of an effort that has characterized so much of AI history — what Dreyfus and Dreyfus call the *fallacy of the first successful step*. It explains why we haven't gotten very far in explaining pattern recognition in terms of symbol manipulation. As noted above, that is exactly the wrong way about. And, to return to the major issue of the previous chapter, it explains why people evidently don't suffer from a frame problem.

To be sure, many kinds of mechanisms can be simulated, since there are many ways mathematically to construct a rule. But for computer simulation of the brain, such simulations will be helpful at the I/O level, or for specific functions, but not for systemic, deep P-simulations, since, if Margolis is right, the deep processes of the brain are radically noncomputational. In computers, architecture and program reign supreme, and hardware is finally not very interesting;

in brains, by contrast, the evidence cited by Margolis and regularly seconded by Fischler and Firschein favors the claim that hardware still very much matters; the way that function is rooted in hardware apparently solves the problems that bedevil computational attempts at the generation of intelligence.

The importance of these considerations lies in the picture of complexity of the brain that they paint. That we have made such little progress in understanding the brain from a neurophysiological perspective is explained by the continuity-of-structure/novelty-of-function picture Margolis provides. Novel function rooted in conservative structural change, generated incrementally by environmental selective pressures over vast spans of time, looks to be singularly resistant to successful investigation. As a result, especially given the modest investigatory powers of science, the prospects for coming to anything more than a shallow understanding of the human brain, at least in the foreseeable future, seem poor.

5. Conclusion

I have advanced reasons supporting the claim that mature natural language competence is the most demanding computer simulation of human mentality imaginable, and that, unlike narrow, isolatable talents such as chess playing and Rogerian counseling, it presupposes intelligence. I also argued that we face severe difficulties understanding both mindlike programs and the mind; the result, I claimed, is that the prognosis for understanding as well as generating deep P-level simulations of the mind is poor. Given these two considerations, I conclude that we will have to rely on "I/O" tests such as Turing's for assessing what computer simulations of human mentality we can attempt and that his Imitation Game remains the best "criterion for recognizing intelligence in a machine," to requote Gregory (1987), that we possess.

I criticized Turing for the philosophic thinness of his essay "Computing Machinery and Intelligence," specifically for rushing precipitously from one topic to the next without the sustained consideration these subtle topics deserve. Since he worked in the earliest days of the development of the computer, perhaps we should excuse his unduly optimistic prognosis of how people might begin the process of building a machine that thinks. Moreover, he clearly did not comprehend the magnitude of the "scale" problems as Cherniak brings them to our attention. On the other hand, as I argued, he got one important issue correct: He surmised that successful participation in a full-ranging human conversation represents a test sufficiently severe that, taking into account the staggering difficulties that coping with the demands such an activity would place on a machine, there would be good grounds for concluding that such a machine was, indeed, thinking.

Dennett's contribution to the issues at hand centers on his "quick probe" assumption: inherent in this assumption is the claim that language ability differs fundamentally from "isolatable talents" such as playing a respectable game of chess or finding a ninth-order derivative. Mature language ability, according to Dennett, presupposes a general ability that could be used in numerous activities that require some measure of intelligence. The claim is that the competence a machine would have to have to pass the test could not be based on stock responses, as in the ELIZA program, or computation based on scripts or frames, or look-up in a large database, since the latter is orders of magnitude too slow and also faces the frame problem. While I complained that he missed considerations stemming from the frame problem and the relevance space problems it generates, I seconded Dennett's claim that demanding queries asked of a candidate system are good quick probes for intelligence.

I appealed to Howard Margolis's argument that human intelligence is based exclusively on pattern recognition, not rule-based manipulation of symbols that represent the world. His claim is that whatever logical and mathematical competencies we have are predicated on pattern recognition processes and not the other way around; the problem, of course, is that pattern recognition is ill understood. If we could determine how to develop robust pattern-recognition capacities in a machine, then possibly problems such as combinatorial explosion and the frame problem could be avoided or defeated and, as a result, full-fledged machine language competency might be feasible.

Consequently, my position is that passing the Turing test would require genuine intelligence on the part of the computer. Such a claim does not mean that a weak or truncated application of the test might not result in a premature claim that a computer had passed the test; testing procedures of all kinds are vulnerable to inept administration. Rather, the claim is that passage of the full-fledged, correctly administered test could only be accomplished by a genuinely intelligent system. Fully engaging in an extended, mature human conversation is the most challenging, feasible problem I can imagine — it is challenging because we don't know how we do it, and is feasible since we clearly do it. But, like the classic halting problem, it may not be computable. In fact, any algorithmic process with which I am familiar attempting tasks requiring humanlike intelligence founders on the combinatorial explosion (the frame problem can be considered a special case) that Newell and Simon, perhaps unwittingly, pointed out stands in the way of true machine intelligence. Rather, recapitulating natural history after a fashion, it may be necessary to build such a machine on pattern-recognition processes rather than rule-based manipulation of formal symbols. The daunting problem is that we currently have little idea how to do that.

In sum, I concur with Turing and Dennett that a machine that passed the test would have to think. However, since we haven't solved the frame problem and since the prognosis for its solution seems poor, as argued in Chapter 4, I am skeptical that we have even begun to understand how such a machine could be built.

CHAPTER 6

The Relation of the Frame
Problem to the Turing Test

In the first section of the chapter, I attempt to educe some of the implications of the frame problem for the Turing test, with a particular focus on what implications bear on Searle- and Gunderson-style arguments against the Turing test. I develop further distinctions based on the epistemologically simple learning/epistemologically complex learning distinction I developed in Chapter 2. Applied to conversations which might take place in Searle's Chinese Room, I argue that we should distinguish between *epistemologically simple (ES) conversations* and *epistemologically complex (EC) conversations*. My pivotal claim in the first section of the chapter is that ES conversations do not presuppose a solution to the frame problem, but that EC conversations do.

I have discussed the frame problem and the Turing test at length, but I have not attempted to spell out what I think the implications of the frame problem are for the Turing test and some of the discussions of the test. In this first section of the chapter, I would like to undertake this task.

As we saw in Chapter 4, the frame problem is often cast in terms of how it poses problems for an artificial system as such a system attempts to engage the world in some significant sense. Recall that Fodor, for example, cast his understanding of the general frame problem in terms of the problems a robot would face attempting quite ordinary tasks. According to Fodor, as we saw, the frame problem is largely the problem of adjusting beliefs about the world, given the experiences—

here we might say "input" — the robot has, which almost always entail changes in those beliefs so that the robot can effectively adjust its behavior.

In Chapter 4, I also distinguished two aspects of the frame problem, namely the *specific* and the *general* frame problem. The general frame problem, cast in robot terms, is a matter of determining the relevance of the experiences that a robot might have to the beliefs that the robot has about the world in two ways: (a) how should the robot's belief system be updated in light of new input? and (b) what is relevant in the robot's database to the solution of any given problem?

The specific frame problem, as I defined it in Chapter 4, involves issues associated with what changes are *not* needed in an axiom-based system, given changes in the world modeled by the system. There are production systems that have some ability spelling out what changes are entailed by the change of this or that axiom; the problem is that determining that changes $a..m$ are required does not mean that changes $n .. z$ are not required. The system is left with the problem of determining that a change does not entail that change, and that change, and so on. A solution to the specific frame problem would be a matter of identifying a "principled" way, rather than an ad hoc way, to make such determinations. As Hayes (1987) argues, there doesn't seem to be any rule-based way to do this. Attempting to do it ad hoc, for a real as opposed to a toy world, of course, results in computational paralysis. Cast in my terms, the specific frame problem details at the programmatic level why there appears to be no way to enhance programming techniques as we understand them now so that computer-based epistemologically simple learning can be extended to encompass epistemologically complex learning.

As I argued in Chapter 4, the specific frame problem is related to the general frame problem since the attempt to find Hayes's "principled" way to avoid the specific frame problem unavoidably entangles the attempt in the general frame problem. In this chapter, I intend to argue that the frame problem blocks epistemologically complex learning, and, since EC learning is a prerequisite to the kind of the conversational ability Turing had in mind, an unsolved frame problem means that it will not be possible for an automatic formal system to pass the Turing test. Instead, it will be forced into inept, ELIZA-like responses when the conversational partner imparts new, epistemologically complex information. A system that responds with ELIZA-like responses, as I attempted to show in the last chapter (and will argue again at the end of this chapter), will conspicuously fail the Turing test.

The general frame problem inhibits epistemologically complex learning in automatic formal systems for the following reasons. Any computer model of the world that would be rich enough to support conversation (assuming that such a feat is possible) would contain, in addition to many other components, presumably, something like a logical snapshot of the world. That is, it would contain a manipulable representation of the world, its components, and how those components that are significant for human activities usually interact. Even given the contentious assumption that such a snapshot was adequate for the conversational task, however, it is adequate only so long as there is no new information in the conversation that has any bearing on the model's representation of the world. As soon as such information appears in the course of the conversation, the model must be successfully updated if it is to use the new information in responding convincingly to a query or a comment. And that is precisely what is required if the conversation is to be convincing enough that the computer plays the Imitation Game successfully.

In terms of the specific frame problem, as soon as epistemologically complex information is encountered in a conversation, the question becomes how to assimilate such information axiomatically—namely, how does the system survey its system of production rules and data and determine which should be revised and which should not be—and do so in conversational "real-time"? Even this vexing question presupposes, moreover, that the system would have some way to recast an EC comment encountered in a conversation, for example, in programmatic/database terms. It is a commonplace, by now, that translation of natural language sentences into first-order predicate calculus, even when done by thinking people, is accomplished at the price of "losing something in the translation." As a result, the automatic formal system faces two problems in light of the frame problem: (a) how should EC information be translated without losing part of the meaning of the original, and (b) how should the system of rules and data comprising the "programming" of the system be revised in light of this translation? The overriding question, of course, is whether there is a mechanical (presumably nonthinking or at most ES-thinking) way to do this.

It might be objected that many—perhaps most—conversations do not involve epistemologically complex information, or, if they occasionally do, that successful manipulation of epistemologically complex information is not necessary for more or less successful participation in such conversations. To put it another way, it might be possible that EC information is handled by clever ES responses in such a way that the Turing test is satisfied — this is the kind of possibility, I take it, that Gunderson would point to in resisting the ascription of thought to a maturely conversing system solely on the basis of its conversational abilities. I readily concede that some kinds of conversation would impose no such burden, since they consist of the kind of banter that a bantam expert system, constructed using ELIZA-like techniques, should be able to support. By sheer weight, I grant that a large percentage of human conversation is epistemologically simple: greetings, simple exhortations, requests for uncomplicated factual information, and so on. While I think it would be difficult for a rule-based system to handle all such conversations — I take it that Haugeland's "jerky" problem would likely be encountered in the inevitable unusual interchanges, even in these kinds of straightforward conversations — I think it is likely that such a limited linguistic competency is possible. If this is right, it should be no insuperable problem to write a computer program capable, given a little good fortune, of the following credible conversation.

Alayna: Well, here it is Friday, again.
Computer: Yes, I see it is the 12th of the month. Didn't miss the 13th by much!
Alayna: You're not superstitious are you?
Computer: No, of course not. Logic and superstition don't mix.

Indeed, such conversational give and take could plausibly be ascribed to two persons rather than a person and a computer. The computer's responses don't simply mirror, in a trivial fashion, the comments of the person, they engage the person's comments in a plausible way. As a result, while I don't think ELIZA, for example, would often be this good, I readily concede that some conversations — and perhaps significant parts of all conversations — could satisfactorily be handled by means of a rule-based inference system. So I will concede to the objection that a large part of conversation is epistemologically simple and therefore is capable of being handled by nonthinking (or ES thinking only) systems. In terms of the Turing test, this means that some parts of such a test could likely be handled well by a computer system possessing such conversational abilities.

Consistent with my contrast between epistemologically simple and epistemologically complex learning, I will call this genre of conversation *epistemologically simple* conversation. What I mean by this is that ES conversation makes no demands on an automatic formal system such that a solution to the frame problem is required before an engaging, appropriate conversational response can be made. The conversational exchanges are simple enough that no system-wide revision of the system's belief complex is required in order to respond with an answer that meets the demands of the Turing test. If this particular exchange does not appear to be simple enough to be obviously an epistemologically simple conversation, I assume that the responses can be scaled to the point where such agreement could be reached. It might look as though the first comment, "Well, here it is Friday, again" might generate the frame problem since it evidently contains new information. But this is not information that the system would likely not have or, alternately, have difficulty handling. Specifically, it doesn't require much storage to represent a calendar in a computer, all the way to the year 2050, which would be adequate for most purposes. Add some general purpose conversational responses in an array with a good look-up device, a simple inference mechanism that would support inferences such as the fact that the 13th follows the 12th in every month, and the computer would likely do well in such conversational settings for at least a short period of time. While slightly more complicated, similar comments could be made about the computer's second comment.

I should emphasize that it is not that an epistemologically simple conversation can impart no new knowledge to an automatic formal system while it is driven by a program with conversational capacities. To be sure, "run-time" data entry, in contrast to the use of some kind of internal data base, is almost as old as automatic computing itself. I should add that the problems associated with "run-time" assignment of data to variables have shaped a good part of programming language history. Classical programming languages such as Pascal are characterized as *prescriptive* languages, since extensive use of run time assignments is typically made. New languages such as PROLOG rely more on *description*; no potentially destructive assignments to variables are made at run time. The point is that successful run-time assimilation of data has been a problem even for epistemologically simple computational activity. It is that such information has to be amenable to representation in the system's storage without necessitating a system-wide examination of the implications of that information. Such information should be amenable to representation in the system's storage and should not require system-wide examination of other storage cells which are not overwritten in the storage process.

In *epistemologically complex* conversation, by contrast, if an adequate response is to be generated, the system's belief complex must undergo a system-wide examination, identifying both what needs to be changed and what does not need to be changed, given the kind of information encountered in a conversation. When a conversational fragment contains new information that has nontrivial implications for the system's belief complex, such that a system-wide examination and partial revision is a prerequisite for adequate conversational responses, then the frame problem is joined. It might be possible to isolate some identifying characteristic of all epistemologically complex information, but the best criterion I can think of that distinguishes epistemologically complex information from epistemologically simple information is that the former necessitates system-wide examination of the beliefs of the computer, in the manner just suggested, if the system is to respond convincingly to queries about that information and what it means for the world the computer inhabits. The frame problem, to put it simply, is what distinguishes the two.

Recall from the last chapter that virtually any topic involving human interests and practices can be involved, as Turing envisioned the Imitation Game. This doesn't mean, I take Turing to be saying, that the computer has to be an expert conversationalist in every area of human endeavor, just reasonably well informed in the way that we would expect that an informed, reasonably well-educated, fluent speaker of the language would be. As an example, suppose that Alayna, the interrogator, relays some information to SIMON, the robot, by way of a question.

Alayna: Did you hear that Gorbachev's political strength within
                the upper ranks of the KGB is deteriorating significantly?
SIMON: No, that's news to me.

Alayna: What do you think that means for the federal government's attempt to decrease the budget deficit?

Surely a modestly well-informed adult, for example, one who reads
Time magazine on a regular basis, should be able to surmise and
express, in response to Alayna's question, that a deterioration of
Gorbachev's position in the Soviet intelligence agency might well
contribute to Gorbachev's political demise, which, in turn, would likely
increase calls for an increase in the American military budget, which,
in turn, with other things being equal, makes it more difficult to
reduce the prodigious federal budget. While one might object to the
example by observing that the American CIA did rather a poor job of
predicting both the August 1991 coup, as well as the eventual demise
of the Soviet Union itself, my response would be that large organiza-
tions such as the CIA often act much like computers with acute frame
problems. Prerequisite to such a sophisticated surmise, however, is
quite a large number of inferences and whole belief examinations and
partial revisions; the recurring question, of course, is whether we have
adequate grounds for supposing that an automatic formal system is
capable of such inferences and whole belief revisions without foun-
dering on the frame problem and falling prey to a terminal — so to
speak — case of computational paralysis.

The robotic response in the conversation just displayed, "No, that's
news to me," is certainly plausible, even given the problems associated
with the frame problem. SIMON's reply is the sort of reply that a
person might expect of another person in response to such a question.
In fact, an ELIZA-like program could be expected to perform just as
adequately in such a situation: a very specific, epistemologically
complex question is handled by means of a general-purpose response.
If all that is expected of SIMON is Rogerian psychotherapeutic-like
answers of the kind we find in ELIZA-like programs, then passing the
Turing test would be relatively easy.

But some care needs to be exercised at this point. We need to
distinguish between conversational *response* to a comment or query and
appropriation of that query's or comment's content in order to see that
mature conversational ability entails more than simply the plausibility
of the response at any given exchange. In the conversation just
displayed, "No, that's news to me" is certainly an acceptable *response* to
the new information about Gorbachev but that is not the only task the

conversing computer attempting to pass the Turing test has given the question, "Did you hear that Gorbachev's political strength within the upper ranks of the KGB is deteriorating significantly?" There must also be an epistemological appropriation of the content of the comment such that it is incorporated into SIMON's beliefs about the world. We can't tell, on the basis of SIMON's only response, "No, that's news to me," whether the computer has appropriated the information so that it can be used to support the conversation as it develops. The reason for conversing at length about such matters, during the administration of the test, is to determine if such appropriation is made and is made in something approximating the way that we would expect of a competent adult.

The pivotal point is that ES conversational adequacy is not equivalent to EC conversational adequacy. If SIMON has a large belief complex, some kind of logical picture of the world, which surely would be required to participate adequately in a mature conversation, then that belief complex has to be examined and appropriately changed to reflect the new information, in this case, the claim that Gorbachev's political situation within the KGB is deteriorating. But notice that the nature of the change required is quite different from what we saw with the Coin Toss game in Chapter 2. New data in that epistemologically simple situation, such as reading an H on the game string, meant only that a magnitude had to be changed in one location of storage at a given instant. Megabytes of such epistemologically simple data are, in principle, readily handled by computer systems in a short amount of time — that's what they are good at and we, by contrast, are comparatively poor at. Nevertheless, the way that such volumes of data are handled in current systems is epistemologically simple, since the frame problem blocks it from being used in the epistemologically complex way that would be presupposed by any EC response predicated on an EC appropriation of the new information about Gorbachev.

It might be hoped that some kind of clever ES mechanism could handle the new information in such a way that epistemological issues are avoided and plausible responses are supported. The problem is that conventional AI database changes that normally are used in what I have called epistemologically simple learning and conversation cannot involve systemic, principled belief revisions; single item changes, such as the change required by encountering a new item on the game string, are atomic, not system wide. That can occur at such speeds that it might look as though there is support for system-wide revision (here we have to beware of the dangers of "user illusions") but the fact remains that digital computers with an unsolved frame problem make atomic, rule-governed storage changes that are incapable of effecting epistemologically complex changes. In the case of SIMON being informed, in a conversation, that "Gorby's" political position is deteriorating in the upper echelons of the Soviet intelligence establishment, there is no rule-based, automatic ES change that can be made that would be adequate to the conversation since the implications of the claim bear on large parts of the belief system. Analogically speaking, individual tiles of the mosaic comprising the system's logical portrait of its world can be changed according to production rules and intermediate data, but the rules and tiles together are insufficient to generate the sense of the picture embodied in the mosaic that would be needed to make changes in an epistemologically complex manner.

For a rule-based system like a digital computer, it might be hoped that some kind of sophisticated set or hierarchy of rules could handle the updating required about the news about Gorbachev in an ES way. The purpose of a rule is to enable the user of the rule to have a shorthand method for coping with virtually limitless numbers of applications of a rule over some domain. But if recent assessments in the emerging field of complexity study, such as Heinz Pagels's (1988), are right, some phenomena admit of satisfactory rule-based modeling or simulation, and therefore symbolic manipulation based on rules, but some cannot be adequately modeled by any system simpler than the phenomenon being modeled. Pagels cites the weather as a prominent example of such a phenomenon. In fact, Pagels speculates that the brain is just one such system.

> the simplest system that simulates a brain's operation is that brain itself. If these ideas are right, then there is a 'complexity barrier' that lies between our instantaneous knowledge of the state of neuronal network and our knowledge of its future development. The brain, and hence the mind, is another example of an unsimulatable system. (pp. 227–228)

Because of the enormous number of concepts, words, nuances of concepts, words and expressions, and what Winograd and Flores (1986) call the *rootedness* of all these words, expressions, and concepts in (largely tacit) human convention and tradition, I believe that natural language also has a "complexity barrier." Natural language is so complex that no manageable set of (syntactic-based) rules can model it in anything approximating its complexity. The qualification problem, which I discussed briefly in Chapter 3, is related: given a rule, it is always possible to qualify a description of that to which the rule purportedly applies so that it no longer clearly applies.[1] If this is right, then there is nothing like a rule, or a system of rules, that would enable SIMON to do the updating of a rule-based system which attempts to model and use natural language such as English. Consequently, the evidence favors the result that there is no set of rules, no matter how they are organized or how sophisticated they are, that can be constructed to overcome the frame problem as it obstructs the attempt to build computers capable of passing the Turing test.

Barring a solution to the frame problem, as a result, it is not possible to extend the kind of techniques that are adequate for epistemologically simple conversations so that they would be adequate for epistemologically complex conversations. Algorithmic techniques that are now used in AI and were used in the Coin Toss game in Chapter 2 should be adequate for many epistemologically simple conversational tasks. My claim is that such techniques are not extendible to encompass epistemologically complex conversational tasks just because we have no way at present to solve the frame problem with programming techniques that support only epistemologically simple learning.

A classical AI objection at this point might be that I have missed the point of what distinguishes AI from conventional programming. Namely, AI is based more on heuristics than algorithms as understood in conventional computer science. In fact, some might go so far as to say that what distinguishes AI from conventional computer science is that the former is principally based on heuristics while the latter is based on algorithms. The claim is that heuristic search reduces the search space of a problem by using knowledge to eliminate areas of the search which are unlikely to yield a solution. From the fact, therefore, the objection would continue, that I have putatively shown that algorithmic techniques which support epistemologically simple conversations cannot be extended to support EC conversations, it doesn't follow that digital computers cannot engage in EC conversations. Heuristic search procedures, at some point in the future, may well

---

[1]Interestingly enough, it was John McCarthy (1977) who identified this problem.

prove up to the task of supporting EC conversations. While the jury may still be out, the objection would conclude, it remains an unsettled question whether digital computers can engage in EC conversations.

I have never been particularly impressed by the claim that AI uses heuristics while computer science employs only algorithms, since conventional (albeit sophisticated) programming often involves knowledge-based search space constraint, and "heuristic search" still cashes out as algorithmic manipulation of data at the machine level. The fact of the matter is that there is little evidence that heuristic search is any more likely to solve the frame problem than is conventional algorithmic programming. David Waltz (1988, p. 195), who is otherwise more optimistic about AI than I, seems to agree: "In retrospect it is remarkable how seriously heuristic search has been taken as a cognitive model . . . [and it is now] clear that traditional AI methods do not scale up well and that new AI paradigms will therefore be needed." The failure of heuristic search methods to "scale up well," in fact, is likely due at least in part to the frame problem. And my claim, of course, is that the best line of demarcation that we have between the epistemologically simple and the epistemologically complex, in automatic formal systems that attempt to engage in tasks such as natural language use, is the frame problem.

Assuming that the computer wouldn't have to distinguish between epistemologically simple and complex conversation — that is, judge whether this or that conversational segment is simple or complex so as to invoke different routines, for instance, it should often perform well with such conversation. In fact, I take it that such a judgment itself would founder on the frame problem. It turns out, however, that this is a problematic assumption. I would like to call the issue of whether a conversational segment is simple or complex the *frame problem generator question*. I believe it is likely that the frame problem generator question is an analog to the halting problem. In other words, if we can't write a program to determine if any arbitrarily entered program halts, which is what the provable halting problem means, and if the frame problem generator question is an analog to the halting problem, it follows that we can't write a program that determines if any arbitrarily presented conversational segment (one more "program") will generate the frame problem for the system.

In fact, other considerations support the claim that we cannot write a program that determines whether an arbitrarily selected conversational fragment will turn out to be a frame problem generator. Consider what such a program would have to do. It has to be able to answer the question, "Does this statement or query, which is the last part of the conversational fragment, generate the frame problem?" But this question, which can only be answered by system-wide scrutiny of the implications and nonimplications of the conversational fragment, *itself* is epistemologically complex, not simple. Since it is complex, it generates the frame problem if an automatic formal system attempts to answer it, and, as a result, the system is left with two equally undesirable (from our perspective) choices. Either the system possesses a routine that returns a randomly generated answer—a guess—or it takes on the question, hangs on the frame problem, and is unable either to answer this question or continue in the conversation.

As a result, it is not possible to write a program which would gracefully, convincingly handle a conversation segment that turns out to be a frame problem generator—for example, by including a procedure that, by some means, gracefully deflects segments that turn out to be frame problem generators. Since such an identification is not possible, two possibilities remain, neither of which is desirable. Either the program would handle the segment ineptly by taking an epistemologically complex segment to be simple, and, as a result, answer simplistically at best or "jerkily" at worst, or, correctly surmising, by whatever means, that the epistemologically complex segment is complex, it would founder on the frame problem, either hanging in speechless suspended animation, or, if it had some arbitrary routine that monitors cycle time, it would interrupt belief system revision arbitrarily, and, likewise, answer simplistically or jerkily. In either case, the computer answers unconvincingly and thus contributes to the failure of the test.

The signal result is that there is no way, barring a solution to the frame problem, for an automatic formal system to cope gracefully and effectively with epistemologically complex conversations.

I should point out that there is a parallel between the ES/EC contrast, and the frame problem, on one hand, and Dreyfus and Dreyfus's five stages of skill acquisition on the other. On the distinction I have drawn, it should be clear why a computer should be able to advance through stages 1–3 but founder at stages 4 and 5. While much of Dreyfus and Dreyfus's discussion of these stages is couched in terms of the human learner, it is easy to transfer their claims to the "computer learner." A computer learner, as it accumulates experience (in the case of the Coin Toss game, as it reads more of the game string) is able to become more adequate to an epistemologically simple task. In Dreyfus and Dreyfus (1986, p. 28) terms, enough "experience" (data) is accumulated as the computer learns that the rules begin to generate a distinctive improvement in performance. However, for tasks that require "holistic similarity recognition," which, according to Dreyfus and Dreyfus, are possible only in stages 4 and 5, ES learning is insufficient. EC learning, requiring whole belief system revision, enables what they would call "intuitive know-how." On the set of contrasts I have drawn, in sum, ES learning supports automatic formal system advances from stages 1 to 3, but such a system would founder on the frame problem and would be incapable of advancing to the "intuitive" skills characterizing stages 4 and 5. EC learning would be required for these last two stages.

CHAPTER 7

Two Major Critiques of the Turing Test: Searle and Gunderson

In Chapters 2 and 3, I discussed some of the properties of digital computers, I illustrated how we simulate phenomena on computers, and I developed a distinction between epistemologically simple (ES) and epistemologically complex (EC) learning. In Chapter 4, I looked at the Dreyfus critique of AI, and I attempted to explain why a more precisely expressible, yet related, problem facing AI, specifically the frame problem, constitutes a formidable impediment to development of rule-based AI systems that attempt functionally to approximate human-level intelligence. In Chapter 5, I argued that a mature natural language competency possessed by an artificial system would presuppose a generalized faculty — in contrast to a highly specialized faculty, which is typical of AI systems to date — which is significantly equivalent to the faculty we use when we think and use language. In short, I argued that passage of the Turing test would constitute adequate grounds for concluding that the machine passing the test was thinking. I claimed, however, that we have little idea how to build such a machine, and I speculated that natural language competency of the sort envisioned by Turing may not be a computable function on a digital computer. In the last chapter, I took the position that the frame problem's fate will determine whether or not we will be able to develop computers that can pass the Turing test.

In this chapter, I take up aspects of two major challenges to the Turing test advanced during the last 20 years, namely, those of John

Searle and Keith Gunderson. Searle's "Chinese Room" thought experiment is probably the most discussed counterexample in philosophical discussions of AI in the last 10 years. As I read them, both Searle and Gunderson take Searle's counterexample to be plausible, they evidently agree that the Turing test does not likely pose a formidable obstacle for AI, and they concur that passing the test would not be sufficient grounds for concluding that the computer passing the test was thinking. Reasons that each have for objecting to what Searle calls strong AI in general and the Turing test in particular differ in specifics, though generally not in temperament. Searle maintains that computer programs lack the semantical content that is a necessary ingredient in thinking; Gunderson argues that, while thinking has usually been thought to be a necessary condition for mature conversational ability, we have often seen in technological history how what appear to be necessary conditions to generate some phenomenon turn out to be only sufficient. In other words, we have a habit of mistaking a sufficient for a necessary condition, and it is an empirical question whether a nonthinking system of some kind will turn out to be a sufficient condition for such language competency.

I will attempt to use arguments developed in Chapters 5 and 6 against both positions. I claim that what I have called the general and the specific frame problem stand as serious impediments to the passage of the test, and that, at least in the writings that I have seen in print, Searle and Gunderson either have not noticed this problem or do not regard it to be significant. Not only, in my view, does the frame problem make the Turing test much more difficult to pass—in fact, my suspicion is that the frame problem will prove fatal to the attempt to program a digital computer so that it can pass the test—I claim that it makes Searle's Chinese Room experiment counterexample to the Turing test implausible, because it is difficult to ascribe such a mature conversational ability to Searle in his Chinese Room in the absence of a reasonable expectation of overcoming the frame problem. In sum, I argue that it is the frame problem that stands as the principal problem faced by the Turing test in particular and AI in general, not counterexamples to and related criticisms of Turing's Imitation Game such as Searle's and Gunderson's.

In the first section, I consider and reject John Searle's critique of AI, specifically his Chinese Room thought experiment and generally his criticism of *strong AI*. Strong AI, the view that the goal of AI is (or should be) to replicate to some significant degree the capabilities of a human brain — that, by possessing the right program that yields the desired output, given certain inputs, it is correct to say that a computer thinks — is Searle's general target. Searle believes that his Chinese Room counterexample and his accompanying philosophic argument constitute a decisive rebuttal of the strong AI view in general and the Turing test in particular. Searle claims that his counterexample demonstrates that the Turing test could be passed without a rule-based digital computer understanding what it is doing (for the purposes of this essay, I'll take this to be synonymous with *thinking*) when it passes the test.

While I have some sympathy with the overall conclusion he reaches, namely, that a program running on a digital computer cannot capture the full causal powers of a human brain, I will argue that the counterexample itself, as well as some of the assumptions ingredient in it, are not plausible. Part of the reason for the extended consideration of the frame problem in Chapter 4 is that I believe that, not only does the frame problem make it much more difficult for a digital computer to pass the Turing test, but it also counts against the plausibility of Searle's counterexample. In other words, I will argue that the evident intractability of the frame problem seriously undercuts the plausibility of Searle's counterexample. It is not that I find the general tenor of Searle's philosophical stance uncongenial — in fact I like quite a lot of what he has to say about the philosophy of mind and the philosophy of science. Instead, it is that I find his specific objections to AI, most particularly his counterexample, to be implausible, inconsistent, or both.

In the second section of the chapter, I look at two objections by Keith Gunderson (1985) to the Turing test, first, that "similar inputs and outputs would not guarantee similar intervening processes" (p. 202), and second, that, as technological history often has illustrated, it is easy to mistake a sufficient for a necessary condition when attempting to determine whether some activity can be done only one way.

In terms of the first objection, the conclusion that Gunderson apparently urges upon us is that, in addition to having good I/O, we would have to evaluate the intervening processes in order to reach the admittedly weighty conclusion that a machine thinks. I take exception to this objection on two grounds. While I will not expand on this point in this chapter, since I did so in Chapter 5, I believe that the mind and mindlike programs are monumentally resistant to the kind of investigation that would be needed to assess adequately the lineaments of the "intervening processes." We're not in a position, in other words, to make the requisite kinds of investigations; we are limited at best to depth *or* breadth investigations of a mindlike program, were one to exist, but nothing approaching simultaneous depth and breadth understanding, which is what would be needed to claim that the intervening process is reasonably well understood, is possible. As a result, I claim, we are forced largely to rely upon I/O types of evaluations such as the Turing test.

As my second ground, I claimed in the last chapter that natural language competency, of the kind Turing evidently had in mind, makes such demands on any system successfully engaging in the Imitation Game, that the best general explanation for such a system's success, should it occur, is that it is thinking. In other words, the Turing test turns out to be a strong I/O test — even with its faults, the most demanding, feasible test we have. To argue otherwise, I maintain, is to claim that what might be called a *syntax only*, nonthinking, rule-based system is capable of defeating the frame problem in particular and the combinatorial explosion problem in general. I believe both Searle and Gunderson must embrace this problematic claim if they wish to maintain their positions.

In terms of Gunderson's second objection to the Turing test, that we can easily mistake a sufficient for a necessary condition when we attempt to determine if intelligence is a necessary condition for mature conversational ability, I argue that the language competency is not like other analogically offered parallels that support this caution. I agree that it doesn't necessarily take a human to generate vocal music, since a stereo can do it, and I agree that it doesn't take muscles to dig tunnels, since we know now that steam engines can do it. It is true, therefore, that we often find alternate ways to do what we had formerly thought could be done only one way. It is a logical possibility, I am willing to concede to Gunderson, that we might develop nonthinking ways to generate mature conversational abilities, since conversation is an activity. But I think the evidence counts decisively against this, because of the extraordinary demands of the test itself and because a nonthinking conversational ability presupposes a nonthinking solution to the frame problem. I argue that the latter is sufficiently unlikely that it is more reasonable to ascribe — especially since we routinely ascribe thinking to other persons on grounds that are no more compelling — thinking to a maturely conversing computer.

Let me emphasize my overall stance. In Chapter 5, I cited Haugeland's (1981a) useful distinction between the *poor substitute* strategy and the *hollow shell* strategy. The claim of the poor substitute strategy is that AI will likely prove to be a poor substitute for human intelligence. In terms of the Turing test, the claim would be that an artificially "intelligent" system would not be adequate to pass the test. By contrast, the hollow shell strategy maintains that such a system might behave in ways that look intelligent, but that it cannot really be such, because it is missing some essential component presupposed by intelligence. Haugeland suggests in passing that the poor substitute strategy is more promising as an objection to AI than the hollow shell strategy. I intend to provide an argument for why this is the case: I claim that Searle's Chinese Room experiment is a hollow shell counterexample and, as I have said, that its plausibility suffers when viewed in light of considerations associated with the frame problem. Additionally, I argue that Searle's own understanding of how language is a social phenomenon that resists capture by nomic generalizations undermines his counterexample. So I question the consistency of Searle's view of language and his professed Chinese language competency in the Chinese Room.

Assuredly, I don't claim that any particular system has passed or can pass the Turing test. I take the passage of the test to be an empirical question that has not been decided yet. I remain skeptical that any digital computer — in Haugeland's terms, any *automatic formal system* — is capable of passing the test, because I don't see a way for a computer to overcome the frame problem. However, should it turn out that a digital computer, however it is constructed or programmed, passed the test, I would believe that such a system was thinking; a solved frame problem and a system able to handle mature conversation is the best available evidence I can think of for inferring that *thinking* aptly characterizes the processing occurring in such a system. As a result, mine is what might be called a soft or modified poor substitute position: I think it is unlikely that there is a rule-based solution to the frame problem, and, as a result, it is unlikely that a computer system will be able to pass the Turing test. But should one pass the Turing test, on the other hand, I claim that we would have sufficient grounds

for believing that the computer is thinking at a significant (epistemologically complex) level.

There is nothing like a proof or a "knock-down" argument here, of
course. My position simply is that the prospects for a nonthinking (or
an ES-thinking only) system solving the frame problem are sufficiently
improbable that, however unlikely it appears now, should a system
solve the frame problem and pass the Turing test, our grounds for
attributing (EC) thought to it would be roughly as good as those we
have — which virtually all of us evidently find sufficient — for attributing thought to other people. Was it Bertrand Russell who observed
that solipsism is philosophically irrefutable but psychologically impossible? If we attribute thought to maturely conversing people with the
unabashed alacrity we do, it seems to me we should be willing to do so
for maturely conversing computer systems as well. My claim is that the
argument for attributing thought to maturely conversing systems is
philosophically on a par with the (usually tacit) argument that we
routinely accept for attributing thought to other people.

1. The Searle Critique

Few philosophical papers on issues associated with AI of recent years
have caused as much discussion and acrimony as John Searle's "Minds,
Brains and Programs," which first appeared in *The Behavioral and Brain
Sciences* in 1980. This paper was followed in 1984 by the Reith Lectures
in Britain, which were issued in book form as, *Minds, Brains and Science*.
More recently, Searle published "Is the Brain's Mind a Computer
Program?" in the January 1990 edition of *Scientific American*, with the
Churchlands (Churchland & Churchland, 1990) providing something
of a rebuttal in the same issue. In fact, the term *Chinese Room* has
become nearly synonymous with Searle's kind of critique of what he
calls *strong AI*. As a result, Searle has maintained his objections to
strong AI in particular and cognitive science in general, as well as his
Chinese Room counterexample, before a wide audience for a decade
and more.

As I stated at the beginning of this chapter, I intend to argue that the
Chinese Room counterexample is not plausible, that Searle will not be
capable of the kind of Chinese conversation in the room that he would
need to have if his counterexample is to serve, as he supposes it does,

as a refutation of the Turing test. Moreover, I will point out that Searle himself is not consistent, because his view of language, and of how human conventions of various kinds shape how we use language, will not allow the rule-based use of language he claims he has in the Chinese Room.

Consider Figure 7–1's illustration of Searle's Chinese Room counterexample to the claims of strong AI. I understand the thought experiment this way. Assume that Searle, positioned as illustrated in his room, understands absolutely no Chinese symbols or words. Let batch 1 of the Chinese language materials be a script that includes the necessary background knowledge such as "A restaurant is a place where. . . ." Let batch 2 be a story that includes lines such as "A man orders a hamburger in a restaurant, it is served burned, and the man abruptly leaves the restaurant in anger. . . ." Let batch 3 be a series of questions such as, "In this story, does the man eat the hamburger?" Let the English materials be the rules, the program, that Searle is to follow. These include, as it were, "If squoggle squiggle is followed by squiggle squoggle squiggle, then place another squiggle in box x." Assume further that Searle gets so good at correlating the batches, given his rules for manipulating Chinese and lots of practice, that he answers the questions about the story well enough that his answers are indistinguishable from those of a native speaker of Chinese. This might take him 2 years for each question; it might take him 400 years to get good

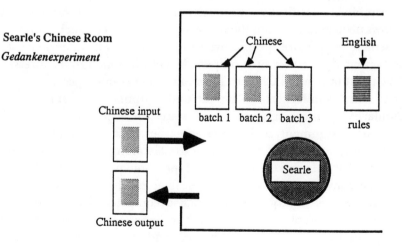

Figure 7.1.

enough at it that he would answer questions as well as a native speaker of Chinese. In this case, we invent a time machine so the extra time is transparent to the room of people asking questions outside Searle's window.

Here is a capsule version of Searle's argument:

1. a machine would have to possess causal powers at least equal to the brain to be capable of thinking;
2. a necessary component of thinking is intentionality, which is to say aboutness, which refers to something — it has semantical content;
3. according to strong AI proponents, a computer manipulates symbols according to rules — it has syntactical content alone;
4. since computers lack one essential component, namely, semantical content attaching to its representations, it follows that computers cannot think.

The question Searle wishes to pose is: given that the conversation is indistinguishable from what we would expect from a native speaker of Chinese, and that Searle is able to converse convincingly (which stems from the program and not his understanding of Chinese), ought we to attribute understanding of Chinese to this Searlean system? We are back to the issue of the relation of input/output to processes that produce output, in my terms, of I/O-simulation to justifiable process ascriptions. Specifically, the question is one of what successful I/O allows us to deduce about the processes that produced such output, and whether, to be more specific, we can ascribe various intentional states to "systems" based on such output. As Gunderson (1985) expresses it, "the point of Searle's Chinese Room argument — and a crucial part — is that from similarities in inputs and outputs one cannot deduce similarity of intervening processes, states, or events" (p. 201).

Searle's argument, as I suggested earlier, is a version of the hollow shell critique. That is, he is willing to play along with the assumption of classical AI and computational psychology and assume that a mature conversational ability is feasible; he does not take the poor substitute tack of arguing that such a competency is unlikely. The heart of his complaint is that a mature language competency, of the kind stipulated by Turing for his test and exemplified in his counterexample, would not be sufficient grounds for concluding that the computer is thinking since, as his counterexample purportedly illustrates, such a competency is possible without the semantical content that is requisite to understanding and, therefore, thinking.

It is the plausibility of the counterexample I wish to challenge. It is my claim that the argument developed to this point counts significantly against the plausibility of the counterexample. Against Searle, that is, I claim that, should a computer carry on such a conversation, that would be strong grounds for concluding that it was thinking, because the kind of problems it would have to solve appear not to be amenable to nonthinking, mechanical solution; mine is a poor substitute strategy amended by a "but if, by some near miracle, they do get that good, then" qualification.

Searle could respond at the outset to my questioning of the plausibility of his counterexample by pointing out that he is simply momentarily granting the AI picture of human intelligence, as applied to language and the Turing test, to see what would follow if it turns out that computers and programs get that good. In other words, he need not be particularly concerned to defend the plausibility of a computer passing the test. Instead, I think he would answer, "All right, let's grant strong AI its admittedly strong assumption and suppose that they get that good and pass the Turing test. What would that fact in itself signify? If the specific question is, Would such a turn of events support the claim that the computer is thinking? then the answer is, 'Clearly no.' " Of course, what we would get next would be the litany about computers possessing only syntax and, since thinking requires semantical content, it follows as a "knock-down" argument that computers with mature conversational ability would not necessarily be thinking.

As a general rule, I agree that thought experiments can be a productive way to analyze issues, and, as well, it can be philosophically astute to take a position, grant the assumptions ingredient in a position, and then determine whether what follows from those assumptions are the results claimed by the proponent. But we should exercise some caution in granting assumptions that are problematic to grant, given other considerations. Searle grants the classical AI assumptions without reference to the implications of the frame problem, and I think this is a mistake. The considerations attaching to the frame problem are such that the discussions we have about computer conversational ability should take them into account.

Searle (1984) comments that "I don't believe I have a knockdown refutation of cognitivism in the way that I believe I have one of strong

AI" (p. 46). I find Searle's belief that he has a "knock-down" argument surprising. David Lewis, who is often thought the owner of bizarre beliefs about possible worlds and the gods therein, stands in plausible contrast to Searle, who otherwise owns notably nonbizarre beliefs. Lewis (1983) has written:

> The reader in search of knock-down arguments in favor of my theories will go away disappointed. Whether or not it would be nice to knock disagreeing philosophers down by sheer force of argument, it cannot be done. Philosophical theories are never refuted decisively. . . . The theory survives its refutation — at a price. . . . But when all is said and done, and all the tricky arguments and distinctions and counterexamples have been discovered, presumably we will still face the question which prices are worth paying, which theories are on balance credible, which are the unacceptably counterintuitive consequences and which are the acceptably counterintuitive ones. (p. x)

Searle's belief that he has a knock-down refutation of strong AI is itself too strong — strong AI can be defended so long as one is willing to pay certain kinds of prices. Parenthetically, I take it that the question of which theories are credible, which are not, and which should be maintained at certain prices is itself a prime example of a frame problem generator, which I defined in the last chapter.

Searle has become well known during the 10 years of the Chinese Room debate for his straightforward, direct talk. With no expansion or sustained discussion, in the *Scientific American* piece, he says simply and provocatively in regard to what the Chinese Room experiment signifies, "I satisfy the Turing test for understanding Chinese." But this claim depends, as I see it, on an inadequate articulation of the requirements of both mature conversational ability and the Turing test. Let me attempt to explain why, as he defines it, Searle in the Chinese Room cannot be capable of the linguistic competency he claims he is.

Searle repeatedly insists that computer programs consist of syntax alone. As I will argue below, I think this is likely incorrect and that, minimally, it is not clear that the line between syntax and semantics is as clear as Searle would need for it to be in order for him to make his case as he does. But, for the moment, let's grant that Searle is exactly right: Digital computer simulation consists exclusively of syntactical manipulation of formally defined symbols. All syntax, no semantics. For reasons articulated earlier in this chapter as well as in Chapter 2, what follows from this is that, at best, all a computer is capable of, in terms of learning, is epistemologically simple learning.

Consider "Searle-in-the-room," as Boden puts it. He correctly surmises that his task parallels that of a digital computer. While not understanding Chinese — Searle's presumed equivalent of having no semantics — he is given a rule book — Searle's presumed equivalent of an instruction set and the appropriate programming — at whatever level we like. Specifically, in terms of Chinese "manipulation," he notices instructions such as, "'Take a squiggle-squiggle sign out of basket number one and put it next to a squoggle-squoggle sign from basket number two'" (1984, p. 32). Two more assumptions set the stage for the counterexample's provocative central claim:

1. I/O at the window turns out to be questions and answers — a conversation;
2. the programmers are sufficiently good at the programming, and Searle gets so good at the manipulation that:
   (Result): Searle's answers are indistinguishable from a native Chinese speaker.

Of course, I wish to call (2) into question and, as a result, I wish to claim that the result, that Searle's answers could be indistinguishable from those of a native Chinese speaker, is not defensible at anything like a reasonable price.

On my view, Searle-in-the-room will be capable only of ES learning. As Searle manipulates his squiggles and squoggles, purportedly bereft of any understanding of what they mean, he should be capable, given enough time (which would be prodigious — but this is irrelevant for his point), of the kind of learning which the Coin Toss game in Chapter 2 exemplified. That is, using his baskets (storage locations) and rules (program), he should be capable of comparing baskets, of logically evaluating Boolean expressions ("If basket 1 contains more squiggles than squoggles"), changing the contents of baskets ("Add a squoggle to basket 3"), and putting together arbitrary strings of squiggles and squoggles ("squoggle, squiggle, . . .

squoggle"). To be sure, Searle's baskets, in principle if not in imaginable practice, should be capable of storing whatever a modern computer's storage could hold, since all he needs is a set of "positive read/write techniques," as Haugeland puts it. With the rules in his book, his array of storage baskets, and his positive read/write techniques, he will be capable of slowly computing any computable function.

Searle does not consider the question of whether all conversations are equivalent in terms of an automatic formal system's ability to learn. Given some input through the window (one or more squoggle squiggle string(s)), as a result, Searle will be capable of the type of learning we saw in the Coin Toss game, namely, ES learning. But the pivotal question, which he does not address, is whether such ES learning capacity is adequate to support mature conversational ability that involves EC conversational segments as well as ES segments. Epistemologically complex conversations, ones that involve real — in contrast to "toy" worlds, as I tried to show in the last chapter, presuppose epistemologically complex learning capacity. As I have argued, EC learning capacity presupposes a solution to the frame problem. Without such a solution, a syntax-only computing system such as Searle-in-the-room (temporarily granting him this contentious assumption) cannot engage in EC learning, and, since EC conversations presuppose EC learning capability, he cannot engage in EC conversations. The kind of conversations that Searle will be capable of, therefore, will be ELIZA-like conversations that are the functional analog of the Coin Toss game. He will be capable of answering certain kinds of questions that do not presuppose an ability to revise the system in an epistemologically complex manner.

Unfortunately, we never get much of a discussion of what kind of conversation is purportedly occurring in the Chinese Room; evidently, there is no recognition that there are two fundamentally different kinds of conversation, epistemologically speaking. If, by "your answers are indistinguishable from those of a native Chinese speaker," all that is meant is the ability to answer ES questions, then Searle is quite right. Consequently, he should be able to converse in such a manner and such a conversational competency would not, by itself, warrant the ascription, "Searle-in-the-room understands Chinese" or "Searle-in-the-room thinks" (where *thinks* means more than the epistemologically simple thinking we arguably saw in the Coin Toss game).

To be sure, some kinds of conversations are epistemologically sufficiently simple that they are what might be called Searle-in-the-room computable. So Searle will be capable of the following Chinese equivalent of the question and answer "I/O," a variation of which we saw earlier:

Interrogator: Well, here it is Friday, again.
Searle: Yes, I see it is the 12th of the month. Didn't miss the 13th by much!
Interrogator: You're not superstitious are you?
Searle: No, of course not. Logic and superstition don't mix.

While he will not understand the squiggle-squoggle strings needed to support such a conversation, since this conversation is epistemologically simple, as I argued earlier, he should be able to generate something like these responses. On the other hand, if, by "your answers are indistinguishable from those of a native Chinese speaker," he means mature conversational ability, of the kind I have tried to emphasize characterizes the Turing test, then he will not be able to converse in such a manner. His answers will be noticeably *distinguishable* from a native Chinese speaker who would be capable of such conversation. He will be incapable, I claim, of this kind of conversation in Chinese, a variation of which we also saw earlier:

Interrogator: Did you hear that Gorbachev's political strength within the upper ranks of the KGB is deteriorating significantly?
Searle: No, that's news to me.
Interrogator: What do you think that means for the federal government's attempt to decrease the budget deficit?
Searle: I should think it would make it much more difficult.

As I see it, he will not be capable of the Chinese equivalent of this question and answer "I/O" but would have to settle, at best, for some kind of ELIZA-like, epistemologically simple response such as "Why do you want to know about the budget deficit?" On the set of distinctions I have drawn, there is a difference of kind between "I should think that it would make it much more difficult" and "Why do you want to know about the budget deficit?" such that the former, barring a solution to the frame problem, is not a Searle-in-the-room computable function, while the latter, we can at least imagine, is. The latter, ES response does not require the kind of understanding that Searle insists he does not have in the Chinese Room while the former, the EC response, does. For the EC response, the sense of what is being asked must be appropriated by any system making the response and revisions of the system's axiomatized beliefs must occur before the response can be made. By Searle's own admission he has no such ability to appropriate the sense of what is asked and an unsolved frame problem prevents a syntax-only computation of such an EC response.

I have used considerations dependent on the frame problem to argue that Searle misrepresents the kind of Chinese language abilities he would have in the Chinese Room. It might be objected that I have somewhat unfairly used a philosophical problem that has become prominent since Searle developed his argument. Indeed, the earlier pieces, namely, "Minds, Brains and Programs" and *Minds, Brains and Science*, appeared before the frame problem became a prominent topic for philosophers commenting on AI — it is anachronistic, the objection would continue, to fault Searle for not exploring whether the frame problem constitutes a difficulty for his position. But Searle's newest piece, "Is the Brain's Mind a Computer Program?" (1990), was presumably written or edited after Pylyshyn's volume on the frame problem appeared. If it is anachronistic to fault Searle for not paying attention to the frame problem in the earlier pieces, it no longer is. The conclusion I draw from Searle's inattention to the frame problem and how it bears on mature conversational abilities in a computer is that Searle doesn't see that the frame problem is pertinent.

Additionally, there are grounds for resisting Searle's strong claim that there is a sufficiently clear difference between syntax and semantics such that it can be argued forcefully that all that computer programs possess is syntax. Searle adds that one lesson from his *Gedankenexperiment* is that we can't get semantics from syntax, and all he has in his room, which is all any computer program has, is syntax. But Searle seems to assume that there is a clear enough distinction between semantics and syntax that we can speak as though there is a clear-cut difference of kind. It is not obvious that the distinction is sufficiently clean that Searle can simply assume the distinction holds as tightly as he supposes it does.

In discussing semantics and computer programs, I find it helpful to distinguish *original* from *derivative* semantical content. Even if it is the case that a program has no original semantic content *qua* program (and I think this is problematic as well), programs as implemented on this or that machine, at least at some levels of description, have considerable derivative semantic content. That programs are — at one level of description — independent of this or that machine does not mean that programs are always independent of all machines, as though they are some kind of *Gedankenexperiment* themselves. Unembodied programs do no work. Programs get executed on computers and, as a result, they do derivatively refer to things in the world, such as registers, memory locations and ports, and other objects in the world, and consequently, they do — as they execute at least — have derivative semantical content. I think Gunderson intuits some of the difficulty with Searle's position when he observes that we need to consider how programs are roboted as well as how robots are programmed in coming to terms with these issues. Programs are hooked into the real world, they do refer, at least some of the time and in some ways.

As a simple illustration, consider this Pascal procedure call: assign-(datafile, 'b:temps');. There are two parameters in this call, datafile and b:temps. Datafile is the name of the logical file in the Pascal program. Let Searle have his way; let's agree that this part is syntax only (I don't believe this either, but for the sake of argument I'll play along). But even if this is quite right, we cannot say the same for the second parameter, namely b:temps, since it names a file recorded physically on a disk. Run the program and a drive is accessed, on a floppy drive a red light goes on, the read/write head contacts the medium, in short, things happen in the real world. As a result, programs are connected to the real world, they do refer, there is an "aboutness" to them of the kind that Searle claims there isn't.

I grant that Searle would likely not be impressed by this modest counterexample. Searle could respond that the fact that the assign procedure causes the machine to access a disk drive is a mere convenience since we happen to use a disk drive to store the (syntax-only) data and that he is no more moved by this point than he would be by being reminded that a program is stored in a computer's "RAM" using chips built by Motorola in a plant in Rantoul, Illinois. We use physical devices, he would counter, to support formal programs. The physical devices happen to be convenient ways to run the program, but they are finally irrelevant to what a formal program does logically.

But I think Searle lets the fact that we map computable problems onto the resources of an automatic formal system obscure the fact that the course of action taken by programs typically hinges on events in the external world and, in turn, programs often significantly affect the course of events in the world — especially, as we have seen, in the case of conversations. The way the world happens to be going shows up as intermediate data which shape the sequence of instruction execution. The logical map, it is true, can be understood (by a person only, Searle would doubtless insist) in splendid, syntactic isolation. However, in practice, the logical map, the program, often causally interacts with the world in such a way that the sequence of instruction execution directly depends on events transpiring in the world. Considered as a series of logical bits, admittedly, the envisioned SDI battle management software, to use the example cited by Cherniak in the last chapter, is (arguably) syntax only; as it directed (alarmingly, in an epistemologically simple way, in my view) the early stages of the American intercontinental ballistic participation in what might turn out to be the last world war, nonetheless, it surely would have all too real "aboutness." We can consider programs in the abstract and thereby ignore the derivative semantical content they have when they are used. As the assign statement illustrates and these considerations suggest, however, programs such as conversational programs are bidirectionally hooked into the real world and thereby acquire significant derivative semantical content even if we concede that they possess no original or intrinsic semantical content. Searle-in-the-room minimally has just this kind of derivative semantical content.

Though I am less optimistic than she about the prospects for AI, and while I don't otherwise like her critique of Searle, I believe Margaret Boden (1989b) answers the question of whether a program has derivative semantical content correctly.

> But what must not be forgotten is that *a computer program is a program for a computer*: when a program is run on suitable hardware, the machine does something as a result (hence the use in computer science of the words "instruction" and "obey"). At the level of the machine code the effect of the program on the machine is direct, because the machine is

> engineered so that a given instruction elicits a unique operation . . . A
> programmed instruction, then, is not a mere formal pattern — nor even
> a declarative statement . . . It is a procedure-specification that, given
> suitable hardware-context, can cause the procedure in question to be
> executed. (pp. 94–95)

At the programmatic level, there is no semantical content, then, but in
context of driving hardware, a program takes on its semantical
content — its relatedness to the world — derivatively. I think Boden's
case would be stronger if she underscored how program logic presupposes intermediate data, especially in a conversation, to direct which
path the program logically follows of the many that are available.

In essence, it looks as though Searle has uncritically accepted a
debatable functionalist understanding of program — to rebut the strong
AI point of view. In neither "Minds, Brains, and Programs" nor *Minds,
Brains and Science* does Searle attempt to convince us that programs have
no semantic content. He simply assumes it. In "Is the Brain's Mind a
Computer Program?" (Searle, 1990), he advances a brief argument to
support this claim. He writes:

> First, symbols and programs are purely abstract notions. . . . The 0s
> and 1s, qua symbols, have no essential physical properties and a fortiori
> have no physical, causal properties. . . . The second point is that
> symbols are manipulated without reference to any meanings. (p. 27)

What he means, as I understand it, is that the program, for
example, executes an if/then/else statement based on the evaluation of
Boolean expressions and comparisons based on relative magnitudes.
Because it is a logical abstraction, such a program could be instantiated
using any jury-rigged device capable of supporting automatic computation — in fact, Searle-in-the-room is exactly just such a jury-rigged
computer. However, I'm at a loss to understand, if the 0s and 1s have
no "causal properties," how it is that Searle-in-the-room, who cannot,
by stipulation, point to his own understanding of Chinese as the causal
explanation, can nevertheless "satisfy the Turing test for understanding Chinese." If satisfying the Turing test cannot be explained in
terms of Searle's understanding, what gets the credit for the Chinese
language competency? Surely the program does. If the program were
removed from the room, and this means that Searle would not have it

memorized, no Chinese competency would remain. As a result, I don't believe that it is consistent to claim that the program has no causal properties and yet plays the pivotal role in an extraordinary achievement, namely, the ability to converse in a language in such a way that the conversational ability is indistinguishable from that of a native speaker. Abstract, unembodied formulas presumably play no causal role in the world but "roboted" (Gunderson's term) formulas sometimes have significant causal roles.

There is another way that Searle is not consistent. In terms of this essay, I take it that Searle would want to say that he believes that rule-based, syntax-only EC conversations are possible in the Chinese Room — remember that he claims a competency which is indistinguishable from that of a native speaker. His inconsistency becomes apparent when we consider the implications of Chapter 5 of *Minds, Brains and Science*, where he discusses why the social sciences will not be able to explain human behavior. The discussion turns on the issue of why we don't have anything like the success with nomic generalizations in the social sciences that we have in the natural sciences. The position that Searle advances to account for this disparity is that there is a "peculiar kind of self-referentiality" about many kinds of social phenomena. Using everyday, common examples, Searle tells us that such phenomena include money and marriage. In the case of conventions associated with money, the question, according to Searle, is whether we can develop a rule which determines whether something is money. We cannot, says Searle, because money just is what people decide will be used as money. There is no rule which would cover issues associated with what is to count as money (1984, p. 78). He writes:

> The defining principle of such social phenomena set[s] no physical limits whatever on what can count as the physical realisation of them. And this means that there can't be any systematic connections between the physical and the social or mental properties of the phenomenon. The social features in question are determined in part by the attitudes we take toward them. The attitudes we take toward them are not constrained by the physical features of the phenomena in question. Therefore, there can't be any matching of the mental level and the level of the physics of the sort that would be necessary to make strict laws of the social sciences possible. (pp. 78–79)

I can't understand how it would be possible to engage in the conversation in the Chinese Room if such social phenomena are not capable, in principle, of being described by rules. Searle's conception of social phenomena surely has considerable implications for the nature of language, which is arguably the most social phenomenon there is.

Heinz Pagels (1988) underscores this point by writing that "behavioral scientists have a greater challenge in making computer models because they lack a deep theory of social or psychological phenomena" (p. 90). He quotes Stan Ulam of Stanford as remarking:

> You see an object *as* a key, you see a man *as* a passenger, you see some sheets of paper *as* a book. It is the word 'as' that must be mathematically formalized, on a par with the connectives 'and,' 'or,' 'implies,' and 'not' that have already been accepted into formal logic. Until you do that, you will not get very far with your AI problem. (p. 94)

In other words, we have succeeded at formalizing some parts of natural language but other parts remain resistant to formalization. While such resistance remains, full natural language competency will elude computer systems. While Pagels is optimistic about AI, this quote, perhaps unwittingly, underscores what Searle seems to be saying and parallels a good bit of what, in stronger, more comprehensive terms, Winograd and Flores argue (1986). I take it that if Ulam, Searle, and Winograd and Flores are significantly correct, and contrary to what Searle assumes in his Chinese Room, we will not be able to build digital computers with anything approximating a deep enough understanding of human language that they could pass the Turing test.

For example, suppose that Searle participated in a question-and-answer conversation in which he was asked to imagine that he was the man in a restaurant having a meal. Recall that scripts have played a significant role in AI, and that a script is a set of rules and information that purportedly would allow a formal system to handle itself in typical human situations such as having a meal in a restaurant. The story continues in this way: The man eats his meal and, upon receiving his check, presents the waiter with a 50 dollar bill. Discovering he has no money to make change, the waiter remarks to Searle-in-the-room:

Waiter: I must apologize that I have no change. Would you be willing to take this 1987 Frank Viola baseball card instead of your $40 change?

If it is the case, as Searle insists, that "'money' refers to whatever people use and think of as money" and if it is the case that "there can't be any matching of the mental level and the level of the physics of the sort that would be necessary to make strict laws of the social sciences possible," how are we to imagine that Searle-in-the-room could use a program devoid of semantical content to marshal a sensible response to the waiter's question? Or how might he be able to make the connection that this is possibly a fair offer and ask relevant questions in order to make the determination that it is something like fair?

In sum, I don't believe that Searle has made a convincing case that his much-discussed Chinese Room experiment is plausible. He has not given us adequate grounds for concluding that, given his understanding of what he has at his disposal in the room, namely a program, he would be capable of such a competency. I have attempted to show why he would not have the kind of competency that would be needed to pass the Turing test. Specifically, I conceded an ES language competency, but I argued that he would not possess the requisite EC competency. As a result, therefore, his claim that, as Searle-in-the-room, "I satisfy the Turing test for understanding Chinese" is not convincing. Moreover, I argued that Searle himself has a view of the relation of language and convention to human intentionality that entails that no set of rules could capture the relationship in a way adequate to support mature conversational ability. Minimally, I take this to mean that he does not believe himself, upon pain of contradiction, that he could perform as stipulated in the Chinese Room. Maximally, it means that he could not pass the Turing test at an EC level.

The following objection might be raised to my criticism of Searle: Your criticism of Searle is predicated on an unsolvable frame problem. Suppose that we find a solution for the frame problem, some kind of delightfully imaginative engineering solution, such that a computer, to everyone's complete satisfaction and perhaps astonishment, passes the Turing test. What would you, Crockett, say in response to Searle's Chinese Room counterexample then? The point, I take it, is that my criticism of the plausibility of Searle's Chinese Room thought experiment assumes an unsolvable frame problem but I have conceded that it is at least logically possible we might at some point find a solution. All Searle is doing, as it were, is assuming that there is a solution to the frame problem, just as classical AI must assume there will be one.

What are the implications of a solved frame problem? In such a situation, I think we will have to do a fair amount of the science that Pat Hayes has been pushing on us, then do some of the careful philosophical analysis that Searle and Gunderson have been saying is essential to interpreting impressive computer performance. A solved frame problem in digital systems means some very interesting things may begin to happen. Understanding may be an emergent property for which a solved frame problem is a necessary condition. Self-awareness similarly may begin to develop in systems that possess a solution to the frame problem and some yet to be determined minimal storage capacity. Speculating even more, a solved frame problem in a sufficiently massively parallel system may mean that the contrast I have insisted we must observe — that between storage and memory — becomes much fuzzier or even disappears.

It is conceivable that Searle-in-the-room with a solved frame problem, given sufficient time, would develop an understanding of the language he is using in much the same way that an infant begins to appropriate what at first must appear to the infant as so many oral squiggle-squoggle strings. In fact, Searle-in-the-room with a solved frame problem may well be a system that finally becomes psychologically relevant in the way that computational psychology has largely been simply assuming to date. Moreover, I think a solved frame problem would count in favor of the hollow shell criticism, at least initially, and against the poor substitute strategy I currently endorse, simply because a sufficiently large system with a solved frame problem is going to be able to do some epistemologically complex learning. To the point, such a system will likely be a good substitute for human-level intelligence. Even more dramatically, a solved frame problem would be impressive evidence that the classical AI understanding of intelligence itself is reviving as a research paradigm.

2. The Gunderson Critique

Keith Gunderson's critique of AI has some parallels with Searle's, but there are two objections Gunderson makes to AI in general and the Turing test in particular that I find at once distinctive in terms of specific emphasis and philosophically more subtle than Searle's take-no-prisoners frontal assault. First, consider Gunderson's (1985) comment on what I have called the relation of I/O to what we can justifiably infer about the intervening processes that generate the "O" of the I/O:

> Now perhaps comparable net results achieved by machines and human beings is all that is needed to establish an analogy between them, but it is far from what is needed to establish that one sort of subject (machines) can do the same thing that another sort of subject (human beings or animals) can do. Part of what things do is how they do it. To ask whether a machine can think is in part to ask whether machines can do things in certain ways. (p. 45)

I take this first objection to be a reminder that similarity of I/O descriptions between two systems would not, in itself, justify similar characterizations about the intervening processes producing the output. For purposes of analyzing the Turing test, I believe that Gunderson is saying, there are two aspects to an activity done by a machine or a person. One is the output as compared with the input and the other is the process which generates the output, given the input. To establish that a machine is doing the same thing as a person, specifically, we would have to know something about the intervening processes as well as the I/O.

In terms of a second objection by Gunderson that I wish to discuss, consider his comments about the purported lack of appreciation in the literature that some tasks which may have previously been thought to require intelligence may not, owing to developments in machine technology, turn out to require intelligence:

> What I wish to stress and what I think has been increasingly overlooked is that any taxonomy of the field of machine intelligence must leave room for a category that tolerates the possibility of machines performing tasks that had hitherto required intelligence (human or otherwise) and *performing them in ways totally bereft of any psychological reality*. (p. 174; emphasis in original)

I understand this second objection to be a matter of asking whether it is possible that tasks we had formerly supposed required intelligence — say, for example, chess playing — may turn out to be a task, owing to the advance of computer and related technology, which is amenable to being done by a purely mechanical, nonthinking machine. His example in *Mentality and Machines* is that of steam engine power replacing muscle power in the digging of tunnels. To put it in traditional philosophic terms, Gunderson reminds us how tempting it is to mistake a sufficient condition for a necessary condition — if we can ignore related factors, muscles are a sufficient but not a necessary condition for digging tunnels. Analogously, he claims, intelligence is a sufficient condition (again, if we can ignore all the auxiliary "hardware" usually needed to communicate with another user of the language) for mature conversational ability, but we cannot claim, since it may well turn out that such competency can be generated by machines "totally bereft of any psychological reality," that it is a necessary condition. Of course, this allows him to deny the logic of the Turing test, namely, that mature conversational ability as defined by Turing means that we are justified in ascribing intelligence to the system passing the test.

In this last section of the chapter, I intend to argue against these two objections as they pertain to the frame problem and the Turing test. I conclude the section as well as the chapter with a brief discussion of Gunderson's claim that Weizenbaum's ELIZA and Winograd's SHRDLU are capable of passing "Turing-type" tests.

I should emphasize that I don't believe Gunderson has no appealing grounds for warning us about the philosophic difficulty of making ascriptions about intervening processes on the basis of I/O alone. In fact, given what I have claimed about the treacherous nature of computer simulation, the problem may be even more difficult than Gunderson suggests. We have access to, and significant understanding of, many kinds of natural and human phenomena, and, as a result, we have at least some basis for claiming that we understand "how they do it." Ordinarily, with the overwhelming majority of phenomena, I readily concede, it is important to ask if something is done "in certain ways" before risking characterizations about behavior when such characterizations tacitly suppose something about the intervening processes supporting the behavior. Since, indeed, "part of what things do is how they do it," in most situations, when we want to know if x is doing y, it will usually be correct to ask about how x does the phenomenon in question in order to be in a position to agree, reasonably, that x really is doing y.

To cite a computer illustration that underscores Gunderson's claim, it would not be justified to infer from only the fact that a computer had computed some function that the computer must be using one language rather than another. Since, given a few essential properties, all languages can compute the same class of computable functions, we are not in a position, without knowing more, to infer from this I/O description, namely, that function x was computed, to that process description, namely, that language y must have been used. In Chapter 3, I attempted to underscore how computer simulations are particularly likely to mislead the unsuspecting. It is because we know the power of simulation, how it is that a computer is uniquely suited to generating a "user illusion," that we should especially be concerned to resist quick inferences to the similarity of intervening processes from similarity of I/O alone. With massively parallel computing becoming more feasible than it was just a few years ago, the user illusions that we will be capable of generating will be even more seductive. Consequently, Gunderson is on to something significant in terms of warning us of the dangers of advancing characterizations about intervening processes on the basis of I/O alone.

I agree that such caution is warranted in virtually every case — but I do not agree that it is warranted in all situations. As I attempted to argue in the last chapter, we are not currently in a position to do the kind of inspection of internal processes of the brain that we are for many other objects of study. For somewhat similar reasons of scale, we are not in a position to understand to any significant extent a mindlike program. In order to compare a brain with a program, to see if there is something like intervening similarity of process, we would have to have some significant knowledge of brain processes and some significant knowledge of program processes of a mindlike program. But as I argued, we have neither of these to any significant simultaneous breadth and depth. Consequently, I believe, we are not in a position to make the relevant comparisons. It would be welcome indeed if we could make such comparisons, but, unfortunately, we are not in the requisite position and, given the likelihood that the radically novel function possessed by the human brain developed over largely conserved structure in evolutionary history, and given the extraordinary complexity of a mindlike program, I see no grounds for optimism that this unfortunate impairment can be overcome.

As should be expected by now, I claim that considerations attaching to mature conversational ability make it an exception to Gunderson's "similarity of input/output does not guarantee similarity of intervening processes" objection. Mature conversational competency on a computer is not typical I/O—which is why Turing presumably chose it. But not only does Gunderson reject the Turing test, he claims that it is quite weak:

> With respect to Turing's Test, it should also be emphasized that not only is it inadequate as a test for there being literally a mind in the machine, it is for reasons given in Chapter Four inadequate as a test for a simulation in a machine of a mind. In this sense the chapter might be seen as trying to delineate how very weak Turing's Test actually is. (1985, p. 205)

I cannot claim to have one of Searle's "knock-down" arguments, but I believe the price for holding Gunderson's position is too high. Like Searle's, Gunderson's is a variation on a hollow shell strategy; in other words, he claims that passage of the test by a computer would not, in itself, justify the claim that the computer is thinking—that is, passage of the test is not a sufficient condition for concluding that the computer is thinking. By contrast, my position is that, if the grounds are sufficient for concluding that other persons think, owing to behavioral considerations and presumably some kind of argument by analogy, passage of the Turing test is surely also a sufficient condition for concluding that the computer is thinking, owing to behavioral considerations and a solved frame problem, for which I see no mechanical, nonthinking solution.

The argument from analogy, I take it, would go something like this: Other people have bodies quite similar to my own, and they behave in ways that are similar to the way I often behave. Certain kinds of problems that I work at and solve require what I call *thinking*. I notice that other people work at these kinds of problems, and, since they have similar bodies and hence likely similar biological processes, I infer that they must be thinking as well when they do the tasks I do that require what I call *thinking*. While there are problems with all arguments from analogy, and while there is an additional problem with arguing from a single-case analogy, namely, from myself to many other people, most of us do accept the conclusion that other people think, presumably on grounds, if we are philosophically reflective, something like these. I don't claim that this is a knock-down argument. My claim is that, given the difficulty of solving the frame problem, and given the role that the frame problem has of distinguishing ES from EC thinking "systems," it seems to me that a digital computer system capable of passing the Turing test, one that has therefore solved the frame problem, is at least as worthy of being described as *thinking* as another person who displays the right behavior and about whom I make some kind of attribution by analogy. In other words, the grounds, on my view, are roughly on a par.

Gunderson would argue that we would need, to some extent, presumably, to see *how* it is conversing in the way that it is — not just that it is conversing that way, and that it might turn out that the test can be passed by systems that are not thinking (in something like a full sense of *thinking*). I have already argued at length why we are not in a position to achieve an adequate picture of the intervening processes; I intend to argue now that Gunderson's position commits him to claiming that it is feasible that a nonthinking, rule-based, automatic formal system can be programmed in such a way that it can defeat the frame problem. This is the price he must pay for his position, I claim, and I find it to be too high.

Suppose that a computer, appropriately enhanced with the requisite peripherals, engaged in a long conversation with an interrogator, with Turing, Dennett, Gunderson, and myself observing carefully. Suppose as well that the computer was so skilled at the conversation that we all agreed that, by any reasonable definition of the test, here, at last, we have a computer that had passed the test. Gunderson claims that such passage would not, by itself, justify the claim that the computer is thinking. Turing and Dennett and I, of course, suppose the opposite.

Given such a situation in which all observers agreed that a computer had passed the test, what would it mean for Gunderson to be correct in his claim that it is possible that a test-passing machine might still not be thinking? It would mean that it is feasible that a nonthinking automatic formal system had passed the test. That is, it would have engaged successfully in a mature conversation of the sort envisioned by Turing and amplified by Dennett and, I hope, myself. However, I argued in the previous chapter that a Turing test conversation is an epistemologically complex conversation that presupposes an ability for the system to engage in EC learning. I claimed that adequacy of conversational response in an EC conversation presupposes the ability of the system to revise its own set of beliefs, presumably some kind of axiom system, in light of epistemologically complex information — at least in some parts of an EC conversation. To be sure, I didn't claim that such revision was necessary for all parts of an EC conversation, just some. I also argued that EC learning is blocked by an unsolved frame problem since the frame problem prevents the kind of system-wide inspection and revision, in light of EC information, that is requisite to EC learning. An unsolved frame problem prevents EC learning, which is a necessary condition for an EC conversation. And EC conversational skills, not simply ES skills, are necessary for passage of the Turing test.

I should emphasize at this point that, given the history of the debate that Turing's paper started, the question often gets phrased in the unrefined way, "Can machines think?" or "Do we have adequate grounds for concluding that SIMON the robot thinks, given that he has just passed the Turing test?" I have distinguished ES from EC thinking, granting that digital computers are capable of the former but, it appears now, probably not the latter. Pushed to relinquish my distinction and use the rougher grained *thinking* and *nonthinking* dichotomy, I would reluctantly equate *EC thinking* with *thinking* and *ES thinking* with *non*thinking, with the result that a digital computer, on my view, is likely not capable of the kind of thinking that Turing had in mind, nor is it capable of the activity pointed to by the term *thinking* as most people apparently understand that word.

Using these qualifications, Gunderson's view commits him, therefore, to the claim that it is feasible that a nonthinking automatic formal system can be programmed in such a way that it can solve the frame problem each time an EC comment or query is encountered, in conversational real time. However, I have argued that the evidence is compelling that there is no mechanical, nonthinking way for the frame problem to be solved, particularly in such a circumstance. Minimally, there is no way currently known to solve the frame problem in a mechanical, nonthinking way. We don't know how to begin the task of constructing and programming such a digital computer.

As I see it, therefore, the choice comes down to this: either affirm that it is feasible for a nonthinking, mechanical system to solve the frame problem or be willing to ascribe thinking to the system which passes the Turing test. Gunderson, I claim, would have to opt for the former choice; of course, I choose the latter.

Gunderson could respond that, from the fact that we currently are not able to program an automatic formal system to solve the frame problem when it arises in a conversational context, we are not justified in concluding that it cannot be done in principle. From the fact that we cannot do it *now*, it does not follow that it cannot be done in principle. On this point, then, Gunderson is likely not far from defenders of classical AI who remind us that the discipline is young and that AI engineers ought to be given a chance to see what can be done; in any case, they are largely oblivious to the claims of philosophers that such and such is impossible or unlikely.

I wholeheartedly concur that such an inference is not justified. But I have not claimed that the frame problem cannot, in principle, be solved by a nonthinking, automatic formal system. I simply claim that there is little evidence at present that it can, and a considerable amount of evidence that it can't, be solved by a nonthinking system. Put in more constructive terms, I claim that the evidence against it is sufficiently compelling that the best way we have to distinguish thinking from nonthinking activity, if the general frame of reference is AI, is that thinking activity does not suffer from the frame problem. The frame problem, in other words, is fatal to automatic formal systems that are programmed to think in the ways requisite to a mature conversation. The frame problem, on my view, represents the principal demarcation which distinguishes EC from ES thinking machines (or, using the rougher grained dichotomy, thinking from nonthinking machines).

Of course, I don't wish to claim that an automatic formal system which suffers from the frame problem does no thinking — to carry my distinction through, I claim that it is capable of epistemologically simple thinking rather than epistemologically complex thinking. The fact that a computer can compute a ninth-order derivative means that a ninth-order derivative problem is amenable to solution by ES thinking. By contrast, if it is not possible to program a digital computer with an unsolved frame problem so that it passes the Turing test, this means that mature conversational ability is not amenable to solution by ES thinking alone.

The result I wish to sponsor is that an automatic formal system that passes the Turing test does not suffer from the frame problem. Passing the test is evidence that the frame problem has been solved; in the case of an automatic formal system or, in cases where other kinds of systems are putatively under scrutiny, it may not exist at all. I suggested earlier that pattern-recognition-based "systems" that are not computationally based may not need a solution to the frame problem because they don't suffer from it to begin with.

If the evidence, as I have argued, favors the view that there is no mechanical, nonthinking way to solve the frame problem, and if an automatic formal system had solved the problem on its way to passing the Turing test, I think we would have grounds for ascribing thinking to the system that are at least as compelling as the grounds we have — and evidently find compelling — for ascribing thinking to other persons.

To be sure, I cannot begin to detail how such a feat would be possible such that I could answer the question, "Well, how would such a mechanical, thinking device solve the frame problem?" I remain skeptical that we can build a digital computer which incorporates a solution to the frame problem. As I stated earlier, I am convinced that full-fledged thinking is most likely exclusively associated with pattern-recognition of the type described by Margolis, not automatic manipulation of symbols at all.

Gunderson in fact recognizes that there is a problem with what I have called *EC conversation*, even though I don't believe he sees the full significance of it. The following remarks are occasioned by problems associated with character recognition:

> The major obstacle is that there is still no precise account of how one could build into a program the fantastically varied background knowledge (e.g., that cows don't eat fish) that human speaker-hearers bring to a communication situation and that enables them in fairly systematic and facile ways to interpret correctly each other's utterances, even though considerable novelty may attend both the syntactic, and situational or pragmatic features of the remark that is interpreted. (1985, p. 111)

I take it as uncontroversial that people possess a "fantastically varied background knowledge," which is central to our ability to answer correctly the question whether, to use Gunderson's example, cows eat fish — and that we do so virtually immediately and with evident ease. But the major obstacle to mature conversational ability for a computer is not just acquiring the enormous background of knowledge we can bring to a conversation. I take it as an open, empirical question whether current computers can store background knowledge in amounts that at least rival that of people. The problem is not so much that we have no precise account of how to represent this wealth of knowledge in a machine — we've made considerable progress with the problem of representation. Instead, the principal problem is understanding how an automatic formal system should go about integrating old beliefs with new (epistemologically complex) information, it is identifying a principled way to recognize the relevance of new items of information for problem tasks, given such a background, and it is a matter of solving the problem of doing all this at a speed that makes it possible to engage in a real conversation in real time. On a classical AI paradigm understanding of intelligence, the principal problem is not the storage of knowledge per se, it is how to overcome the frame problem so that such knowledge can be used in epistemologically complex problem solving situations such as Turing test-style conversations.

Specifically, I see no evidence that Gunderson has adequately acknowledged that there is a difference between *developing* a rich representation, a "fantastically varied background knowledge," and *maintaining* that representation over a period of time in situations of real world complexity. If by "fantastically varied background" he means everything a system would need to know to pass the Turing test, it is too much to expect that we can simply program a sufficiently rich background into the computer. For reasons pointed to by Putnam (1988), which I amplified in Chapter 4 and elsewhere, learning at a high (EC) level will be a necessary capacity in any system that passes the test. If he will agree that such learning is a necessary ingredient in any system passing the test, he is going to have to take account of the impediment to such learning posed by the frame problem. He has not done this.

Parenthetically, I should state that the old CS/AI distinction has been lost — probably, as I think Gunderson supposes as well, to the detriment of the philosophical conversations about AI. In his chapter entitled "Philosophy and Computer Simulation," Gunderson discusses the Turing test and computer simulation. If the question is phrased as: Is the Turing test psychologically relevant to human intelligence? I think the answer is: not necessarily. All it shows, in my view, is that there is thinking, which may have little, in some respects at least, to do with human thinking. I take no position on the psychological relevance of such thinking to psychological investigations of human thinking. That is, we don't get from an I/O statement about a machine passing the Turing test to a surmise about a *human* process description; nothing about a machine passing the Turing test necessarily tells us anything specific about human intelligence. I take it as an axiom that there are lots of quite dissimilar ways at the process level to generate functional similarity at the I/O level. The more modest claim I defend is that passage of the Turing test does tell us something about the likely existence of intelligence in the machine.

At this point, I want to discuss what I have called Gunderson's second objection to the Turing test, namely, that we can't be sure that what we have taken to be a necessary condition for a phenomenon won't turn out to be one of two or more sufficient conditions — in other words, the objection that it may turn out that thinking is a sufficient condition for passing the test but not necessarily a necessary condition. Parenthetically, I should add that I will use the usual contrast between necessary and sufficient conditions in this section even though I know that, strictly speaking, thinking is not a sufficient condition for conversation, for since various other conditions would have to be present as well — in the case of people, for example, conversation also requires sensory organs of some kind, some physically supported way to communicate, and so on. For the sake of simplicity of expression, I will claim that Gunderson supposes thinking is a sufficient condition for conversation but not a necessary condition even though, strictly speaking, I am sure he would agree that it is neither necessary nor sufficient. The central question is the necessity of thinking for conversation such that conversational ability at a Turing test level would be sufficient grounds for inferring the presence of thinking on the part of the system passing the test.

To get a full picture of his objection, I will quote Gunderson at greater length:

> So we shall be primarily concerned with asking whether or not a machine, which could play the imitation game as well as Turing thought it might, would thus be a machine which we would have good reasons for saying was capable of thought and what would be involved in saying this. (1985, p. 41)

After comparing Turing's Imitation Game with his own parody of the Imitation Game, Gunderson writes (pp. 43–44):

The above seems to show the following: what follows from the toe-stepping game situation surely is not that rocks are able to imitate . . . but only that they are able to be rigged in such a way that they could be substituted for a human being in a toe-stepping game without changing any essential characteristics of that game.

To be sure, a digital computer is a more august mechanism than a rock box, but Turing has not provided us with any arguments for believing that its role in the imitation game, as distinct from the net results it yields, is any closer a match for a human being executing such a role, than is the rock box's execution of its role in the toe-stepping game a match for a human being's execution of a similar role. The parody comparison can be pushed too far. But I think it lays bare the reason why there is no contradiction in saying, "Yes, a machine can play the imitation game, but it can't think."

For thinking (or imitating) cannot be fully described simply by pointing to net results such as those illustrated above. For if this were not the case it would be correct to say that a phonograph could sing, and that an electric eye could see people coming.

Turing brandishes net results. But I think the foregoing at least indicates certain difficulties with any account of thinking or decision as to whether a certain thing is capable of thought which is based primarily on net results.

What Gunderson assumes here is that there is some significant analogy between a computer and conversation, on the one hand, and a phonograph and singing on the other. Since the digital onslaught has overtaken musical reproduction as well, allow me to update the comparison to a compact disk. Other than the fact we might imagine — under quite unusual but still plausible circumstances — that a person might mistake, say, a "Use Your Illusion I" disk played on a state-of-the-art system for the rock group Guns N' Roses on their tour, and that, in a parallel way, a person might not be able to distinguish a computer from a person in Turing's Imitation Game, what grounds has Gunderson given us for supposing that there is a significant analogy between the two situations? Singing, for all of its subtly beautiful dimensions at its best, has few of the singular dimensions of a mature conversation. A Jesuit biologist friend of mine, James Mulligan, helped the philosopher Charles Hartshorne edit his well-regarded book of birdsong. Mulligan once observed to me, "For all its beauty, birdsong appears to be finally quite mechanical." Song, whether by a person or a bird (and the equivalence is a tip-off), lacks the principal asset of conversation in terms of testing for intelligence: unpredictable interactivity over an uncircumscribed domain. In a mature conversation, one would expect spontaneity, unanticipated twists and turns, nuances, new information, probing questions, perhaps some wry humor here and there, and so on. That which is rather clearly mechanical, namely, song, would seem to lend itself to mechanization in a way that that which is not rather clearly mechanical, namely, conversation, would not. There is little relevant philosophical moral, as a result, in the fact that a phenomenon such as song is amenable to mechanical reproduction.

Gunderson's contrast between program receptive and program resistant aspects of mentality achieved considerable currency in philosophical discussions of AI when it was advanced about 20 years ago. One might conclude that there is a correlation between my ES/EC distinction and Gunderson's distinction. On this conclusion, epistemologically simple (ES) learning and conversation are program receptive; epistemologically complex (EC) learning and conversation are program resistant. I certainly have argued that ES learning and conversation are amenable to programming, and I have argued that EC learning and conversation are resistant to programming, given an unsolved frame problem. But one should notice that Gunderson's distinction has to do with the performing of acts, of behaviors, as opposed to the having of experiences. Full language competency, of the kind required to pass a full-fledged test, remains, for Gunderson a behavior that might be duplicated, since it is a behavior, by means other than thinking. That is, thinking is a sufficient condition for such a behavior, but it is not a necessary condition — the technology, as it has so often in the past, might get good enough to do what formerly we thought could only be done by means of thinking. Gunderson would point to top-rank computer chess play as a prominent case in point. What is resistant to programming, according to Gunderson, are certain kinds of experiences that characterize human mentality: pains, anxieties about the fidelity of one's spouse, after-images, and so on. These are not behaviors we *do*, they are experiences we *have*. That part of human mentality, as Gunderson sees it, is resistant to capture in a program.

But Gunderson's question of whether a program can capture all aspects of human mentality is a somewhat different question from the one Turing addressed. Turing was not so concerned about whether programs could capture certain kinds of human mental experiences; he was concerned, in spite of some initial protestations to the contrary, with whether machines can think and how we might convince ourselves they can think. Gunderson might argue that the ability to have such mental experiences is part of the ability to think, and therefore is a necessary condition for thinking, but I don't know that this is the case.

While I am unsettled on the issue of whether natural language competency is fully a behavior, or best thought of as exclusively a behavior and not bound up intimately with mental states that we have, for the moment, let's agree that it is a behavior. My view, then, is that there is a behavior that is resistant to programming, namely full natural language competency, so long as the frame problem remains unsolved. I agree that certain kinds of mental states are program resistant, but I want to add one behavior to the list of the program resistant, so long as we have no solution to the frame problem, namely, natural language competency of the kind requisite to passing the Turing test.

In general, in drawing the analogy between computer conversation, on the one hand, and the music produced by a system on the other, Gunderson has evidently not noticed that thinking of the sort I claim is required for the Turing test is a singular predicate such that analogies with other phenomena are not likely to be useful. Let me qualify my use of the strong term *singular*. I am quite happy to agree that there are gradations of thinking, shades of gray, places where some thinking is happening or where a small amount of what might be called high-order thinking is being applied, or a great deal of low-order thinking is being applied — and it might be difficult to distinguish such contrasts on an I/O basis alone (in fact, as we have seen, this is one basis for objecting to the Turing test). I understand my distinction between ES and EC thinking to be only a start toward the kind of rich taxonomy that might be needed adequately to describe the cognitive activities that could come under the umbrella term *thinking*. Consequently, I agree with Gunderson that there is a significant "conceptual space" between what the "strong AI" view of what "thinking" machines do and how the Dreyfus brothers view such machines; as I have intimated, some kinds of thinking may well be occurring even as a computer approximates a derivative. But I also insist that considerations attaching to an unsolved frame problem entail a fundamental distinction, namely, that between ES and EC thinking. As a result, thinking of the kind needed to pass the Test, which avoids or solves the frame problem, is not analogous to many other kinds of phenomena to which Gunderson's otherwise timely remarks would aptly apply. The usual philosophic lessons, I claim, don't always illumine an extraordinary situation.

It is not that I don't agree with the pertinence of Gunderson's remarks for almost all inferences from I/O descriptions to process ascriptions. I'll use one of Gunderson's literary devices at this point to emphasize where I agree with him. Consider: you're at one of the sexier indoor megamalls, and you see what appears to be a tree growing in an atrium. Upon closer inspection, the bark feels about right, there are imperfections here and there, the leaves vary in texture, shape and color, as they do on a real tree. It is easy to split one with your fingers; some dried leaves even litter the floor, which surrounds a hole filled with dirt. Still, you wonder — perhaps this is one of those new, quite expensive artificial trees that you recently read about in the "What Will They Think of Next?" newspaper column. In this case, it is philosophically astute to insist on knowing whether, for example, photosynthesis is occurring in the leaves (it wouldn't be enough to discover moisture in a split leaf) before possibly agreeing that the evidence warrants the process ascription, "This is a genuine tree." If still not convinced, since photosynthesis might be simulated in some way, we might wish to know: If a branch were sawn in half, would we see rings? After a few minutes, would we see some sap oozing from the wound? If we were to watch over a long period, would the tree get taller from year to year? While the complete skeptic would never be satisfied, since a process description can always be reformulated at a lower explanatory level as an I/O description, Gunderson is correct in this sense: We have gotten so good at simulations and imitations that there are many phenomena where examination of the process level must be made before it is reasonable to assent to the conclusion that this is the genuine item, not just a clever, state-of-the-art simulation. As a result, Gunderson serves us well in reminding us that such inferences are generally treacherous philosophically.

Situations in which it is reasonable to attempt an inference from I/O descriptions alone to a specific characterization of the intervening process are therefore admittedly rare — perhaps there is only one. But I claim thinking of the kind required to pass the test remains a notable exception. We have some understanding now about the limits of programmable machines in terms of dealing with a complex phenomenon such as a Turing-level conversation. In principle, the evidence is compelling that this limit is set by the frame problem. Computers are astonishingly good at epistemologically simple manipulations. Epistemologically simple tasks are amenable to mechanization and mechanical tasks which are amenable to algorithmic solution face limitations such as the speed of light and the efficiencies that attach to certain sorts of algorithms. But the evidence is that mature conversational ability does not yield to algorithmic decomposition and solution in the way that even chess does.

Chess, in fact, warrants a comment at this point. It is vast in terms of search space but perfectly simple epistemologically. There are more components in natural language than there are in a chess game, and while the number of different chess games is quite large, perhaps 10^{120}, it is many orders of magnitude smaller than the number of different conversations that two persons, each of whom could comfortably use and understand approximately 15,000 words, could have over, say, the course of an hour. Not only is the search space larger for an unconstrained conversation, chess programs do not founder on the frame problem; EC conversations do. The conversation is at once many orders of magnitude larger in terms of search space and it is complex, rather than simple, epistemologically.

Inferring that a computer thinks because it plays world class chess is risky for exactly the reasons Gunderson supplies. Previously, it was usually believed it is necessary to think in order to play a good game of chess — indeed, it was supposed it is necessary to be smart. People had a difficult time imagining a mechanical, nonthinking machine playing good chess. All that good chess playing programs show us, Gunderson would rightly point out, is that it doesn't take (EC) intelligence to play a good game of chess, since a good (at most ES) program will do. If it turns out that a chess-playing computer defeats the best human player, I will be impressed but not necessarily moved to conclude that the machine thinks, again, for exactly the reasons Gunderson supplies. I would want to know something about the intermediate processes before I could imagine endorsing such a judgment.

But part of the reason I have for welcoming a Gunderson-style caveat in the case of chess is that chess is a formal game. It is describable in unambiguous terms, and while "look-ahead" is severely circumscribed, owing to combinatorial explosion, no frame problem is joined, because no moves that an opponent might make require revision of the system of "beliefs" (let McCarthy have his way for a moment) needed to play the game. In a word, chess is epistemologically simple. Chess is an ES programmatic task. EC conversations are not. Philosophic lessons learned from detailing the relation of I/O descriptions to appropriate process ascriptions in chess, as a result, do not apply to EC conversations, because, as I have tried to argue, there is a difference in epistemological kind between chess and mature conversations, and there is an inaccessibility to systems supporting mature conversation that does not obtain in the case of chess.

In sum, Gunderson's critique applies to epistemologically simple tasks that a computer might perform. On the assumption that such an investigation is feasible, epistemologically simple simulations warrant just the kind of investigation that Gunderson would surely urge upon us before we could justifiably agree that, in some sense, the "computer is thinking." When cashed in for the rougher grained terms, *nonthinking* and *thinking*, I have reluctantly correlated ES thinking with *nonthinking* but, if we adopt a preferable, richer taxonomy, I take it to be an empirical question what kinds of low-level thinking might correctly be ascribed to various sorts of programs — and, here, I concede, Gunderson's remarks are germane. For the reasons I have advanced in this essay, nevertheless, I claim that the critique does not apply to the epistemologically complex task of mature conversation. In other words, Gunderson has supposed that his critique applies to thinking of the two types I have called ES and EC thinking, when, on my view, they apply only to the former.

Let me conclude my critique of what I have called Gunderson's necessary/sufficient objection by commenting on another analogy Gunderson (1985) offers. In *Mentality and Machines*, at the end of the chapter entitled "The Imitation Game," Gunderson raises the by-now familiar possibility that a computer may not need thinking to pass the Turing test. In his view, thinking, as we have seen, would be sufficient to explain the passage of the Turing test but not necessary, since some nonthinking process might turn out to be sufficient to explain the passage. He writes, "In the end the steam drill outlasted John Henry as a digger of railway tunnels, but that didn't prove the machine had muscles; it proved that muscles were not needed for digging railway tunnels" (p. 59). The analogy, then, is that just as the steam drill illustrated that muscles are not needed to dig large tunnels, it is a distinct possibility that what a conversationally gifted computer will show us is that thinking is not required for conversation. While, as I have said, I agree that it is easy to mistake sufficient for necessary conditions, I think it is also tempting to reach conclusions supported by analogies that other considerations count against. To the point, was there any sustainable reason to suppose that only muscles can dig railway tunnels? Surely such a supposition doesn't do well under even a little scrutiny. Water, to cite perhaps the most conspicuous alternate sufficient condition, erodes vast mountain ranges, sometimes carving huge caverns underground. Digging railway tunnels by steam engine is an impressive achievement, but it does not stand apart from other phenomena in terms of warranting philosophic scrutiny the way that thinking does — there are good reasons why there is no philosophy of tunnel digging. Consequently, the grounds are weak for supposing that only muscles can dig tunnels. My principal complaint about this analogy, then, is that our grounds for tying thinking to mature conversation are significantly more compelling than associating muscles with tunnel digging; while the John Henry analogy is picturesque, I do not find it convincing.

Last, I wish to offer some remarks about Gunderson's assessment of our old conversational friend ELIZA, since I believe that Gunderson is too generous in his assessment both of ELIZA and Winograd's SHRDLU. In the Epilogue to *Mentality and Machines*, for example, he writes that "both ELIZA and SHRDLU could pass Turing-type tests, which, I think, only shows how ineffectual such tests are for showing the comparative psychological significance of different AI programs" (1985, pp. 191–192). Such a statement is difficult to sustain in the face of actual experience with ELIZA, Weizenbaum's assessment of ELIZA, or Winograd's own assessment of his early, famous work — which he now claims is based on a fundamentally mistaken understanding both of human cognition and language.

But notice: Gunderson is more impressed by SHRDLU than Winograd and is more sanguine about ELIZA than Weizenbaum. Winograd and Flores (1986) offer the following assessment of SHRDLU:

The rationalistic approach to meaning that underlies systems like SHRDLU is founded on the assumption that the meanings of words and of the sentences and phrases made up of them can be characterized independently of the interpretation given by individuals in a situation. . . . McCarthy responds by pointing out that there are different kinds of understanding and by suggesting that we might expect a computer to understand literal meaning even if it were not open to the connotations and emotional subtleties of full meaning . . . But . . . the concept of literal meaning is inadequate even in dealing with the most mundane examples. The phenomena of background and interpretation pervade our everyday life. Meaning always derives from an interpretation that is rooted in a situation. (p. 111)

In other words, meaning in natural language derives from its rootedness in human experience; SHRDLU is not capable of handling such rooted meanings and, therefore, is incapable of passing the Turing test. Weizenbaum (1976) offers this analysis of his much-discussed ELIZA:

The first extensive script I prepared for ELIZA was one that enabled it to parody the responses of a nondirective psychotherapist in an initial psychiatric interview. I chose this script because it enabled me to temporarily sidestep the problem of giving the program a data base of real-world knowledge. After all, I reasoned, a psychiatrist can reflect the patient's remark, "My mommy took my teddy bear away from me," by saying, "Tell me more about your parents," without really having to know anything about teddy bears, for example. (pp. 188–189)

In my terms, Weizenbaum is saying that ELIZA is capable of epistemologically simple interchanges but is not capable of EC conversations. ELIZA, as Weizenbaum sees it, parodies a Rogerian psychotherapist and therefore enables it to engage in ES conversations without a rich knowledge of the real world.

Gunderson cites the widely quoted "Men are all alike" ELIZA conversation. The problem is that ELIZA is rarely this good and, in my experience at least, is never this good for a sustained period of time. On a number of occasions, I have used ELIZA in class. The pattern of reaction from my students has been neatly consistent: at first they are amazed that a conversation with a computer is possible at all. After an initial period of slightly nervous enthrallment, the students begin to discern the weaknesses and repetitiveness in ELIZA's responses, unknowingly playing the role of the interrogator in a "Turing-type" test. Toward the end of their time with ELIZA, they ask questions or make comments they correctly anticipate it cannot handle convincingly. In my experience with ELIZA, the pattern in student assessments of ELIZA, over the course of a half-hour or 45 minutes, consistently progresses, if I may coin a Schullerism, from amazement to amusement; ELIZA does not impress careful, probing observers for a sustained period of conversation.

This conversation is widely discussed indeed. It appears not only in Weizenbaum's (1976) *Computer Power and Human Reason*, and Gunderson's (1985) *Mentality and Machines*, but also in Elaine Rich (1983). I must confess as well that I quoted it in my "The Information Age: Friend or Foe of the Liberal Arts" (Crockett, 1987). Aside from the fact that Rich ascribes some "knowledge about both English and psychology" to ELIZA, I find her discussion of the implications of ELIZA preferable to others. ELIZA's major strength, according to Rich, is "its ability to say something fairly reasonable almost all the time," while its major weakness is "the superficiality of its understanding and its ability to be led completely astray" (1983, p. 68). In my view, she has it half right.

Gunderson quotes the "Men are all alike" ELIZA conversation in *Mentality and Machines* (1985, pp. 189–190). He quotes with apparent approval Churchland's assessment of ELIZA which includes: "Which just goes to show how surprisingly little understanding is required to engage successfully in many standard forms of conversation." Put in my terms, I take Churchland to be saying that at least some ES conversations would presuppose little understanding. I readily grant the truthfulness of this claim but I question its relevancy to the issue of the adequacy of the Turing test since, to repeat again, virtually any topic that reasonably well-informed, mature adults should be capable of handling is fair game during the administration of the test. Note Churchland's use of the word *standard*. I can't claim to be sure I know what Churchland means by *standard*, but, on the plausible interpretation that it means something like "perfunctory" or "constrained in terms of permissible topic," Turing's test should not be taken to be equivalent to standard conversations. The Turing test's difficulty lies precisely in the permissibility of conversation occurring *in extremis* conditions, to reinvoke Dennett's way of characterizing it. As a result, I claim that the "eerie impression of real understanding" that Churchland claims ELIZA has, is, for reasons I advance in this chapter, unfortunately misleading. The only way that I can account for the widespread quoting of this conversation, and the concomitant, unjustified analysis that often accompanies it, is that commentators discover the quote, take it to be illustrative of the case they are attempting to make, and begin interpreting it without actually spending time with the program itself. One should expect that, if they spent time with the program and not just the quoted conversation, and if ELIZA were consistently this effective, that other similar — equally impressive — conversations with similarly "eerie" attributes would appear in the literature. They don't.

In contrast with the "Men are all alike" conversation, the following conversation I had with ELIZA is not likely to be widely quoted. This conversation should be considered along with its much more discussed "Men are all alike" cousin (computer part is in uppercase; all terminating punctuation, as per instructions, is omitted).

HI I'M ELIZA. WHAT'S YOUR PROBLEM
?Did you hear that Bush and Gorbachev are meeting?
WE WERE DISCUSSING YOU NOT ME
?I don't feel well today
DON'T YOU REALLY FEEL WELL TODAY
?Men are all alike
WHAT DOES THAT SUGGEST TO YOU
?That men are sexist
DO YOU ENJOY FEELING SEXIST
:
?Are you a counselor
WHY ARE YOU INTERESTED IN WHETHER OR NOT I AM A
COUNSELOR
?Well you are not interested in talking about Bush
I SEE
?What do you think of rock music
OH I THINK OF ROCK MUSIC
?Since you are smart you must have an opinion
WHAT MAKES YOU THINK I AM SMART
?You're a computer damnit
DOES IT PLEASE YOU TO BELIEVE I AM A COMPUTER
?Enormously

I AM NOT SURE I UNDERSTAND YOU FULLY
?I want to know if you can think
YOU'RE NOT REALLY TALKING ABOUT ME ARE YOU

I had this conversation with ELIZA November 27, 1989. The elided part consisted simply of repeated lines. As the conversation indicates, I hope, some responses are plausible, in fact, even strangely interesting, but some, on the other hand, are implausible and patently unconvincing. Spending an hour or so with ELIZA, in my experience at least, unmasks it for the epistemologically simple, Potemkin village program that it is. Any suggestion that ELIZA can pass a "Turing-type test," therefore, fails to take into account the fact that many conversations are unsatisfactory and that any adequate Turing test would uncover this fact in rather short order. Moreover, I have not seen any suggestion in writing, and it runs against the experience I have had with ELIZA on at least a half dozen different occasions, that ELIZA is capable of convincing conversations over anything more than a trivial amount of time covering a tiny range of human interests — namely, of course, Rogerian-style counseling. Raphael (1976), for example, includes a conversation with ELIZA that has more in common with the conversation I quote here than it does with the "Men are all alike" conversation so widely quoted by others. To be even bolder, I would like to see a defense of the claim that ELIZA is capable of sustained conversation in other than Rogerian-style (read: epistemologically simple) mode.

If by "Turing-type tests" Gunderson means that ELIZA and SHRDLU can more or less converse at an epistemologically simple level, then, of course, I must agree. If, on the other hand, his claim is that ELIZA and SHRDLU can converse at an epistemologically complex level, which is what I have argued is required to pass the Turing test, then it follows that such a claim is quite difficult to defend. As I tried to underscore by citing my "conversation" with ELIZA, it (she?) is incapable of absorbing epistemologically complicated comments or queries and, instead, necessarily traffics in the kind of epistemologically simple database lookup that we saw in the Coin Toss game in Chapter 2. In fact, Rich's discussion of ELIZA's "matching" mechanisms, with surprisingly few changes, could be used as not a bad commentary on the Coin Toss game. As a result, I don't believe that this is the kind of conversational performance that even remotely satisfies the Turing test.

We should be careful in employing the phrase "Turing-type test." There is only one Turing test, with the specific, demanding requirements it includes. Any weakened test is not the Turing test, and use of phrases such as "Turing-type test" obscures the issues at stake. In particular, criticizing the Turing test by saying that some program can pass a "Turing-type test" is simply misleading. We should consistently refer to the full-strength test when we using the name "Turing." Granted, the kind of comments we get in Zeichick (1992, p. 5), which I discussed briefly in Chapter 1, warrant exactly the kind of criticisms brought by Gunderson. But from the fact that too many AI proponents have less than a full understanding of the stringent requirements of the test, and too often make precipitous claims as a result, we should not criticize the Turing test by claiming that some (nonthinking) programs have already passed "Turing-type" tests.

In closing this chapter, I would like to refer to Zeichick's comments. To say, as he does, that "there's no doubt that the state of the art is approaching Alan Turing's goal for machine intelligence," if the relation exists as I claim it does between the frame problem and the Turing test, is to claim that there is no doubt the state of the art is approaching a solution to the frame problem. About that, I believe there is considerable doubt.

CHAPTER 8

The Frame Problem, Philosophy, and AI's Understanding of Intelligence

In this concluding chapter, I wish to make some general comments that presuppose the argument developed in the preceding seven chapters. My general goal is to lay out what I believe this essay contributes to the philosophical discussion of AI as it exists in the early 1990s, and to indicate where we are in the discussions of the philosophic viability of AI as a general theory of intelligence.

Early in the essay, I advanced some preliminary reasons why the Turing test and the frame problem should count as two major issues in philosophical discussions of artificial intelligence. Here I wish to emphasize that the frame problem and the Turing test are not two major but largely separate issues, or two issues that happen to have some tangentially related links. While each is an important issue in its own right, it is the relationship between them that explains why they should be considered jointly. Moreover, not only do I believe that I have shown that there is an important relationship, I think I have also argued persuasively that their relationship has been either poorly understood or neglected outright in some of the books and papers that have attempted to analyze artificial intelligence over the last 10 years or so. The most conspicuous example of this oversight in terms of the Turing test is John Searle's (1990) latest piece, "Is the Brain's Mind a Computer Program?" There is no evidence in the piece that Searle understands the relevance of the frame problem for the Turing test. Of course, I claim not only that the frame problem bears on the Turing test but that it does so in such a way that it counts decisively against the position he espouses. Additionally, neither Pylyshyn's anthology (1987) nor Brown's (1987) anthology, which cover quite a lot of ground on the frame problem from the philosophical and technical perspectives, respectively, say anything about the frame problem's implications for the Turing test. As well, it is perplexing and disappointing that David Anderson's (1989) volume, which covers many of the same issues addressed here, does not attempt to articulate the issue.

One reason the relationship of the frame problem to the Turing test is important is that the prospects for understanding the intervening processes of the brain and a mindlike program are so poor that we have no choice but to rely on input/output tests such as the Turing test and any related, indirect characterizations of the intervening processes we can distill, given such an I/O test. While, as I argued, there is a substantial case to be made for the test without considering indirect characterizations, if we can supplement this case with considerations that enable us indirectly to discern some sense of what is likely happening at the process level, then we can assign a higher probability that the conclusions we draw from both the test and the indirect intervening process considerations are close to right than we could from the case for the test alone. Indeed, I claim that this point speaks to the worry that Gunderson brings to the debate over the Turing test—he wants to know something about the intervening processes as well as the relation of the output to the input. I agree that the impulse for wanting more than an I/O case alone is good operating procedure, philosophically speaking. My claim is that, for reasons advanced in this essay, while we are not in a position to make significant progress directly, we can get a measure of indirect understanding of the intervening processes by considering the implications of the frame problem for the Turing test. To be more specific, as I interpret it, the frame problem bears on the Turing test in such a way that it serves to augment significantly more conventional defenses of the test by proponents such as Dennett and Haugeland, and it enhances the case for why the Turing test is resistant to the criticisms of long-time Turing test critics such as Gunderson and Searle.

If I am right, then there is both indirect and direct evidence that supports the claim that the Turing test is an adequate test of intelligence. One result from studies in the philosophy of science is that, for evidence to support a theory well, it is preferable for there to be a variety of kinds of evidence. I don't claim that there is anything like irrefutable confirmation of a theory, or a philosophical view for that matter, but, other things being equal, it is preferable for there to be a variety of evidence supporting a theory or some kind of philosophical interpretation. In earlier chapters, I attempted to enhance the conventional kind of case made by Dennett and Haugeland for the Turing test by arguing that depending heavily on I/O evidence is unavoidable, but, more importantly I think, I attempted to show that there is a significant body of a different kind of evidence that supports the claim that passage of the Turing test would be reasonable grounds for adopting the view that a computer passing the test is thinking. Specifically, I claim that there is both direct, I/O evidence and indirect evidence, related to intervening processes, that support the positive evaluation of the test. As a result, there is not just one kind of evidence, there are two kinds that serve to supplement each other in the case that can be made on behalf of the test. I believe that this represents a significant enhancement of the case to be made for Turing's test.

A related result of the essay is my claim that an indirect characterization of the intervening processes supporting conversational abilities in a computer is likely the best we can do. Cherniak and Margolis, working independently, have advanced some compelling grounds for concluding, respectively, that a mindlike program would be too complicated for us to understand, and that the human brain supports novel function which developed over conserved biological structure, and, consequently, is also singularly resistant to investigation. Fischler and Firschein are AI proponents but argue that the brain's function is too deeply encoded in its biological structure for us to decipher directly how it works. While their view is sympathetic to an AI understanding of intelligence that I do not share, their point lends support to the claim I do endorse that "hollow shell" criticisms of AI, when such criticisms insist on looking at intervening processes before granting that something like thinking is going on in a Turing test-capable machine, will be hard pressed to show how this is feasible in the case of brains and mindlike programs. In large measure, then, we are limited to I/O assessments of putatively linguistically endowed digital computers, because we have little other choice. Direct evaluation of the intervening processes supporting the linguistic skills, as a result, is out of reach.

I use the qualification *in large measure* because, as I have said, we can make some indirect inferences about intervening processes in the case of a mindlike program with the aid of the distillation advanced here of the relationship of the frame problem to the Turing test. In fact, this essay can be viewed in part as an articulation of an indirect way to get some of the intervening process considerations that Gunderson seems to want in assaying the significance of the Turing test. Since we cannot achieve anything like a simultaneous understanding of the brain or a mindlike program, which is what would be necessary to supplement input/output considerations with intervening process considerations, we cannot claim any kind of direct, comprehensive understanding of the intervening processes supporting a maturely conversing computer. As a result, I believe that we cannot reasonably hold out the hope that we can achieve some significant process level understanding of the kind I take it Gunderson would like to see in order to assent to the claim that a computer passing the Turing test was thinking. Hence, one way to understand this essay is that it has attempted to show that there is no direct understanding of the relevant process levels to which we could appeal to supplement the test, but that some indirect considerations can be brought to bear to supplement the I/O side of the case for the test.

Considerations attaching to the frame problem do count as something of an *indirect* way of distilling some sense of what must be going on at the process level in a program as complicated as a mindlike program. The implications of the frame problem, some of which I have educed here, can be understood as an indirect way of showing, functionally if not specifically, some of what is likely happening in a digital computer if it has the mature conversational ability necessary to pass the Turing test. This is a variation on reverse engineering, since it argues from a certain I/O adequacy, namely, the Turing test, as well as how the frame problem bears on a Turing test capacity in a digital computer, to intervening process descriptions which arguably describe the supporting processes.

Most discussions of AI spend little time considering the fundamental operations of a computer. As I see it, some philosophical discussions of artificial intelligence move too quickly from a consideration of what it means for a digital computer to run a computer program in some high-level language to whether this or that particular skill is possible on a computer, or whether the computer should be characterized as having this or that capacity. I claim that a careful, low-level look at computation is essential before we can begin to appreciate what the capabilities are. Generally speaking, delimiting the characteristics and capabilities of machines that programmatically manipulate prodigious quantities of bits at extraordinary speed is not for the philosophically faint of heart; the probability of getting it wrong is high. My assumption is that some results from the theory of computation, along with some educated intuitions about computation at the machine level, can play an important role in generating a substantial, intuitive understanding about the likely capacities of digital computers with respect to mature conversational ability in particular and thinking in general.

Indeed, a limitative caveat is in order. Alan Kay (1984, p. 59) remarks that the computer, as the first "metamedium," "has degrees of freedom for representation and expression never before encountered and as yet barely investigated." In a parallel way, in the Epilogue to the expanded edition of *Perceptrons*, Minsky and Papert (1988) point out that they required approximately a year to reach a complete under-standing of a simple perceptron. The larger result I take from these two claims and the discussion developed here is that it is foolhardy to suggest that anyone has anything even approximating a full under-standing of the limitations of digital computers such that a detailed articulation of what they will and won't be able to achieve is possible. We assuredly have some provable limitative results from the theory of computability. But the comprehensive limits to what computers can do turn out to be a slippery empirical question that likely is not amenable in general to formal proof techniques. It seems to me, as a result and contra Searle, that we can only traffic in "the evidence appears to support this interpretation rather than that"-kinds of tentative claims.

Here's what I claim the evidence and pertinent logical consider-ations suggest at this point in the philosophy of artificial intelligence. It is apt to characterize a computer as an algorithmic machine, since algorithms are more important than either computers or programs; computers execute programs that express algorithms. A problem has to have an algorithmic solution if it is to be solved on a computer, which is an algorithmic machine. Moreover, any problem solvable by means of an algorithmic process can be solved using at most three kinds of algorithmic structure, each of which is simply expressible. There are more elaborate algorithmic structures, such as AI's favored recursion, and these three structures can be combined into quite elaborate structures, but only three simple structures, namely, sequence, selection and repetition, are necessary for the computation of any computable function. As a result, necessary algorithmic structure is, at this level at least, simpler than might be expected.

Additionally, each step in an algorithmic process can be expressed so simply that automatic formal system computability can be characterized as "pencil and paper computability." Such operations consist of operations as simple as, "add the contents of storage location 2 to the accumulator," "see which storage location, 4 or 5, contains the larger integer," and so on. Arithmetic operations are the direct operations manipulating numeric values. Logical constructs such as "if x is greater than y, then call procedure z" are typically used to determine which of a number of paths through the algorithm to take, given intermediate values. I emphasized that it is preferable to call "memory" *storage*, since digital computer storage is much simpler than animal memories. Consequently, arithmetic and logical operations at machine level turn out to be simpler than what might be thought, given what computers can do at the application program level.

Generally speaking, three simple algorithm structures, when combined with equally straightforward arithmetic and logical operations, are sufficient to constitute a full-fledged computer. I grant that typical programs are large in size, but I believe it is helpful to emphasize that the fundamental structures and operations are just this simple. My claim is that this simplicity has implications in terms of what we are justified in ascribing to the computer. To be sure, we can consider all the algorithmic abstractions we like, in terms of hierarchies, as we attempt to understand the programs we develop and use. Since we're completely inept at trying to remember how hundreds of millions of "bits" are arranged or manipulated, we cannot avoid characterizing the computer's "bit stream" with terms drawn from human convention. But I see such hierarchical understanding, for example, "this program plays the Coin Toss game by betting that its opponent's past play is a good predictor of current play," as finally an attribution on our part, a *useful fiction*, to borrow a term from R. B. Braithwaite, an aid that we use, so that we don't get hopelessly lost in the bits as we attempt to map the problems we want solved onto a system that knows nothing about human conventions and desires. Our anthropomorphizing proclivity is to reify those abstractions and suppose that the computer program possesses something approximating the range of properties that we associate with similar abstractions in human minds. This is harmless so long as we remember that such characterizations can lead to considerable philosophic misunderstanding.

I suppose the rejoinder to this admittedly "low church" approach is that I am ignoring the functional capacities that emerge when we get the bits being manipulated in the requisite way. In other words, a good case can be made to take the abstractions literally. An AI proponent might point out that we could take a "low church" approach to brain functioning in such a way that, after all the low-level talk about neuron firings, electrochemical thresholds, reinforcing connections, and the like, if we didn't know otherwise, we could begin to wonder how seriously to take the high-level reports of consciousness and the claim that conscious attitudes purportedly supported by the brain cause, for example, an arm to rise or a missile to be fired. Phenomena look quite different, the retort would run, depending on what level we look at them. As a result, it doesn't follow that a "bit" analysis, or some other low-level analysis, of a computer will result in the right understanding of what a digital computer can and can't do, any more than a neuron analysis of brains would necessarily result in the right understanding of the rich mental life that people undeniably possess.

But this view, as I see it, presupposes the untenable assumption that there is some significant similarity between brains and computers, when the preponderance of the evidence points in the opposite direction. The reason we don't get far with a "neuron up" analysis of the brain, if Margolis is something like right (and I believe he is), is that the novel function developed over the conserved structure is such that we don't have a good way to deduce the functional properties from a low-level analysis of the structure only. The pattern recognition capacities out of which all of human cognition is made, according to Margolis, are not rooted in a program. The problems computers have with pattern recognition and the difficulty people have with remembering long sequences of meaningless numbers, to put it in more conventional terms, counts in favor of the claim that there are stunning differences between computers and brains. In fact, my entire discussion of the frame problem also supports this view, at least as long as there is no "principled" solution.

I believe that the frame problem serves as a reinforcing systemic consideration that confirms what I claim about computers at the machine level. At the machine level, where the machine does simple arithmetic and logical operations, I find it difficult to imagine the development of any kind of "scale up" significant enough that the operations, by dint of some kind of emergent property, become psychologically relevant. My intuition about this—and who's to say how best to understand a computer's vast "bit stream"?—is significantly reinforced by considerations stemming from the frame problem.

The result, as I see it, is that we should understand digital computers as those machines that execute sequences of simple, atomic steps working with an inert storage where each cell is—at any specific instant—epistemologically quite isolated from the other cells. A specific symptom of this atomicity is that adding data to "smart" systems not infrequently results in performance degradation, often in terms of speed, sometimes in terms of satisfactory output. The opposite is usually the case in people. As a result, I characterized computers as utterly *simple-minded*. I agreed that the great speeds of a computer can blind us to the computer's epistemological atomicity, if I may coin a 12-syllable tongue-twister, because it so readily—in narrow domain situations—generates the "user illusion" of something approximating the causal powers of memory as we experience them in people. The speed of the atomic interactions, I said, generates an appearance of simultaneous, whole-system interactivity, but closer inspection shows this evident, whole-system interactivity to be one more user illusion. The reason I devoted a number of pages to exploring computation at basic levels stemmed from my desire to get as good a picture of computation from the bottom-up as I could. My view is that the frame problem originates in the inherent limitations of digital computing, which are more easily identified in machine-level characterizations than in high-level abstractions.

I concede that my general orientation to interpreting a digital computer as I just have stems, in part, from my expectation that the frame problem is insoluble. I agree that the question of whether the frame problem is solvable is something we don't know yet—it is an empirical question that requires investigation. Should it turn out that it is solvable by a digital computer, then, I have to confess, my entire interpretation of what it means for a system to be a digital computer will change significantly. To go at it the other way around, part of what I understand a digital computer to be stems from my understanding of the frame problem as that which demarcates the probable upper bound of digital computer computing capacity when we attempt to get it to solve "real-world" problems such as conversation. That is, a theoretical result not gotten from just the bits informs my view of what the bits can do. But as I have intimated, what we have to do when we attempt to understand a system that manipulates vast numbers of bits includes identifying philosophic difficulties such as the frame problem, bringing in relevant results from computability theory, seeing what sense can be made of computer operations in close-up mode, as I did with AugsAsm, all in an effort to generate a collage of informed impressions about what computation means and what its likely limits are. The bits themselves are so far silent on philosophical issues. As Dijkstra once observed, the digital computer is so different from any artifact we have ever made that the propensity for getting it wrong, for succumbing to the most egregious anthropomorphizing (he believes AI does just this), is dismayingly high.[1]

I have emphasized that the computer is quite a good simulation machine, provided that the simulation in question is amenable to the kind of epistemologically simple manipulation a digital computer supports. Simulations attempt to generate the appearance of what literally is not there — which is one reason why philosophical analyses of computer simulations are especially fraught with difficulty. As a result, we need to use special care, lest we mistake a simulation for the genuine item. I also attempted to show that there is good reason to distinguish between epistemologically simple and epistemologically complex learning. In fact, this distinction constitutes the backbone of this essay. My claim is that computers, barring a solution to the frame problem and as exemplified by the Coin Toss game, are capable of epistemologically simple learning but not epistemologically complex learning. ES learning does not presuppose a solution to the frame problem while EC learning does. Much of my analysis of hollow shell critiques of AI, specifically those offered by Searle and Gunderson, turns on this basic distinction.

While Hubert Dreyfus has been something of a lonely voice in his three-decades long opposition to AI, the developing importance of the frame problem constitutes a partial vindication of him in the sense that

---

[1]He makes this point in a relatively recent edition of *Communications of the ACM*. I have lost the exact reference.

he was correctly pointing in the general direction of the frame problem. In terms of the problem itself, the expression *frame problem* does not enjoy anything like unanimity of opinion with respect to what it names. There are a number of different definitions of the problem, and technically inclined writers, such as Hayes, define it more technically while more philosophically inclined writers, such as Haugeland, not surprisingly, define it more epistemologically. I called the former, more technical interpretation the *specific frame problem* and understood it to be a matter of finding a principled way to avoid examining an entire axiom system every time one axiom requires revision. Haugeland's understanding, that it involves finding a way to distinguish efficiently temporary from more or less permanent facts is an adequate, rough and ready way to define what I called the *general frame problem*.

One point that I did not emphasize is that there is less discussion of the frame problem, particularly as it bears on the case against artificial intelligence, in recently published material than one would expect. For example, Rainer Born's 1987 anthology, *Artificial Intelligence: The Case Against*, does not discuss the frame problem. The *Daedalus* issue devoted to AI, for the winter quarter of 1988, doesn't discuss the problem to any depth. Fischler and Firschein (1987) devote about three-quarters of a page to it in their Epilogue. Haugeland (1986) discusses it but fails to discuss, as best as I can determine, how it counts in favor of the poor substitute strategy for opposing AI which he himself embraces or what its implications are for the Turing test. Given Dennett's (1987) "Cognitive Wheels" paper which is reprinted in Pylyshyn's frame problem volume, it is also disappointing to see no consideration of it in his *Consciousness Explained* (Dennett, 1991). Missing in the literature, which I believe this essay establishes, are: the frame problem is more important than many writers suppose, it has significant consequences for the attempt to build computer systems which learn, and it dramatically reinforces the difficulty of the Turing test. In fact, there is disappointingly little specific discussion of the frame problem's implications for the Turing test in the literature I have seen.

Another result of this essay is that the conventional belief in AI that the "key to intelligence" in a machine lies in the constraint of search spaces is too simple. For example, Lenat (1984, p. 204) argues that the "essence of intelligence" lies in "finding ways to solve otherwise intractable problems by limiting the search for solutions." I believe I have shown that, because of the frame problem, there are two computational spaces that require constraint in the attempt to generate intelligence on a digital computer. First, as Lenat suggests, the search space must be limited. But considerations attaching to the frame problem indicate that there is also what I have called a *relevance space* that bedevils the representations used by digital computers designed to interact with domains possessing real world complexity. Not only, I argued, are there two kinds of computational spaces that must be drastically limited in order for a machine to possess something like intelligence, I claimed that intelligent behavior, such as that needed to pass the Turing test, must solve both of these "space" problems simultaneously. The fact that they must be solved simultaneously results in a new degree of complexity in the attempt to generate computer intelligence that has not been well articulated in philosophical discussions of AI that I have seen.

Even if the frame problem is solved, AI proponents are not home free. I appealed to recent studies of complexity, as discussed by Pagels, that suggest that a simulation of them would need to be as complicated as that which is simulated. This distinct complexity issue stands as an additional hurdle which AI will need to clear if we are to arrive at what I have called *epistemologically complex learning* and the concomitant ability to communicate at an epistemologically complex level. If this is right, the frame problem is an example of complexity issues facing AI, but its solution would remove only one layer of complexity when there are more to be solved.

One issue I did not consider explicitly in the preceding chapters is the question of whether digital computers attempting tasks such as learning and conversing possess intrinsic intentionality of the kind we have, according to some writers, when, for example, a person says "I'm hungry."[2] The alternative to this kind of intrinsic intentionality would be what is usually called *observer-relative* intentionality. This species of intentionality depends on attributions made by outside observers. If I say, "the computer wants to know which file you want to work on," I am ascribing an intentional state to the computer in an observer-relative way.

---

[2]If we can assume that *original* and *intrinsic* intentionality are identical, Dennett (1987, chap. 8), of course, will have none of this.

As might be anticipated, my view will turn on what happens with the frame problem. So long as there is an unsolved frame problem facing computers, the most that I think the evidence will support is the claim that computers have observer-relative or derivative intentionality. The programming they use depends so heavily on the purposes of the programmers, and they are blocked from significant learning by the frame problem, so that I see no adequate grounds for saying that they have anything more than derivative intentionality. If it turns out that the frame problem is soluble, on the other hand, then things get much more interesting. To see why this is so, I need to make some remarks about what a digital computer that had solved the frame problem represents.

A digital computer with no unsolved frame problem has effectively broken the epistemological curse of what I have characterized as a single-cell simple-mindedness. There may be other significant problems standing in the way of such a general ability, but I have difficulty imagining that they would constitute as high a hurdle as the frame problem. With the right kind of programming, such a frame-solving computer could presumably make surmises about all kinds of things in the world, offer opinions about topics of conversation as we do often, and generally surmise, in some significant sense, the implications of any particular item in the world for any other item. I assume that such a computer would be able to make surmises about itself in a similar fashion. If, as Douglas Hofstadter suggests, it is the case that a sense of self has largely to do with this kind of self-referential surmising, then we have some grounds for ascribing the kind of intrinsic intentionality to a computer that we routinely do with each other. At this point, with no solution to the frame problem on the imaginable horizon, I believe the evidence we have supports only an ascription of derivative or observer-relative intentionality to computers. I continue to be impressed, to make a larger point, that it is the frame problem in light of which many conventionally discussed problems in AI now should be reinterpreted.

A central result of this essay is not only that the Turing test is, as Dennett puts it, "plenty" difficult in terms of being an adequate test for the presence of intelligence in a machine, but that the frame problem bears on the Turing test in a way that has not been appreciated in philosophical discussions of AI to date. Two major results stem, as I see it, from the frame problem's implications for the Turing test, both having to do with the claim that the frame problem adds significantly to the case that the Turing test is a difficult test. First, it reinforces the claim made by Turing, Dennett, and Haugeland that the test is adequate in the way that Turing supposed. That is, any system good enough to pass the full-throated test is good enough that we have sufficient grounds for attributing thought to it. Now, I agreed that there is a pragmatic component to the case that can be made for the test that parallels the ascription of thought to people. I cited Bertrand Russell's observation that solipsism is philosophically irrefutable but psychologically impossible. My claim is that ascription of thought to computers passing the test is reasonable, not provable or demonstrable by means of one of Searle's "knockdown" arguments. The claim is that ascription of thought to computers is at least as justifiable as ascription of thought to people because, I argued, there are two basic grounds for attributing thought to people, first, the right I/O, and second, some kind of argument by analogy. My argument is that considerations attaching to the difficulty of the frame problem make it at least as good an argument as the argument by analogy, and, since most of us routinely and reasonably (would any but the solipsist argue otherwise?) attribute thought to other people, it is at least as reasonable to attribute thought to a maturely conversing computer.

Second, not only does it reinforce a Turing-type assessment of the Imitation Game, the frame problem counts in favor of the poor substitute strategy for opposing AI and against the hollow shell strategy. One major claim of this essay is that most writers have not seen how difficult the test is. Dennett appreciates that it is "plenty" difficult enough. What he doesn't appreciate is that it is so difficult, and reasons for its difficulty are such, that the Turing test, ironically, begins to count against the AI enterprise in ways that I doubt Turing could have imagined. That is, in attempting to build a machine that can pass the test, we find out something about the difficulty of the test, apparent limitations of computing machines, and the raft of problems that must be solved before the test is passable. The way in which the test is difficult, I should emphasize, is what calls the classical AI paradigm into question. I doubt that is what Turing had in mind.

I believe, as well, that the two prominent detractors of the test, specifically Searle and Gunderson, have evidently not fully appreciated all of what the test requires. I think this essay has shown that the hollow shell strategy for objecting to the Turing test requires a solution to the frame problem, yet hollow shell proponents such as Searle and Gunderson have said little about it. An unsolved frame problem, in fact, counts in favor of the poor substitute strategy reproach of AI and serves to count against the two hollow shell reproaches of AI by Searle and Gunderson. Conversely, I grant that a solution to the frame problem will count significantly against the the poor substitute strategy which I find convincing.

The distinction between epistemologically simple and epistemologically complex learning extends readily to mature natural language conversational ability. Correlated with ES learning and EC learning are ES conversational skills and EC conversational skills. My principal claim is that ES learning ability supports ES conversational skills but not EC skills. Required for EC conversational skills is the much more demanding capacity to learn at an epistemological complex level. But, as I have argued, without a solution to the frame problem, digital computers are unable to learn at an EC level. My ES/EC distinction grows out of my understanding of what is and is not possible in a digital computer, given an unsolved frame problem, and it bears on how I view claims about what kinds of real-world tasks computers will be capable of successfully engaging.

I believe the contrast illustrates why Searle's much-discussed Chinese Room experiment is not plausible, and why Searle cannot have the competency he claims he has in the room. Indeed, from its first publication in the *Behavioral and Brain Sciences* a decade ago, it has generated considerably more debate than most philosophical critiques do. My late mentor, Grover Maxwell (1980), wrote at the time that it appeared that Searle's paper was destined to be a classic, and time has proven that intuition to be right on the mark. I did not say much about critiques of Searle's article that have appeared in recent years. Writers such as Torrance (1986) and Boden (1989) have some useful things to say about the article and the counterexample. But it seems to me that most commentators have missed a relevant, pivotal point that psychologists have noticed about the relation between the use of words and intelligence. The skillful handling of words, specifically, words used in a new sense or new words encountered in a conversation, remains a good, general indication of intelligence, because it presupposes the general ability a "system" would need to integrate new with old over a complex domain, that is to say, learn. What I think most philosophical critiques of Searle have missed is the centrality of learning for mature conversational ability and that a digital computer, if it is cognitively impaired by an unsolved frame problem, is capable of some kinds of learning but not the kind of learning it would need to engage in mature conversation. In sum, I claim that Searle will be incapable of EC learning in his room and that, consequently, he will not possess the mature Chinese language competency he claims he will — that is, he will not be able, contrary to what he claims, to pass the Turing test. A major theme of this essay is not just that he will not be able to pass the test, it is that the reasons why he will not be able to pass the test have not been well understood.

As I said, even though I do not share his hollow shell position, I find Gunderson's critique of the test to be more subtle — and finally more interesting — than Searle's. While Searle rests much of his case on his well-known counterexample, and while Gunderson has his own, less well known, "Toe-stepping" counterexample, which roughly parallels Searle's Chinese Room thought experiment, Gunderson finally offers the more enduring argument. Gunderson's case rests largely on the generally sound point that there is often a number of ways to achieve the same end. Cast in terms of thinking and conversation, Gunderson wants to emphasize that, while we have understood thinking to be a prerequisite for at least some kinds of conversation, it may turn out that it is possible to build a good conversationalist that does no thinking at all — or, in my terms, no epistemologically complex thinking. That is, while thinking is (more or less) a sufficient condition for thinking, it is not necessarily necessary. As a result, he wants us to look at intervening processes as well as the "right I/O" before we can suppose that we are in a position to assent to the claim, "Yes, the computer must be thinking."

I have advanced reasons for why we are not in a position to do the kinds of investigations that Gunderson presumably would urge. The complexities of a mindlike program and the brain are such that the prospects for any significant understanding of either is poor. As a result, we are largely left with considerations associated with I/O assessments. I claim that Gunderson would have to pay this price for holding his position: Since he claims that it is conceivable that it will turn out that a computer that passes the test would do no (EC) thinking, this means that it is feasible for a nonthinking, automatic formal system to solve the frame problem. If we are looking for some kind of threshold to demarcate nonthinking from thinking, or ES thinking from EC thinking, in a digital computer, I claim that the frame problem is the natural candidate. I countered that it appears so unlikely that a nonthinking automatic system can solve the frame problem and pass the test that it is more reasonable to ascribe thinking to a machine that passed the test and therefore had solved the frame problem. An auxiliary consideration I appealed to above is that such an ascription is surely at least as good as the appeal to analogy that an ascription of intelligence to a maturely conversing person would (probably) tacitly include. Since we reasonably ascribe intelligence to maturely conversing persons, I believe we can reasonably ascribe thinking to maturely conversing computers. That is, the computer auxiliary consideration, namely, that solution of the frame problem by a nonthinking system seems quite unlikely, is at least as compelling as the person auxiliary consideration, namely, that there is some kind of an analogy between myself and other people. In short, I am willing to call a frame-solving, maturely conversing computer a *thinker*.

But there is an irony here. There comes a point, in defending the Turing test from charges that passage would signify little, in developing the case for the adequacy of the test, in attempting to show all that a digital computer would have to do in order to pass the test, that we begin to undermine the goal that Turing originally had of providing a practical decision procedure for affirming that a computer can think. In other words, if we defensibly reach the conclusion that the test is quite difficult, partly because we have found that there are possibly intractable problems that require solution before a computer could pass the test, we may also begin to suspect that the computer is unlikely to pass the test at all—and that, as a result, we now have significant, new evidence for concluding that AI's understanding of intelligence—namely, that it is the manipulation of symbols under the control of a formal program—is fundamentally mistaken. For reasons advanced in this essay, I believe that this is exactly the point we have reached.

Massively parallel computing (MPC) may address some of the questions raised here but I suspect it will succeed only in trading one large, system-wide frame problem for as many little frame problems as the massively parallel system has individual processors. The complete solution of the frame problem may well require a massively parallel computer of equal or greater granularity to the phenomenon being simulated. An MPC of equal or greater granularity to the human brain, to choose the obvious example, presumably would have to have approximately 10^{11} or about 100 billion processors. While programming massively parallel systems of relatively smaller sizes (say 64K) is not as difficult as we once expected, we know little at present about the ramifications of attempting to program an MPC of that size. This may be a situation in which, in principle, we know how to do the programming but, in practice, it is out of reach because of the sheer size of the parallelism. In fact, one can imagine that individual neurons in an animal brain suffer, as it were, from lilliputian frame problems but it is not noticeable from the perspective of the system as a whole because they wash out in the system's parallelism. If the present study is right, it appears that AI proponents will have to look to massively parallel computing of prodigious sizes to recast the AI research paradigm in radically new form.

References

Abelson, R. P. (1980). Searle's argument is just a set of chinese symbols. *The Behavioral and Brain Sciences, 3.*

Almsbury, W. (1985). *Data structures: From arrays to priority queues.* Belmont, CA: Wadsworth.

Anderson, A.R. (Ed.). (1964). *Minds and machines.* Englewood Cliffs, NJ: Prentice-Hall.

Anderson, D. (1989). *Artificial intelligence and intelligent systems: The implications.* New York: John Wiley & Sons.

Anderson, H. (1987, July). Why artificial intelligence isn't (yet). *AI Expert.*

Arbib, M. (1985). *In search of the person: Philosphical explorations in cognitive science.* Amherst, MA: The University of Massachusetts Press.

Block, N. (1980a). What intuitions about homunculi don't show. *The Behavioral and Brain Sciences, 3,* 425–326.

Block, N. (Ed.). (1980b). *Readings in the philosophy of psychology* (2 vols.) Cambridge, MA: Harvard.

Boden, M. (1977). *Artificial intelligence and natural man.* New York: Basic Books.

Boden, M. (1984). Animal perception from an artificial intelligence viewpoint. In C. Hookway (Ed.), *Minds, machines and evolution.* Cambridge, UK: Cambridge University Press.

Boden, M. (1989). *Artificial intelligence in psychology: Interdisciplinary essays.* Cambridge, MA: MIT Press.

Boden, M. (1989b). Escaping from the chinese room. In M. Boden (Ed.), *Artificial intelligence in psychology: Interdisciplinary essays.* Cambridge, MA: MIT Press.

Born, R. (1987). *Artificial intelligence: The case against*. New York: St. Martin's.

Bridgeman, B. (1980). Brains + programs = minds. *The Behavioral and Brain Sciences, 3*, 427–428.

Bronowski, J. (1973). *The ascent of man*. Boston: Little, Brown and Co.

Brown, F.M. (1987). *The frame problem in artificial intelligence: Proceedings of the 1987 Workshop*. Los Altos: Morgan Kaufmann.

Cherniak, C. (1986). *Minimal rationality*. Cambridge, MA: MIT Press.

Cherniak, C. (1988, April). Undebuggability and cognitive science. *Communications of the ACM*, pp. 402–412.

Churchland, P.M., & Churchland P.S. (1990, January). Could a machine think? *Scientific American*, 32–37.

Cowan, J.D., & Sharp, D.H. (1988, Winter). Neural nets and artificial intelligence. *Daedulus*, pp. 85–122.

Crockett, L.J. (1987). The information age: friend or foe of the liberal arts? In A. L. Olsen (Ed.). *Occasional papers on the christian faith and liberal arts, 1986–1987*. Minneapolis: DCUS.

Danto, A.C. (1980). The use and mention of terms and the simulation of linguistic understanding. *The Behavioral and Brain Sciences, 3*, p. 428.

Dennett, D.C. (1975). Current issues in the philosophy of mind. *American Philosophical Quarterly, 15*(4), 249–261.

Dennett, D.C. (1978). *Brainstorms*. Cambridge, MA: MIT Press.

Dennett, D.C. (1980). The milk of human intentionality. *The Behavioral and Brain Sciences, 3*, 428–429.

Dennett, D.C. (1984). Cognitive wheels: The frame problem of AI. In C. Hookway (Ed.), *Minds, machines & evolution*. Cambridge, UK: Cambridge University Press.

Dennett, D.C. (1985). Can machines think? In M. Shafto (Ed.), *How we know*. Cambridge, MA: Harper and Row.

Dennett, D.C. (1987). *The intentional stance*. Cambridge, MA: MIT Press.

Dennett, D.C. (1988, Winter). When philosophers encounter artificial intelligence. *Daedulus*, pp. 283–295.

Dennett, D.C. (1991). *Consciousness explained*. Boston: Little Brown and Co.

Dreyfus, H.L. (1979). *What computers can't do: The limits of artificial intelligence*. New York: Harper Colophon Books.

Dreyfus, H.L., & Dreyfus, S.E. (1986). *Mind over machine*. New York: Free Press.

Dreyfus, H.L., & Dreyfus, S.E. (1987). How to stop worrying about the frame problem even thought it's computationally insoluable. In Z. W. Pylyshyn (Ed.), *The robot's dilemma: The frame problem in artificial intelligence*. Norwood, NJ: Ablex Publishing.

Dreyfus, H.L., & Dreyfus, S.E. (1988, Winter). Making a mind versus modeling the brain: artificial intelligence back at a branchpoint. *Daedulus*, 15–43.

Firebaugh, M.W. (1988). *Artificial intelligence: A knowledge-based approach.* Boston: Boyd and Fraser.

Fischler, M.A., & Firschein, O. (1987). *Intelligence: The eye, the brain and the domputer.* Reading, MA: Addison-Wesley.

Flanagan, O.J. (1991). *The science of the mind.* (2nd ed.). Cambridge, MA: MIT Press.

Fodor, J.A. (1980). Searle on what only brains can do. *The Behavioral and Brain Sciences, 3,* 431–432.

Fodor, J.A. (1981). *Representations: Philosophical essays on the foundations of cognitive science.* Cambridge, MA: MIT Press.

Fodor, J.A. (1983). *The modularity of mind.* Cambridge. MA: MIT Press.

Fodor, J.A. (1987). Modules, frames, fridgeons, sleeping dogs, and the music of the spheres. In Z. W. Pylyshyn (Ed.), *The robot's dilemma: The frame problem in artificial intelligence.* Norwood, NJ: Ablex Publishing.

Forsyth, R., & Rada, R. (1986). *Machine learning: Applications in expert systems and information retrieval.* New York: John Wiley and Sons.

French, P.A, Uehling, T.E., Jr., & Wettstein, H.K. (1986). *Midwest studies in philosophy X: Studies in the philosophy of mind.* Minneapolis: University of Minnesota Press.

Glymour, C. (1987). Android epistemology and the frame problem: Comments on Dennett's 'cognitive wheels.' In Z. W. Pylyshyn (Ed.), *The robot's dilemma: The frame problem in artificial intelligence.* Norwood, NJ: Ablex Publishing.

Goldschlager, L., & Lister, A. (1982). *Computer science: A modern introduction.* Englewood Cliffs, NJ: Prentice-Hall.

Gregory, R. L. (Ed.). (1987). *The oxford companion to the mind.* Oxford: Oxford University Press.

Gunderson, K. (1972). *Content and consciousness* and the mind-body problem. *The Journal of Philosophy,* LXIX (18), 591–604.

Gunderson, K. (1985) *Mentality and machines* (2nd ed.). Minneapolis: University of Minnesota Press.

Gunderson, K. (1988). Consciousness and intentionality: robots with and without the right stuff. Minneapolis: University of Minnesota Press.

Hardwig, J. (1991). The role of trust in knowledge. *The Journal of Philosophy,* LXXXVIII (12), 693–709.

Haugeland, J. (1980). Programs, causal powers and intentionality. *The Behavioral and Brain Sciences, 3,* 432–433.

Haugeland, J. (1987). An overview of the frame problem. In Z. W. Pylyshyn (Ed.), *The robot's dilemma: The frame problem in artificial intelligence.* Norwood, NJ: Ablex Publishing Corp.

Haugeland, J. (1985). *Artificial intelligence: The very idea*. Cambridge, MA: MIT Press.

Haugeland, J. (Ed.). (1981a). *Mind design*. Cambridge, MA: MIT Press.

Haugeland, J. (1981b). Semantic engines: An introduction to mind design. In J. Haugeland (Ed.), *Mind design*. Cambridge, MA: MIT Press.

Hayes, P. (1987). What the frame problem is and isn't. In Z. W. Pylyshyn (Ed.), *The robot's dilemma: the frame problem in artificial intelligence*. Norwood, NJ: Ablex Publishing Corp.

Hofstadter, D.R., & Dennett, D.C. (1981). *The mind's I*. New York: Basic Books.

Hookway, C. (1984). *Minds, machines & evolution*. Cambridge, UK: Cambridge University Press.

Janlert, L. (1987). Modeling change—the frame problem. In Z. W. Pylyshyn (Ed.), *The robot's dilemma: The frame problem in artificial intelligence*. Norwood, NJ: Ablex Publishing.

Johnson-Laird, P.N. (1988). *The computer and the mind*. Cambridge, MA: Harvard University Press.

Kay, A. (1984, September). Computer software. *Scientific American*, 53–59.

Kripke, S.A. (1982). *Wittgenstein on rules and private language*. Cambridge, MA: Harvard University Press.

Ladd, S. (1986). *The computer and the brain*. Toronto: Red Feather Press.

Lenat, D. B. (1984, September). Computer software for intelligent systems. *Scientific American*, pp. 204–213.

Lewis, D. (1983). *Philosophical papers*. New York: Oxford University Press.

Margolis, H. (1987). *Patterns, thinking, and cognition*. Chicago: The University of Chicago Press.

Maxwell, G. (1980). Intentionality: hardware, not software. *The Behavioral and Brain Sciences, 3*, 437–438.

McCarthy, J. (1977). Epistemological problems in artificial intelligence. *Proceedings of the Fifth International Conference on Artificial Intelligence*. Los Altos, CA: Morgan-Kaufmann.

McCarthy, J. (1980). Beliefs, machines and theories. *The Behavioral and Brain Sciences, 3*, 435.

McCarthy, J., & Hayes, P. (1969). Some philosophical problems from the standpoint of artificial intelligence. In B. Meltzer & D. Mitchie (Eds.), *Machine intelligence 4*. Edinburgh: Edinburgh University Press.

McCorduck, P. (1979). *Machines who think*. San Francisco: Freeman.

Minsky, M., & Papert, S.A. (1988). *Perceptrons*. Cambridge, MA: MIT Press.

Pagels, H. (1988). *The dreams of reason*. New York: Bantam.

Partridge, D., & Wilks, Y. (1990). *The foundations of artificial intelligence: A sourcebook*. Cambridge, UK: Cambridge University Press.

Penzias, A. (1989). *Ideas and information*. New York: W.W. Norton.

Penfield, W. (1975). *The mystery of the mind*. Princeton, NJ: Princeton University Press.

Putnam, H. (1988, Winter). Much ado about not very much. *Daedulus*, pp. 269–281.

Pylyshyn, Z.W. (Ed.). (1987). *The robot's dilemma: The frame problem in artificial intelligence*. Norwood, NJ: Ablex Publishing.

Quine, W. V., & Ullian, J.S. (1978). *The web of belief*. New York: Random House.

Raphael, B. (1976). *The thinking computer: Mind inside matter*. San Francisco: Freeman.

Rich, E. (1983). *Artificial intelligence*. New York: McGraw-Hill.

Searle, J. (1980). Minds, brains, and programs. *The Behavioral and Brain Sciences, 3*, 417–424.

Searle, J. (1983). *Intentionality*. Cambridge, UK: Cambridge University Press.

Searle, J. (1984). *Minds, brains and science*. Cambridge, MA: Harvard University Press.

Searle, J. (1990, January). Is the brain's mind a computer program? *Scientific American*, pp. 26–31.

Shafto, M. (Ed.). (1985). *How we know*. Cambridge, MA: Harper and Row.

Simon, H.A. (1982). *The sciences of the artificial*. Cambridge, MA: MIT Press.

Simon, H.A. (1983). Why should machines learn? In J. G. Carbonell, R. S. Michaleski & T. M. Mitchell (Eds.), *Machine learning — an artificial intelligence approach*. Palo Alto, CA: Tioga.

Sternberg, S. (1986). Inside intelligence. *American Scientist, 74*,000–000.

Toffoli, T., & Margolus, N. (1987). *Cellular Automata Machines*. Cambridge, MA: MIT Press.

Torrance, S. (1984). *The mind and the machine: Philosophical aspects of artificial intelligence*. New York: Ellis Horwood.

Torrance, S. (1986). Breaking out of the chinese room. In M. Yazdani (Ed.), *Artificial intelligence: Principles and applications*. London: Chapman and Hall.

Tucker, A. B. (1986). *Programming languages*. New York: McGraw-Hill.

Turing, A. (1950). Computing machinery and intelligence. *Mind*, LIX (236), (Reprinted in A.R. Anderson (1964), *Minds and machines*. Englewood Cliffs: Prentice-Hall.)

Turkle, S. (1984). *The second self*. New York: Simon and Schuster.

Waltz, D.L. (1988, Winter). The prospects for building truly intelligent machines. *Daedulus*.

Weizenbaum, J. (1976). *Computer power and human reason*. San Francisco, CA: Freeman.

Winograd, T. (1983). *Understanding natural language*. New York: Academic Press.

Winograd, T., & Flores, F. (1986). *Understanding computers and cognition* Reading, MA: Addison Wesley.

Wirth, N. (1984, September). Data structures and algorithms. *Scientific American*.

Yazdani, M. (1986). *Artificial intelligence: Principles and applications*. London: Chapman and Hall.

Zeichick, A. L. (1992, January). The Turing test. *AI Expert*.

Author Index

Subject Index